Save!

Also by Alan Silverstein

Save!

Alan Silverstein's Guide to Mortgage Payment Tables

First published in 1993 by
Stoddart Publishing Co. Limited
34 Lesmill Road
Toronto, Canada
M3B 2T6
(416) 445-3333

Canadian Cataloguing in Publication Data

Silverstein, Alan, 1951-
Save! : Alan Silverstein's guide to
mortgage payment tables

ISBN 0-7737-5562-4

1. Mortgage loans — Canada — Tables.
2. Interest — Canada — Tables.   3. Mortgage
loans — Canada.   I. Title.   II. Title: Alan
Silverstein's guide to mortgage payment tables.

HG1634.S54 1993   332.8'0212   C92-095573-8

Cover design: Brant Cowie/ArtPlus
Typesetting: Tony Gordon Ltd.
Printed and bound in Canada

*Although great care was taken in the preparation of
these tables, there is no warranty of complete accuracy.*

Contents

Glossary

Accelerated Payment Mortgage. A mortgage that is paid weekly, bi-weekly or semi-monthly *and* where one extra mortgage payment is automatically made to the lender each year. It is the only type of fast-pay mortgage that saves borrowers any significant amount of money.

Amortization. The period of time needed to pay off a mortgage if there are no prepayments and no late payments.

Blended Payment. Where the same amount of money (principal and interest) is paid to the lender each payment period; each time a payment is made, the principal component increases while the interest component decreases. The payment period can be monthly, weekly, bi-weekly or semi-monthly.

Calculated Half-Yearly, Not in Advance. The confusing, but "normal" way interest on Canadian mortgages is calculated. "Calculated half-yearly" means half the stated interest rate is paid to the lender every six months. "Not in advance" means that interest is paid at the end of the payment period, not at the beginning (as is usually the case with rent); also known as "calculated semi-annually, not in advance." When a mortgage is paid more frequently (monthly, bi-weekly or semi-monthly) than the interest is calculated (half-yearly), an "interest factor" must be used.

Fast-Pay Mortgage. Any type of mortgage paid more frequently than monthly, be it weekly, bi-weekly or semi-monthly.

Interest. The amount charged by a lender to a borrower as "rent" for the use of the lender's money.

Interest Factor. The number used to calculate the interest component of a mortgage payment.

Minimum Amortized Mortgage Payment. Where a mortgage is paid weekly, bi-weekly or semi-monthly, but the payment is calculated using a 25-year amortization; the least effective type of fast-pay mortgage.

Mortgage. Security for the repayment of a debt; an elaborate form of an IOU that is registered against the title to the borrower's property.

Principal. The amount originally borrowed from a lender.

Regular Fast-Pay Mortgage. Where a mortgage is paid weekly, bi-weekly or semi-monthly but no extra mortgage payments are made to the lender each year. As the regular annual payment is divided into smaller pieces, it does not save borrowers much money.

Term. The life of the mortgage; the period of time until the mortgage matures.

Weekly Mortgages. (Also known as weekly payment mortgages.) Where the mortgage payment is made weekly instead of monthly; of the three types of weekly mortgages available (accelerated, regular and minimum amortized), only the accelerated type will significantly reduce the time needed to retire the loan, and the amount of interest payable.

Introduction

Although interest rates plummeted in 1992, borrowers are still complaining — but for a different and most pleasant reason. Rates have fallen so low, existing amortization books are out-of-date!

Besides, no Canadian amortization book reflects the widespread use of weekly, bi-weekly and semi-monthly mortgages, the so-called "fast-pay" loans embraced by a large number of borrowers. **Because lenders calculate these loans in three different ways with widely varying results, many people have been paying their mortgages more often than monthly with little actual saving in time and money.**

The mortgage payment tables in this book reflect the new interest rate reality. By providing details of the different weekly, bi-weekly and semi-weekly payment plans, borrowers can finally ensure that they fully benefit when arranging a fast-pay loan. Rates range from 4% to 18% in increments of 1/8%, all calculated in the standard Canadian manner of half-yearly, not in advance.

Unlike traditional amortization books that list an overwhelming series of numbers, all the data for an interest rate appear neatly presented on just one page.

How to Use This Book

Current amortization books contain many different principal amounts. This book takes a simpler approach, using only one figure for each interest rate — $1,000. The payment for any principal amount can easily be determined, regardless of how often the mortgage is paid, based on this one number. For this reason, it will be helpful to have a pen, calculator and paper nearby when using this book.

How Does This Work?

Let's calculate the *blended monthly payment* for a mortgage of $75,000 at 10% per year, payable monthly, amortized over 25 years. According to the 10% table, 25-year amortization (page 65), the blended monthly payment of principal and interest for a $1,000 loan is $8.94487. Multiply this figure by $75,000, then divide it by $1,000 for the correct monthly payment — $670.86525 (rounded off to $670.87).

If this was an *accelerated weekly payment mortgage*, according to the same 10% table, 25-year amortization, the blended weekly payment of principal and interest for a $1,000 loan would be $2.23622. Multiply this figure by $75,000, then divide by $1,000 for the correct weekly payment — $167.7165 (rounded to $167.72).

Obviously the payment will vary depending on the balance owing, the applicable interest rate, the amortization chosen, and how often the mortgage is repaid.

To help with this, only six amortizations appear in the tables (from 5 years to 30 years) at 5-year intervals. Virtually all mortgages are booked based on one of these periods, the most popular being 25 years, even when they're being paid weekly, bi-weekly or semi-monthly. While this makes the book considerably easier to use, little of substance has been lost for the vast majority of borrowers. Space also appears in the Appendix at the end of this book where you can easily prepare your own payment schedule regardless of how often the mortgage is paid or the amount paid each time.

All calculations for weekly/bi-weekly/semi-monthly payments are based on a "365-day year" used by Canadian institutional lenders.

While the information in this book has been carefully prepared, there is no warranty of total accuracy. Actual numbers may also vary due to rounding.

1

Weekly, Bi-weekly and Semi-monthly Mortgages — Appearances Can Be Deceiving

Mortgages paid weekly, bi-weekly and semi-monthly are supposed to save Canadian borrowers thousands of dollars of interest. They do — but not always. And that can be an unpleasant surprise to the unwary. **Despite what many people assume, just because a mortgage is paid faster than monthly does not automatically result in significant savings.** What really matters is how the amount to be paid — be it weekly, every two weeks or twice a month — is determined.

Without any standards or guidelines on how they should be calculated, three different types of fast-pay mortgages are being offered by Canadian lenders today. For simplicity, all three payment types will be described in what follows as "weekly mortgages."

The *accelerated weekly payment mortgage* does what borrowers expect: significantly reduces the high cost of mortgage financing and the time needed to fully pay it off. The second, *regular weekly payment mortgage,* is a pale alternative that accomplishes little, while the last, *minimum amortized weekly payment mortgage,* is nothing more than a shuffling of the deck.

Monthly Payment Mortgage (A)

To see how effective the various types of weekly mortgages are, it's necessary to have a yardstick against which to compare other calculations. Assume $100,000 is borrowed at 10% per year amortized over 25 years and repaid monthly. The monthly payment calculated from the 10% table for this conventional mortgage is $894.49. Over 25 years the total interest payable on this loan would be $168,343.

Accelerated Weekly (B), Bi-weekly (E) and Semi-monthly (H) Payment Mortgages

To most borrowers, properly structuring a weekly payment mortgage means paying 1/4 of the normal monthly payment every week (or 1/2 of that payment every two weeks for a bi-weekly payment mortgage). Calculated this way, the weekly payment would be $223.62 and the bi-weekly payment $447.24. Paid weekly to maturity the loan would be paid off in 18.68 years (see 10% table, 25-year amortization, line B) instead of 25 years. A bi-weekly payment to maturity would retire the loan in 18.73 years (see 10% table, 25-year amortization, line E). The savings over six years? About $50,000 in interest.

Why the significant savings? Although there are 12 months in a year, there are 13 4-week periods. This type of mortgage ensures that an extra monthly payment will be paid each year in addition to the regular payment. Every penny of that extra payment is used to reduce the outstanding principal. In turn, this lowers the total interest payable for the loan.

The beauty of this "genuine" form of weekly mortgage payment is its simplicity. It *automatically* arranges for the extra payment to be made each year, and in small, manageable amounts ($17.20 every week or $34.40 every two weeks).

A slightly different approach is needed to calculate the semi-monthly payments (line H). In order to have this built-in extra payment, the monthly payment must be multiplied by 13, with the result divided by 24. Again, one extra month's mortgage payment will be paid each year, the total applied to the principal amount.

The $100,000 mortgage in the example has a monthly payment $894.49. To accelerate this payment, multiply this amount by 13 and divide by 24. This gives a semi-monthly payment of $484.51 and retires the loan in just 18.84 years.

Regular Weekly (C), Bi-weekly (F) and Semi-monthly Payment Mortgages

Most lenders today have dubbed the above types of weekly, bi-weekly and semi-monthly loans "accelerated payment" mortgages. How do some major institutional lenders butcher the pure accelerated payment approach? Instead of taking the normal *monthly* payment and dividing it by four for a weekly payment or two for a bi-weekly payment, they take the total *annual* payment and divide it by 52 or 26. For a semi-monthly payment, the monthly payment is multiplied by 12 only, and then divided by 24. No extra built-in payment is paid each year.

Obviously a mortgage calculated this way will have a lower payment. For example, the weekly payment falls from $223.62 to $206.42; the amount paid bi-weekly will be $412.84, not $447.24; and the semi-monthly payment moves from $484.51 to $447.24. Incidentally the money saved is principal and not interest, since the difference in the numbers is the built-in prepayment of principal that borrowers get with an accelerated payment.

How much time will be saved off the conventional 25 years if a mortgage is paid weekly but without the built-in annual prepayment? Not much. Calculated this way borrowers must still pay for 24.46 years (weekly), 24.55 years (bi-weekly) and 24.78 years (semi-monthly) instead of 25 years before retiring the loan. Dollar-wise, the savings over 25 years are just a few thousand dollars. Sleight of hand perhaps, but still technically it's a weekly/bi-weekly/semi-monthly mortgage payment!

Since this approach carves the regular annual payment into smaller pieces, it's known as a *regular fast-pay payment*. Loan type "C" is the regular weekly payment, "F" is the regular bi-weekly payment, while the regular semi-monthly payment is type "J."

Minimum Amortized Weekly (D), Bi-weekly (G) and Semi-monthly (K) Payment Mortgages

But wait. The odd lender offers borrowers even less under the banner of weekly mortgages! Here the payment is simply recalculated using a 25-year amortization (to $205.34 for a weekly mortgage, $411.07 for a bi-weekly mortgage, and $446.33 for a semi-monthly mortgage). The lowest payment of all, and also the least effective.

How much time is needed to pay off the loan? If you guessed 25 years, you're right! Once again the reduced payment is a savings of principal, not interest, since the missing money is the built-in prepayment of principal (not interest). But once again, despite what it doesn't do — it's still a weekly payment mortgage!

For a minimum amortized weekly payment see line "D"; for the minimum amortized bi-weekly and semi-monthly payments see lines "G" and "K" on the charts.

How to Negotiate an Accelerated Payment Mortgage

How can borrowers ensure they get an accelerated payment mortgage? Here's a simple answer. When negotiating a mortgage, don't discuss weekly, bi-weekly or semi-monthly payments at the outset. Find out what the normal monthly payment would be, amortized over 25 years, and verify that figure with the information on line "A" of the applicable rate and amortization (in our example, $894.49). And don't worry if the number is out by a few cents. Close enough is good enough.

When finalizing the loan, divide that figure by four for a weekly mortgage and two for a bi-weekly mortgage. For a semi-monthly payment mortgage, multiply the monthly payment by 13, and divide the result by 24. Once again, verify that figure with the information on the applicable line of the same chart (line B, E or H depending on payment), ignoring differences in pennies.

If the numbers match, or nearly match — book the mortgage. So if you're told in our example that the weekly payment will be $223.62, the bi-weekly payment $447.24 or the semi-monthly payment $484.51, you're getting the real thing — an accelerated mortgage payment. Anything significantly less is a trap to be avoided. You could be deceived into arranging a loan that is called a weekly mortgage and that is paid every week, but ultimately accomplishes next to nothing.

Tracking Your Payments

Once the loan is advanced, keep track of your payments using the chart appearing in the Appendix. Instructions there will help you create a customized payment schedule reflecting the exact amount borrowed, the interest rate, the amount paid, and how often the payments are due. Having this information will be extremely useful at renewal time, when most borrowers have no way of verifying the number given to them as the balance outstanding on their loan. And who wants to renew a mortgage blindly, without knowing what is actually owing?

2

Preparing Your Own Payment Schedule

When the payment is blended, the amount paid for principal and interest *together* remains the same each payment period — be it monthly, weekly, bi-weekly or semi-monthly. But the make-up of the payment changes, with more money allocated to principal and less to interest over time. This means borrowers have a difficult time calculating how much of each payment is interest and how much is principal, not to mention the balance owing at any given time.

An amortization or payment schedule helps provide the answers. While computerized schedules can be ordered, that becomes expensive when a mortgage is paid more frequently than monthly, if the amount paid is changed, or if the loan is renewed often (every six months or one year).

How to Prepare a Payment Schedule

Armed with the following information:

a) the balance owing after the most recent payment was made (this will be the amount borrowed for new mortgages)
b) the interest rate, and how frequently it is calculated (this book assumes the mortgage is calculated half-yearly and not in advance, the norm for Canadian mortgages)
c) the amount of the blended payment (principal and interest only; ignore any tax component in the mortgage payment)
d) how frequently it is paid (monthly, weekly, bi-weekly or semi-monthly)

e) the date of the *next* payment
f) the interest factor for the interest rate and type of payment

plus the pen, calculator and pad of paper, borrowers can create their own customized payment schedule right in this book! (See Appendix.)

Assembling items (a) through (e) shouldn't be too difficult. If all the information isn't available, check your mortgage document or consult your lender.

Interest Factor

But what about item (f), the interest factor for the interest rate and type of payment?

No need to worry. Starting at page 133 are the *interest factors* for loans of $1,000 at various interest rates calculated half-yearly and not in advance for weekly, bi-weekly and semi-monthly mortgages — the very information needed for (f).

What, though, is an interest factor? It's a number used to calculate the interest component of a mortgage payment based on how often the mortgage is paid (whenever a mortgage is paid more often (monthly, weekly, bi-weekly or semi-monthly) than the interest is calculated — half-yearly — an interest factor is needed). Once the interest component has been satisfied, any additional amount paid each payment becomes the principal component of that payment. This principal component in turn reduces the balance owing on the loan, the number on which future calculations are based.

To help understand the situation, let's examine the interest factors (in dollars) for a loan of $1,000 at 10% from the interest factor table:

monthly interest factor	$8.16485
weekly interest factor	$1.87316
bi-weekly interest factor	$3.74982
semi-monthly interest factor	$4.07412

To determine the interest component of a mortgage payment, it's necessary to multiply the appropriate interest factor by the balance owing and then divide the result by $1,000, regardless of how frequently it is paid. In other words:

$$\frac{interest\ factor \times balance\ owing}{\$1000} = interest\ component$$

So if $100,000 is the amount owing on the mortgage, the interest component for this month's payment is the monthly interest factor ($8.16485), multiplied by the balance owing ($100,000), divided by $1,000, or:

$$\frac{\$8.16485 \times \$100,000}{\$1000} = \$816.485$$

rounded to $816.49. The amount paid that month greater than $816.49 is the principal component of that monthly payment.

Now look at the table for 10% loans with monthly payments (payment type A). If the loan is amortized over 25 years, the blended monthly payment is $894.49 (see page 4 for an explanation of this calculation). As noted above, the interest component of that month's payment is $816.49. Deduct $816.49 from the monthly payment of $894.49, and the remainder ($78.00) is the principal component of that month's payment. This $78.00 principal component will reduce the balance owing at the end of the first month to $99,922.00.

For the second month, repeat the process based on the new, reduced balance owing of $99,922.00. Since the interest factor remains the same, the interest component of the second month's payment now is $8.16485 (interest factor) multiplied by $99,922.00 divided by $1,000, or $815.85. Since the $894.49 blended monthly payment remains constant, the principal component of the second month's payment is $894.49 less $815.85 — namely $78.64. When this $78.64 is deducted from the balance owing at the end of the first month, the balance owing at the end of the second month falls from $99,922.00 to $99,843.36.

Similar calculations can be made for blended weekly, bi-weekly or semi-monthly mortgages too, regardless of their payment type. Assume the $100,000 loan was an accelerated weekly payment loan (type "B") originally amortized over 25 years that will be retired in just 18.68 years. The blended weekly payment: $223.62. But the interest component is only $187.32 (derived by multiplying the weekly interest factor of $1.87316 by $100,000 and dividing it by $1,000, or:

$$\frac{\$1.87316 \times \$100,000}{\$1000} = \$187.316$$

and then rounding up the result. The principal component of that blended payment: $223.62 less $187.32, or $36.30, which reduces the balance owing at the end of the first week to $99,963.70.

Many mortgages today allow borrowers to increase their payments over time, a move which will result in significant savings. But then it becomes difficult to calculate how much of each new blended payment is interest and how much is principal. Well, this is not a problem here: **Even if the amount paid does not appear in the book, exactly the same steps are taken to allocate that new payment between interest and principal, and to determine the balance owing on the mortgage**.

For example, say $235.00 is selected as the blended weekly payment on an accelerated weekly payment loan of $100,000. As the interest component once again is $187.32, the principal component of that first payment would be $235.00 less $187.32, or $47.68. The balance owing at the end of the first week on this loan: $99,952.32 ($100,000 less $47.68).

Week two repeats the process, this time based on the reduced balance owing of $99,952.32. Since the weekly interest factor is $1.87316, the interest component of the second week's payment would be $1.87316 multiplied by $99,952.32 divided by $1,000, or:

$$\frac{\$1.87316 \times \$99,952.32}{\$1000} = \$187.23$$

Since the $235.00 blended weekly payment remains the same, the difference between it and the $187.23 interest component for the second week's payment is the principal component of the second week's payment — $47.77. Therefore after the second week's payment is made, the balance owing falls by $47.77, from $99,952.32 to $99,904.55.

Here's what a customized payment schedule would look like for this loan, if the first payment was made January 1:

Payment Number	Date	Payment Made	Interest Component	Principal Component	Balance Owing
1	Jan 01	$235.00	$187.32	$47.68	$99,952.32
2	Jan 08	235.00	187.23	47.77	99,904.55
3	Jan 15	235.00	187.14	47.86	99,856.69
4	Jan 22	235.00	187.05	47.95	99,808.74
5	Jan 29	235.00	186.96	48.04	99,760.70

When doing the calculations, remember: the balance owing at the end of one payment (whether it be a monthly or one of the fast-pay alternatives) is multiplied by the appropriate interest factor and then divided by $1,000 to get the interest component for the next payment. When that interest component is deducted from the blended payment, the result is the principal component for the next payment. To get the balance owing at the end of this second payment deduct the principal component for the second payment from the balance owing at the end of the first payment . . . and so on.

Don't forget: space is provided at the end of the book where you can prepare your own unique customized payment schedule.

3

Blended
Payment
Schedules

4%

BLENDED PAYMENTS IN DOLLARS OF PRINCIPAL AND IN-
TEREST FOR A LOAN OF $1,000 AT 4% PER YEAR, CALCULATED
HALF-YEARLY, NOT IN ADVANCE

TYPE OF PMT	PMTS EACH YEAR	PMT EACH PERIOD	YEARS TO RETIRE LOAN	TYPE OF PMT	PMTS EACH YEAR	PMT EACH PERIOD	YEARS TO RETIRE LOAN
5 YEAR AMORTIZATION				**10 YEAR AMORTIZATION**			
A	12	$18.40166	5.00	A	12	$10.10887	10.00
B	52	4.60042	4.57	B	52	2.52722	9.05
C	52	4.24654	4.99	C	52	2.33282	9.98
D	52	4.24003	5.00	D	52	2.32867	10.00
E	26	9.20083	4.57	E	26	5.05444	9.06
F	26	8.49308	4.99	F	26	4.66563	9.98
G	26	8.48329	5.00	G	26	4.65911	10.00
H	24	9.96757	4.57	H	24	5.47564	9.06
J	24	9.20083	5.00	J	24	5.05444	9.99
K	24	9.19324	5.00	K	24	5.05026	10.00
15 YEAR AMORTIZATION				**20 YEAR AMORTIZATION**			
A	12	$7.38039	15.00	A	12	$6.04246	20.00
B	52	1.84510	13.44	B	52	1.51062	17.70
C	52	1.70317	14.96	C	52	1.39441	19.93
D	52	1.69976	15.00	D	52	1.39133	20.00
E	26	3.69019	13.44	E	26	3.02123	17.71
F	26	3.40633	14.97	F	26	2.78883	19.94
G	26	3.40080	15.00	G	26	2.78372	20.00
H	24	3.99771	13.46	H	24	3.27300	17.74
J	24	3.69019	14.98	J	24	3.02123	19.97
K	24	3.68715	15.00	K	24	3.01874	20.00
25 YEAR AMORTIZATION				**30 YEAR AMORTIZATION**			
A	12	$5.26020	25.00	A	12	$4.75519	30.00
B	52	1.31505	21.83	B	52	1.18880	25.81
C	52	1.21389	24.90	C	52	1.09735	29.85
D	52	1.21097	25.00	D	52	1.09452	30.00
E	26	2.63010	21.84	E	26	2.37759	25.83
F	26	2.42779	24.91	F	26	2.19470	29.87
G	26	2.42287	25.00	G	26	2.18987	30.00
H	24	2.84928	21.88	H	24	2.57573	25.88
J	24	2.63010	24.96	J	24	2.37759	29.95
K	24	2.62793	25.00	K	24	2.37563	30.00

TYPES OF PAYMENTS: A—monthly; B—accelerated weekly; C—
regular weekly; D—minimum amortized weekly; E—accelerated
bi-weekly; F—regular bi-weekly; G—minimum amortized bi-
weekly; H—accelerated semi-monthly; J—regular semi-monthly;
K—minimum amortized semi-monthly

4.125%

BLENDED PAYMENTS IN DOLLARS OF PRINCIPAL AND INTEREST FOR A LOAN OF $1,000 AT **4.125%** PER YEAR, CALCULATED HALF-YEARLY, NOT IN ADVANCE

TYPE OF PMT	PMTS EACH YEAR	PMT EACH PERIOD	YEARS TO RETIRE LOAN	TYPE OF PMT	PMTS EACH YEAR	PMT EACH PERIOD	YEARS TO RETIRE LOAN
5 YEAR AMORTIZATION				**10 YEAR AMORTIZATION**			
A	12	$18.45716	5.00	A	12	$10.16734	10.00
B	52	4.61429	4.57	B	52	2.54183	9.05
C	52	4.25934	4.99	C	52	2.34631	9.98
D	52	4.25262	5.00	D	52	2.34202	10.00
E	26	9.22858	4.57	E	26	5.08367	9.05
F	26	8.51869	4.99	F	26	4.69262	9.98
G	26	8.50857	5.00	G	26	4.68586	10.00
H	24	9.99763	4.57	H	24	5.50731	9.06
J	24	9.22858	5.00	J	24	5.08367	9.99
K	24	9.22073	5.00	K	24	5.07934	10.00
15 YEAR AMORTIZATION				**20 YEAR AMORTIZATION**			
A	12	$7.44206	15.00	A	12	$6.10733	20.00
B	52	1.86051	13.42	B	52	1.52683	17.67
C	52	1.71740	14.96	C	52	1.40938	19.93
D	52	1.71386	15.00	D	52	1.40618	20.00
E	26	3.72103	13.43	E	26	3.05366	17.68
F	26	3.43480	14.97	F	26	2.81877	19.94
G	26	3.42906	15.00	G	26	2.81345	20.00
H	24	4.03111	13.44	H	24	3.30814	17.71
J	24	3.72103	14.98	J	24	3.05366	19.97
K	24	3.71786	15.00	K	24	3.05107	20.00
25 YEAR AMORTIZATION				**30 YEAR AMORTIZATION**			
A	12	$5.32818	25.00	A	12	$4.82618	30.00
B	52	1.33205	21.78	B	52	1.20654	25.73
C	52	1.22958	24.89	C	52	1.11373	29.84
D	52	1.22654	25.00	D	52	1.11078	30.00
E	26	2.66409	21.80	E	26	2.41309	25.75
F	26	2.45916	24.91	F	26	2.22747	29.87
G	26	2.45404	25.00	G	26	2.22243	30.00
H	24	2.88610	21.83	H	24	2.61418	25.81
J	24	2.66409	24.96	J	24	2.41309	29.95
K	24	2.66183	25.00	K	24	2.41104	30.00

TYPES OF PAYMENTS: A—monthly; B—accelerated weekly; C—regular weekly; D—minimum amortized weekly; E—accelerated bi-weekly; F—regular bi-weekly; G—minimum amortized bi-weekly; H—accelerated semi-monthly; J—regular semi-monthly; K—minimum amortized semi-monthly

4.25%

BLENDED PAYMENTS IN DOLLARS OF PRINCIPAL AND IN-
TEREST FOR A LOAN OF $1,000 AT **4.25%** PER YEAR, CALCU-
LATED HALF-YEARLY, NOT IN ADVANCE

TYPE OF PMT	PMTS EACH YEAR	PMT EACH PERIOD	YEARS TO RETIRE LOAN	TYPE OF PMT	PMTS EACH YEAR	PMT EACH PERIOD	YEARS TO RETIRE LOAN
5 YEAR AMORTIZATION				**10 YEAR AMORTIZATION**			
A	12	$18.51273	5.00	A	12	$10.22598	10.00
B	52	4.62818	4.57	B	52	2.55660	9.04
C	52	4.27217	4.99	C	52	2.35984	9.98
D	52	4.26522	5.00	D	52	2.35540	10.00
E	26	9.25637	4.57	E	26	5.11299	9.05
F	26	8.54434	4.99	F	26	4.71968	9.98
G	26	8.53389	5.00	G	26	4.71269	10.00
H	24	10.02773	4.57	H	24	5.53907	9.05
J	24	9.25637	5.00	J	24	5.11299	9.99
K	24	9.24826	5.00	K	24	5.10851	10.00
15 YEAR AMORTIZATION				**20 YEAR AMORTIZATION**			
A	12	$7.50400	15.00	A	12	$6.17255	20.00
B	52	1.87600	13.41	B	52	1.54314	17.64
C	52	1.73169	14.96	C	52	1.42443	19.93
D	52	1.72802	15.00	D	52	1.42110	20.00
E	26	3.75200	13.41	E	26	3.08627	17.65
F	26	3.46338	14.96	F	26	2.84887	19.94
G	26	3.45743	15.00	G	26	2.84335	20.00
H	24	4.06466	13.43	H	24	3.34346	17.68
J	24	3.75200	14.98	J	24	3.08627	19.97
K	24	3.74871	15.00	K	24	3.08357	20.00
25 YEAR AMORTIZATION				**30 YEAR AMORTIZATION**			
A	12	$5.39660	25.00	A	12	$4.89768	30.00
B	52	1.34915	21.73	B	52	1.22442	25.65
C	52	1.24537	24.89	C	52	1.13023	29.84
D	52	1.24221	25.00	D	52	1.12716	30.00
E	26	2.69830	21.75	E	26	2.44884	25.67
F	26	2.49074	24.91	F	26	2.26047	29.86
G	26	2.48542	25.00	G	26	2.25523	30.00
H	24	2.92316	21.79	H	24	2.65291	25.73
J	24	2.69830	24.96	J	24	2.44884	29.95
K	24	2.69594	25.00	K	24	2.44669	30.00

TYPES OF PAYMENTS: A—monthly; B—accelerated weekly; C—
regular weekly; D—minimum amortized weekly; E—accelerated
bi-weekly; F—regular bi-weekly; G—minimum amortized bi-
weekly; H—accelerated semi-monthly; J—regular semi-monthly;
K—minimum amortized semi-monthly

4.375%

BLENDED PAYMENTS IN DOLLARS OF PRINCIPAL AND IN-
TEREST FOR A LOAN OF $1,000 AT **4.375%** PER YEAR, CALCU-
LATED HALF-YEARLY, NOT IN ADVANCE

TYPE OF PMT	PMTS EACH YEAR	PMT EACH PERIOD	YEARS TO RETIRE LOAN	TYPE OF PMT	PMTS EACH YEAR	PMT EACH PERIOD	YEARS TO RETIRE LOAN
5 YEAR AMORTIZATION				**10 YEAR AMORTIZATION**			
A	12	$18.56838	5.00	A	12	$10.28480	10.00
B	52	4.64209	4.57	B	52	2.57120	9.04
C	52	4.28501	4.99	C	52	2.37342	9.98
D	52	4.27784	5.00	D	52	2.36882	10.00
E	26	9.28419	4.57	E	26	5.14240	9.04
F	26	8.57002	4.99	F	26	4.74683	9.98
G	26	8.55923	5.00	G	26	4.73960	10.00
H	24	10.05787	4.57	H	24	5.57093	9.05
J	24	9.28419	4.99	J	24	5.14240	9.99
K	24	9.27582	5.00	K	24	5.13776	10.00
15 YEAR AMORTIZATION				**20 YEAR AMORTIZATION**			
A	12	$7.56620	15.00	A	12	$6.23812	20.00
B	52	1.89155	13.39	B	52	1.55953	17.61
C	52	1.74605	14.95	C	52	1.43957	19.92
D	52	1.74224	15.00	D	52	1.43611	20.00
E	26	3.78310	13.40	E	26	3.11906	17.62
F	26	3.49209	14.96	F	26	2.87913	19.94
G	26	3.48593	15.00	G	26	2.87341	20.00
H	24	4.09836	13.41	H	24	3.37898	17.65
J	24	3.78310	14.98	J	24	3.11906	19.97
K	24	3.77969	15.00	K	24	3.11625	20.00
25 YEAR AMORTIZATION				**30 YEAR AMORTIZATION**			
A	12	$5.46545	25.00	A	12	$4.96967	30.00
B	52	1.36636	21.68	B	52	1.24242	25.57
C	52	1.26126	24.88	C	52	1.14685	29.83
D	52	1.25797	25.00	D	52	1.14365	30.00
E	26	2.73273	21.70	E	26	2.48483	25.59
F	26	2.52252	24.90	F	26	2.29369	29.85
G	26	2.51699	25.00	G	26	2.28824	30.00
H	24	2.96045	21.74	H	24	2.69190	25.65
J	24	2.73273	24.96	J	24	2.48483	29.94
K	24	2.73026	25.00	K	24	2.48259	30.00

TYPES OF PAYMENTS: A—monthly; B—accelerated weekly; C—
regular weekly; D—minimum amortized weekly; E—accelerated
bi-weekly; F—regular bi-weekly; G—minimum amortized bi-
weekly; H—accelerated semi-monthly; J—regular semi-monthly;
K—minimum amortized semi-monthly

4.5%

BLENDED PAYMENTS IN DOLLARS OF PRINCIPAL AND IN-
TEREST FOR A LOAN OF $1,000 AT **4.5%** PER YEAR, CALCU-
LATED HALF-YEARLY, NOT IN ADVANCE

TYPE OF PMT	PMTS EACH YEAR	PMT EACH PERIOD	YEARS TO RETIRE LOAN	TYPE OF PMT	PMTS EACH YEAR	PMT EACH PERIOD	YEARS TO RETIRE LOAN
5 YEAR AMORTIZATION				**10 YEAR AMORTIZATION**			
A	12	$18.62410	5.00	A	12	$10.34379	10.00
B	52	4.65603	4.56	B	52	2.58595	9.03
C	52	4.29787	4.99	C	52	2.38703	9.97
D	52	4.29048	5.00	D	52	2.38228	10.00
E	26	9.31205	4.57	E	26	5.17190	9.03
F	26	8.59574	4.99	F	26	4.77406	9.98
G	26	8.58462	5.00	G	26	4.76659	10.00
H	24	10.08806	4.57	H	24	5.60289	9.04
J	24	9.31205	4.99	J	24	5.17190	9.99
K	24	9.30342	5.00	K	24	5.16710	10.00
15 YEAR AMORTIZATION				**20 YEAR AMORTIZATION**			
A	12	$7.62868	15.00	A	12	$6.30405	20.00
B	52	1.90717	13.38	B	52	1.57601	17.58
C	52	1.76046	14.95	C	52	1.45478	19.92
D	52	1.75652	15.00	D	52	1.45119	20.00
E	26	3.81434	13.38	E	26	3.15203	17.60
F	26	3.52093	14.96	F	26	2.90956	19.93
G	26	3.51455	15.00	G	26	2.90363	20.00
H	24	4.13220	13.40	H	24	3.41469	17.62
J	24	3.81434	14.98	J	24	3.15203	19.97
K	24	3.81080	15.00	K	24	3.14910	20.00
25 YEAR AMORTIZATION				**30 YEAR AMORTIZATION**			
A	12	$5.53473	25.00	A	12	$5.04216	30.00
B	52	1.38368	21.63	B	52	1.26054	25.49
C	52	1.27725	24.88	C	52	1.16357	29.82
D	52	1.27383	25.00	D	52	1.16025	30.00
E	26	2.76736	21.64	E	26	2.52108	25.51
F	26	2.55449	24.90	F	26	2.32715	29.85
G	26	2.54875	25.00	G	26	2.32149	30.00
H	24	2.99798	21.69	H	24	2.73117	25.57
J	24	2.76736	24.96	J	24	2.52108	29.94
K	24	2.76480	25.00	K	24	2.51874	30.00

TYPES OF PAYMENTS: A—monthly; B—accelerated weekly; C—
regular weekly; D—minimum amortized weekly; E—accelerated
bi-weekly; F—regular bi-weekly; G—minimum amortized bi-
weekly; H—accelerated semi-monthly; J—regular semi-monthly;
K—minimum amortized semi-monthly

4.625%

BLENDED PAYMENTS IN DOLLARS OF PRINCIPAL AND IN-
TEREST FOR A LOAN OF $1,000 AT **4.625%** PER YEAR, CALCU-
LATED HALF-YEARLY, NOT IN ADVANCE

TYPE OF PMT	PMTS EACH YEAR	PMT EACH PERIOD	YEARS TO RETIRE LOAN	TYPE OF PMT	PMTS EACH YEAR	PMT EACH PERIOD	YEARS TO RETIRE LOAN
5 YEAR AMORTIZATION				**10 YEAR AMORTIZATION**			
A	12	$18.67990	5.00	A	12	$10.40296	10.00
B	52	4.66997	4.56	B	52	2.60074	9.02
C	52	4.31075	4.99	C	52	2.40068	9.97
D	52	4.30313	5.00	D	52	2.39578	10.00
E	26	9.33995	4.57	E	26	5.20148	9.03
F	26	8.62149	4.99	F	26	4.80137	9.98
G	26	8.61003	5.00	G	26	4.79365	10.00
H	24	10.11828	4.57	H	24	5.63494	9.04
J	24	9.33995	4.99	J	24	5.20148	9.99
K	24	9.33105	5.00	K	24	5.19652	10.00
15 YEAR AMORTIZATION				**20 YEAR AMORTIZATION**			
A	12	$7.69142	15.00	A	12	$6.37033	20.00
B	52	1.92286	13.36	B	52	1.59258	17.55
C	52	1.77494	14.95	C	52	1.47008	19.92
D	52	1.77087	15.00	D	52	1.46636	20.00
E	26	3.84571	13.37	E	26	3.18517	17.57
F	26	3.54989	14.96	F	26	2.94015	19.93
G	26	3.54328	15.00	G	26	2.93400	20.00
H	24	4.16619	13.38	H	24	3.45060	17.59
J	24	3.84571	14.98	J	24	3.18517	19.97
K	24	3.84205	15.00	K	24	3.18213	20.00
25 YEAR AMORTIZATION				**30 YEAR AMORTIZATION**			
A	12	$5.50443	25.00	A	12	$5.11513	30.00
B	52	1.40111	21.58	B	52	1.27878	25.41
C	52	1.29333	24.87	C	52	1.18041	29.81
D	52	1.28979	25.00	D	52	1.17696	30.00
E	26	2.80222	21.59	E	26	2.55756	25.43
F	26	2.58666	24.89	F	26	2.36083	29.84
G	26	2.58071	25.00	G	26	2.35495	30.00
H	24	3.03573	21.64	H	24	2.77067	25.49
J	24	2.80222	24.96	J	24	2.55756	29.94
K	24	2.79955	25.00	K	24	2.55513	30.00

TYPES OF PAYMENTS: A—monthly; B—accelerated weekly; C—
regular weekly; D—minimum amortized weekly; E—accelerated
bi-weekly; F—regular bi-weekly; G—minimum amortized bi-
weekly; H—accelerated semi-monthly; J—regular semi-monthly;
K—minimum amortized semi-monthly

4.75%

BLENDED PAYMENTS IN DOLLARS OF PRINCIPAL AND INTEREST FOR A LOAN OF $1,000 AT **4.75%** PER YEAR, CALCULATED HALF-YEARLY, NOT IN ADVANCE

TYPE OF PMT	PMTS EACH YEAR	PMT EACH PERIOD	YEARS TO RETIRE LOAN	TYPE OF PMT	PMTS EACH YEAR	PMT EACH PERIOD	YEARS TO RETIRE LOAN
5 YEAR AMORTIZATION				**10 YEAR AMORTIZATION**			
A	12	$18.73577	5.00	A	12	$10.46230	10.00
B	52	4.68394	4.56	B	52	2.61557	9.02
C	52	4.32364	4.99	C	52	2.41438	9.97
D	52	4.31580	5.00	D	52	2.40931	10.00
E	26	9.36789	4.56	E	26	5.23115	9.02
F	26	8.64728	4.99	F	26	4.82875	9.98
G	26	8.63548	5.00	G	26	4.82080	10.00
H	24	10.14854	4.57	H	24	5.66708	9.03
J	24	9.36789	4.99	J	24	5.23115	9.99
K	24	9.35872	5.00	K	24	5.22603	10.00
15 YEAR AMORTIZATION				**20 YEAR AMORTIZATION**			
A	12	$7.75443	15.00	A	12	$6.43696	20.00
B	52	1.93861	13.35	B	52	1.60924	17.52
C	52	1.78948	14.95	C	52	1.48545	19.91
D	52	1.78527	15.00	D	52	1.48160	20.00
E	26	3.87722	13.35	E	26	3.21848	17.53
F	26	3.57897	14.96	F	26	2.97090	19.93
G	26	3.57214	15.00	G	26	2.96454	20.00
H	24	4.20032	13.37	H	24	3.48669	17.56
J	24	3.87722	14.98	J	24	3.21848	19.97
K	24	3.87342	15.00	K	24	3.21533	20.00
25 YEAR AMORTIZATION				**30 YEAR AMORTIZATION**			
A	12	$5.67456	25.00	A	12	$5.18858	30.00
B	52	1.41864	21.52	B	52	1.29715	25.32
C	52	1.30951	24.87	C	52	1.19736	29.80
D	52	1.30584	25.00	D	52	1.19378	30.00
E	26	2.83728	21.54	E	26	2.59429	25.34
F	26	2.61903	24.89	F	26	2.39473	29.83
G	26	2.61286	25.00	G	26	2.38864	30.00
H	24	3.07372	21.59	H	24	2.81048	25.41
J	24	2.83728	24.95	J	24	2.59429	29.94
K	24	2.83450	25.00	K	24	2.59175	30.00

TYPES OF PAYMENTS: A—monthly; B—accelerated weekly; C—regular weekly; D—minimum amortized weekly; E—accelerated bi-weekly; F—regular bi-weekly; G—minimum amortized bi-weekly; H—accelerated semi-monthly; J—regular semi-monthly; K—minimum amortized semi-monthly

4.875%

BLENDED PAYMENTS IN DOLLARS OF PRINCIPAL AND IN-
TEREST FOR A LOAN OF $1,000 AT **4.875%** PER YEAR, CALCU-
LATED HALF-YEARLY, NOT IN ADVANCE

TYPE OF PMT	PMTS EACH YEAR	PMT EACH PERIOD	YEARS TO RETIRE LOAN	TYPE OF PMT	PMTS EACH YEAR	PMT EACH PERIOD	YEARS TO RETIRE LOAN
5 YEAR AMORTIZATION				**10 YEAR AMORTIZATION**			
A	12	$18.79172	5.00	A	12	$10.52181	10.00
B	52	4.69793	4.56	B	52	2.63045	9.01
C	52	4.33655	4.99	C	52	2.42811	9.97
D	52	4.32848	5.00	D	52	2.42289	10.00
E	26	9.39586	4.56	E	26	5.26090	9.02
F	26	8.67310	4.99	F	26	4.85622	9.98
G	26	8.66096	5.00	G	26	4.84802	10.00
H	24	10.17885	4.56	H	24	5.69931	9.02
J	24	9.39586	4.99	J	24	5.26090	9.99
K	24	9.38643	5.00	K	24	5.25563	10.00
15 YEAR AMORTIZATION				**20 YEAR AMORTIZATION**			
A	12	$7.81770	15.00	A	12	$6.50393	20.00
B	52	1.95443	13.33	B	52	1.62598	17.49
C	52	1.80409	14.95	C	52	1.50091	19.91
D	52	1.79973	15.00	D	52	1.49693	20.00
E	26	3.90885	13.34	E	26	3.25197	17.50
F	26	3.60817	14.96	F	26	3.00181	19.93
G	26	3.60112	15.00	G	26	2.99523	20.00
H	24	4.23459	13.35	H	24	3.52296	17.53
J	24	3.90885	14.98	J	24	3.25197	19.97
K	24	3.90493	15.00	K	24	3.24870	20.00
25 YEAR AMORTIZATION				**30 YEAR AMORTIZATION**			
A	12	$5.74510	25.00	A	12	$5.26251	30.00
B	52	1.43627	21.47	B	52	1.31563	25.24
C	52	1.32579	24.86	C	52	1.21443	29.80
D	52	1.32199	25.00	D	52	1.21071	30.00
E	26	2.87255	21.49	E	26	2.63125	25.26
F	26	2.65158	24.88	F	26	2.42885	29.83
G	26	2.64520	25.00	G	26	2.42254	30.00
H	24	3.11193	21.53	H	24	2.85053	25.33
J	24	2.87255	24.95	J	24	2.63125	29.93
K	24	2.86967	25.00	K	24	2.62861	30.00

TYPES OF PAYMENTS: A—monthly; B—accelerated weekly; C—
regular weekly; D—minimum amortized weekly; E—accelerated
bi-weekly; F—regular bi-weekly; G—minimum amortized bi-
weekly; H—accelerated semi-monthly; J—regular semi-monthly;
K—minimum amortized semi-monthly

5%

BLENDED PAYMENT IN DOLLARS OF PRINCIPAL AND INTEREST FOR A LOAN OF $1,000 AT **5%** PER YEAR, CALCULATED HALF-YEARLY, NOT IN ADVANCE

TYPE OF PMT	PMTS EACH YEAR	PMT EACH PERIOD	YEARS TO RETIRE LOAN	TYPE OF PMT	PMTS EACH YEAR	PMT EACH PERIOD	YEARS TO RETIRE LOAN
5 YEAR AMORTIZATION				**10 YEAR AMORTIZATION**			
A	12	$18.84774	5.00	A	12	$10.58149	10.00
B	52	4.71193	4.56	B	52	2.64537	9.00
C	52	4.34948	4.99	C	52	2.44188	9.97
D	52	4.34118	5.00	D	52	2.43650	10.00
E	26	9.42387	4.56	E	26	5.29075	9.01
F	26	8.69896	4.99	F	26	4.88377	9.98
G	26	8.68648	5.00	G	26	4.87531	10.00
H	24	10.20919	4.56	H	24	5.73164	9.02
J	24	9.42387	4.99	J	24	5.29075	9.99
K	24	9.41417	5.00	K	24	5.28530	10.00
15 YEAR AMORTIZATION				**20 YEAR AMORTIZATION**			
A	12	$7.88124	15.00	A	12	$6.57125	20.00
B	52	1.97031	13.31	B	52	1.64281	17.46
C	52	1.81875	14.95	C	52	1.51644	19.91
D	52	1.81425	15.00	D	52	1.51232	20.00
E	26	3.94062	13.32	E	26	3.28563	17.47
F	26	3.63749	14.96	F	26	3.03288	19.92
G	26	3.63022	15.00	G	26	3.02608	20.00
H	24	4.26900	13.34	H	24	3.55943	17.50
J	24	3.94062	14.98	J	24	3.28563	19.96
K	24	3.93656	15.00	K	24	3.28224	20.00
25 YEAR AMORTIZATION				**30 YEAR AMORTIZATION**			
A	12	$5.81605	25.00	A	12	$5.33691	30.00
B	52	1.45401	21.41	B	52	1.33423	25.15
C	52	1.34217	24.86	C	52	1.23159	29.79
D	52	1.33823	25.00	D	52	1.22774	30.00
E	26	2.90802	21.43	E	26	2.66845	25.17
F	26	2.68433	24.88	F	26	2.46319	29.82
G	26	2.67773	25.00	G	26	2.45665	30.00
H	24	3.15036	21.48	H	24	2.89082	25.24
J	24	2.90802	24.95	J	24	2.66845	29.93
K	24	2.90503	25.00	K	24	2.66571	30.00

TYPES OF PAYMENTS: A—monthly; B—accelerated weekly; C—regular weekly; D—minimum amortized weekly; E—accelerated bi-weekly; F—regular bi-weekly; G—minimum amortized bi-weekly; H—accelerated semi-monthly; J—regular semi-monthly; K—minimum amortized semi-monthly

5.125%

BLENDED PAYMENTS IN DOLLARS OF PRINCIPAL AND INTEREST FOR A LOAN OF $1,000 AT **5.125%** PER YEAR, CALCULATED HALF-YEARLY, NOT IN ADVANCE

TYPE OF PMT	PMTS EACH YEAR	PMT EACH PERIOD	YEARS TO RETIRE LOAN	TYPE OF PMT	PMTS EACH YEAR	PMT EACH PERIOD	YEARS TO RETIRE LOAN
5 YEAR AMORTIZATION				**10 YEAR AMORTIZATION**			
A	12	$18.90383	5.00	A	12	$10.64135	10.00
B	52	4.72596	4.56	B	52	2.66034	9.00
C	52	4.36242	4.99	C	52	2.45570	9.97
D	52	4.35390	5.00	D	52	2.45015	10.00
E	26	9.45192	4.56	E	26	5.32067	9.00
F	26	9.72485	4.99	F	26	4.91139	9.98
G	26	8.71203	5.00	G	26	4.90269	10.00
H	24	10.23958	4.56	H	24	5.76406	9.01
J	24	9.45192	4.99	J	24	5.32067	9.99
K	24	9.44195	5.00	K	24	5.31507	10.00
15 YEAR AMORTIZATION				**20 YEAR AMORTIZATION**			
A	12	$7.94503	15.00	A	12	$6.63891	20.00
B	52	1.98626	13.30	B	52	1.65973	17.43
C	52	1.83347	14.94	C	52	1.53206	19.90
D	52	1.82883	15.00	D	52	1.52780	20.00
E	26	3.97252	13.31	E	26	3.31945	17.44
F	26	3.66694	14.95	F	26	3.06411	19.92
G	26	3.65944	15.00	G	26	3.05709	20.00
H	24	4.30356	13.32	H	24	3.59608	17.47
J	24	3.97252	14.98	J	24	3.31945	19.96
K	24	3.96833	15.00	K	24	3.31596	20.00
25 YEAR AMORTIZATION				**30 YEAR AMORTIZATION**			
A	12	$5.88741	25.00	A	12	$5.41177	30.00
B	52	1.47185	21.36	B	52	1.35294	25.06
C	52	1.35863	24.85	C	52	1.24887	29.78
D	52	1.35456	25.00	D	52	1.24488	30.00
E	26	2.94371	21.38	E	26	2.70588	25.08
F	26	2.71727	24.87	F	26	2.49774	29.81
G	26	2.71044	25.00	G	26	2.49097	30.00
H	24	3.18902	21.43	H	24	2.93137	25.16
J	24	2.94371	24.95	J	24	2.70588	29.93
K	24	2.94060	25.00	K	24	2.70303	30.00

TYPES OF PAYMENTS: A—monthly; B—accelerated weekly; C—regular weekly; D—minimum amortized weekly; E—accelerated bi-weekly; F—regular bi-weekly; G—minimum amortized bi-weekly; H—accelerated semi-monthly; J—regular semi-monthly; K—minimum amortized semi-monthly

5.25%

BLENDED PAYMENTS IN DOLLARS OF PRINCIPAL AND IN-
TEREST FOR A LOAN OF $1,000 AT **5.25%** PER YEAR, CALCU-
LATED HALF-YEARLY, NOT IN ADVANCE

TYPE OF PMT	PMTS EACH YEAR	PMT EACH PERIOD	YEARS TO RETIRE LOAN	TYPE OF PMT	PMTS EACH YEAR	PMT EACH PERIOD	YEARS TO RETIRE LOAN
5 YEAR AMORTIZATION				**10 YEAR AMORTIZATION**			
A	12	$18.96000	5.00	A	12	$10.70138	10.00
B	52	4.74000	4.56	B	52	2.67534	8.99
C	52	4.37539	4.99	C	52	2.46955	9.97
D	52	4.36663	5.00	D	52	2.46385	10.00
E	26	9.48000	4.56	E	26	5.35069	9.00
F	26	8.75077	4.99	F	26	4.93910	9.98
G	26	8.73761	5.00	G	26	4.93014	10.00
H	24	10.27000	4.56	H	24	5.79658	9.01
J	24	9.48000	4.99	J	24	5.35069	9.99
K	24	9.46977	5.00	K	24	5.34491	10.00
15 YEAR AMORTIZATION				**20 YEAR AMORTIZATION**			
A	12	$8.00904	15.00	A	12	$6.70691	20.00
B	52	2.00227	13.28	B	52	1.67673	17.40
C	52	1.84825	14.94	C	52	1.54775	19.90
D	52	1.84347	15.00	D	52	1.54336	20.00
E	26	4.00455	13.29	E	26	3.35345	17.41
F	26	3.69650	14.95	F	26	3.09550	19.92
G	26	3.68877	15.00	G	26	3.08825	20.00
H	24	4.33826	13.31	H	24	3.63291	17.44
J	24	4.00455	14.98	J	24	3.35345	19.96
K	24	4.00022	15.00	K	24	3.34983	20.00
25 YEAR AMORTIZATION				**30 YEAR AMORTIZATION**			
A	12	$5.95918	25.00	A	12	$5.48708	30.00
B	52	1.48980	21.30	B	52	1.37177	24.97
C	52	1.37520	24.84	C	52	1.26625	29.77
D	52	1.37099	25.00	D	52	1.26213	30.00
E	26	2.97959	21.32	E	26	2.74354	25.00
F	26	2.75039	24.87	F	26	2.53250	29.80
G	26	2.74334	25.00	G	26	2.52551	30.00
H	24	3.22789	21.37	H	24	2.97217	25.07
J	24	2.97959	24.94	J	24	2.74354	29.92
K	24	2.97637	25.00	K	24	2.74058	30.00

TYPES OF PAYMENTS: A—monthly; B—accelerated weekly; C—
regular weekly; D—minimum amortized weekly; E—accelerated
bi-weekly; F—regular bi-weekly; G—minimum amortized bi-
weekly; H—accelerated semi-monthly; J—regular semi-monthly;
K—minimum amortized semi-monthly

5.375%

BLENDED PAYMENTS IN DOLLARS OF PRINCIPAL AND IN-
TEREST FOR A LOAN OF $1,000 AT **5.375%** PER YEAR, CALCU-
LATED HALF-YEARLY, NOT IN ADVANCE

TYPE OF PMT	PMTS EACH YEAR	PMT EACH PERIOD	YEARS TO RETIRE LOAN	TYPE OF PMT	PMTS EACH YEAR	PMT EACH PERIOD	YEARS TO RETIRE LOAN
5 YEAR AMORTIZATION				**10 YEAR AMORTIZATION**			
A	12	$19.01625	5.00	A	12	$10.76157	10.00
B	52	4.75406	4.55	B	52	2.69039	8.99
C	52	4.38837	4.99	C	52	2.48344	9.97
D	52	4.37938	5.00	D	52	2.47757	10.00
E	26	9.50812	4.56	E	26	5.38079	8.99
F	26	8.77673	4.99	F	26	4.96688	9.98
G	26	8.76322	5.00	G	26	4.95767	10.00
H	24	10.30047	4.56	H	24	5.82919	9.00
J	24	9.50812	4.99	J	24	5.38079	9.99
K	24	9.49762	5.00	K	24	5.37484	10.00
15 YEAR AMORTIZATION				**20 YEAR AMORTIZATION**			
A	12	$8.07341	15.00	A	12	$6.77524	20.00
B	52	2.01835	13.27	B	52	1.69381	17.36
C	52	1.86309	14.94	C	52	1.56352	19.90
D	52	1.85816	15.00	D	52	1.55898	20.00
E	26	4.03670	13.27	E	26	3.38762	17.38
F	26	3.72619	14.95	F	26	3.12704	19.92
G	26	3.71822	15.00	G	26	3.11956	20.00
H	24	4.37310	13.29	H	24	3.66992	17.41
J	24	4.03670	14.97	J	24	3.38762	19.96
K	24	4.03224	15.00	K	24	3.38388	20.00
25 YEAR AMORTIZATION				**30 YEAR AMORTIZATION**			
A	12	$6.03135	25.00	A	12	$5.56285	30.00
B	52	1.50784	21.25	B	52	1.39071	24.88
C	52	1.39185	24.84	C	52	1.28373	29.76
D	52	1.38750	25.00	D	52	1.27947	30.00
E	26	3.01567	21.27	E	26	2.78143	24.91
F	26	2.78370	24.86	F	26	2.56747	29.79
G	26	2.77642	25.00	G	26	2.56024	30.00
H	24	3.26698	21.32	H	24	3.01321	24.98
J	24	3.01567	24.94	J	24	2.78143	29.92
K	24	3.01234	25.00	K	24	2.77835	30.00

TYPES OF PAYMENTS: A—monthly; B—accelerated weekly; C—
regular weekly; D—minimum amortized weekly; E—accelerated
bi-weekly; F—regular bi-weekly; G—minimum amortized bi-
weekly; H—accelerated semi-monthly; J—regular semi-monthly;
K—minimum amortized semi-monthly

5.5%

BLENDED PAYMENTS IN DOLLARS OF PRINCIPAL AND INTEREST FOR A LOAN OF $1,000 AT **5.5%** PER YEAR, CALCULATED HALF-YEARLY, NOT IN ADVANCE

TYPE OF PMT	PMTS EACH YEAR	PMT EACH PERIOD	YEARS TO RETIRE LOAN	TYPE OF PMT	PMTS EACH YEAR	PMT EACH PERIOD	YEARS TO RETIRE LOAN
5 YEAR AMORTIZATION				**10 YEAR AMORTIZATION**			
A	12	$19.07257	5.00	A	12	$10.82194	10.00
B	52	4.76814	4.55	B	52	2.70549	8.98
C	52	4.40136	4.99	C	52	2.49737	9.97
D	52	4.39215	5.00	D	52	2.49134	10.00
E	26	9.53628	4.56	E	26	5.41097	8.98
F	26	8.80272	4.99	F	26	4.99474	9.97
G	26	8.78886	5.00	G	26	4.98527	10.00
H	24	10.33097	4.56	H	24	5.86188	8.99
J	24	9.53628	4.99	J	24	5.41097	9.98
K	24	9.52550	5.00	K	24	5.40485	10.00
15 YEAR AMORTIZATION				**20 YEAR AMORTIZATION**			
A	12	$8.13798	15.00	A	12	$6.84391	20.00
B	52	2.03450	13.25	B	52	1.71098	17.33
C	52	1.87800	14.94	C	52	1.57936	19.89
D	52	1.87292	15.00	D	52	1.57469	20.00
E	26	4.06899	13.26	E	26	3.42196	17.35
F	26	3.75599	14.95	F	26	3.15873	19.91
G	26	3.74779	15.00	G	26	3.15102	20.00
H	24	4.40807	13.28	H	24	3.70712	17.38
J	24	4.06899	14.97	J	24	3.42196	19.96
K	24	4.06439	15.00	K	24	3.41809	20.00
25 YEAR AMORTIZATION				**30 YEAR AMORTIZATION**			
A	12	$6.10391	25.00	A	12	$5.63906	30.00
B	52	1.52598	21.19	B	52	1.40977	24.79
C	52	1.40860	24.83	C	52	1.30132	29.75
D	52	1.40411	25.00	D	52	1.29692	30.00
E	26	3.05196	21.21	E	26	2.81953	24.82
F	26	2.81719	24.86	F	26	2.60264	29.79
G	26	2.80967	25.00	G	26	2.59518	30.00
H	24	3.30629	21.26	H	24	3.05449	24.90
J	24	3.05196	24.94	J	24	2.81953	29.91
K	24	3.04851	25.00	K	24	2.81634	30.00

TYPES OF PAYMENTS: A—monthly; B—accelerated weekly; C—regular weekly; D—minimum amortized weekly; E—accelerated bi-weekly; F—regular bi-weekly; G—minimum amortized bi-weekly; H—accelerated semi-monthly; J—regular semi-monthly; K—minimum amortized semi-monthly

5.625%

BLENDED PAYMENTS IN DOLLARS OF PRINCIPAL AND INTEREST FOR A LOAN OF $1,000 AT **5.625%** PER YEAR, CALCULATED HALF-YEARLY, NOT IN ADVANCE

TYPE OF PMT	PMTS EACH YEAR	PMT EACH PERIOD	YEARS TO RETIRE LOAN	TYPE OF PMT	PMTS EACH YEAR	PMT EACH PERIOD	YEARS TO RETIRE LOAN
5 YEAR AMORTIZATION				**10 YEAR AMORTIZATION**			
A	12	$19.12896	5.00	A	12	$10.88248	10.00
B	52	4.78224	4.55	B	52	2.72062	8.97
C	52	4.41437	4.99	C	52	2.51134	9.97
D	52	4.40493	5.00	D	52	2.50514	10.00
E	26	9.56448	4.55	E	26	5.44124	8.98
F	26	8.82875	4.99	F	26	5.02268	9.97
G	26	8.81454	5.00	G	26	5.01296	10.00
H	24	10.36152	4.56	H	24	5.89468	8.99
J	24	9.56448	4.99	J	24	5.44124	9.98
K	24	9.55343	5.00	K	24	5.43495	10.00
15 YEAR AMORTIZATION				**20 YEAR AMORTIZATION**			
A	12	$8.20281	15.00	A	12	$6.91291	20.00
B	52	2.05070	13.23	B	52	1.72823	17.30
C	52	1.89296	14.94	C	52	1.59529	19.89
D	52	1.88773	15.00	D	52	1.59047	20.00
E	26	4.10141	13.24	E	26	3.45646	17.31
F	26	3.78591	14.95	F	26	3.19058	19.91
G	26	3.77747	15.00	G	26	3.18263	20.00
H	24	4.44319	13.26	H	24	3.74450	17.35
J	24	4.10141	14.97	J	24	3.45646	19.96
K	24	4.09667	15.00	K	24	3.45246	20.00
25 YEAR AMORTIZATION				**30 YEAR AMORTIZATION**			
A	12	$6.17687	25.00	A	12	$5.71571	30.00
B	52	1.54422	21.13	B	52	1.42893	24.70
C	52	1.42543	24.83	C	52	1.31901	29.74
D	52	1.42080	25.00	D	52	1.31446	30.00
E	26	3.08844	21.15	E	26	2.85786	24.72
F	26	2.85086	24.85	F	26	2.63802	29.78
G	26	2.84311	25.00	G	26	2.63032	30.00
H	24	3.34581	21.21	H	24	3.09601	24.81
J	24	3.08844	24.94	J	24	2.85786	29.91
K	24	3.08487	25.00	K	24	2.85455	30.00

TYPES OF PAYMENTS: A—monthly; B—accelerated weekly; C—regular weekly; D—minimum amortized weekly; E—accelerated bi-weekly; F—regular bi-weekly; G—minimum amortized bi-weekly; H—accelerated semi-monthly; J—regular semi-monthly; K—minimum amortized semi-monthly

5.75%

BLENDED PAYMENTS IN DOLLARS OF PRINCIPAL AND INTEREST FOR A LOAN OF $1,000 AT **5.75%** PER YEAR, CALCULATED HALF-YEARLY, NOT IN ADVANCE

TYPE OF PMT	PMTS EACH YEAR	PMT EACH PERIOD	YEARS TO RETIRE LOAN	TYPE OF PMT	PMTS EACH YEAR	PMT EACH PERIOD	YEARS TO RETIRE LOAN
5 YEAR AMORTIZATION				**10 YEAR AMORTIZATION**			
A	12	$19.18542	5.00	A	12	$10.94318	10.00
B	52	4.79636	4.55	B	52	2.73580	8.97
C	52	4.42741	4.99	C	52	2.52535	9.97
D	52	4.41772	5.00	D	52	2.51899	10.00
E	26	9.59271	4.55	E	26	5.47159	8.97
F	26	8.85481	4.99	F	26	5.05070	9.97
G	26	8.84025	5.00	G	26	5.04071	10.00
H	24	10.39210	4.55	H	24	5.92756	8.98
J	24	9.59271	4.99	J	24	5.47159	9.98
K	24	9.58138	5.00	K	24	5.46513	10.00
15 YEAR AMORTIZATION				**20 YEAR AMORTIZATION**			
A	12	$8.26790	15.00	A	12	$6.98224	20.00
B	52	2.06697	13.22	B	52	1.74556	17.26
C	52	1.90798	14.93	C	52	1.61129	19.89
D	52	1.90260	15.00	D	52	1.60632	20.00
E	26	4.13395	13.23	E	26	3.49112	17.28
F	26	3.81595	14.95	F	26	3.22257	19.91
G	26	3.80727	15.00	G	26	3.21439	20.00
H	24	4.47844	13.25	H	24	3.78205	17.32
J	24	4.13395	14.97	J	24	3.49112	19.96
K	24	4.12907	15.00	K	24	3.48700	20.00
25 YEAR AMORTIZATION				**30 YEAR AMORTIZATION**			
A	12	$6.25022	25.00	A	12	$5.79280	30.00
B	52	1.56256	21.07	B	52	1.44820	24.60
C	52	1.44236	24.82	C	52	1.33680	29.73
D	52	1.43758	25.00	D	52	1.33210	30.00
E	26	3.12511	21.09	E	26	2.89640	24.63
F	26	2.88472	24.85	F	26	2.67360	29.77
G	26	2.87673	25.00	G	26	2.66565	30.00
H	24	3.38554	21.15	H	24	3.13776	24.72
J	24	3.12511	24.94	J	24	2.89640	29.91
K	24	3.12142	25.00	K	24	2.89298	30.00

TYPES OF PAYMENTS: A—monthly; B—accelerated weekly; C—regular weekly; D—minimum amortized weekly; E—accelerated bi-weekly; F—regular bi-weekly; G—minimum amortized bi-weekly; H—accelerated semi-monthly; J—regular semi-monthly; K—minimum amortized semi-monthly

5.875%

BLENDED PAYMENTS IN DOLLARS OF PRINCIPAL AND INTEREST FOR A LOAN OF $1,000 AT **5.875%** PER YEAR, CALCULATED HALF-YEARLY, NOT IN ADVANCE

TYPE OF PMT	PMTS EACH YEAR	PMT EACH PERIOD	YEARS TO RETIRE LOAN	TYPE OF PMT	PMTS EACH YEAR	PMT EACH PERIOD	YEARS TO RETIRE LOAN
5 YEAR AMORTIZATION				**10 YEAR AMORTIZATION**			
A	12	$19.24196	5.00	A	12	$11.00406	10.00
B	52	4.81049	4.55	B	52	2.75101	8.96
C	52	4.44045	4.99	C	52	2.53940	9.97
D	52	4.43054	5.00	D	52	2.53287	10.00
E	26	9.62098	4.55	E	26	5.50203	8.97
F	26	8.88090	4.99	F	26	5.07880	9.97
G	26	8.86599	5.00	G	26	5.06855	10.00
H	24	10.42273	4.55	H	24	5.96053	8.97
J	24	9.62098	4.99	J	24	5.50203	9.98
K	24	9.60937	5.00	K	24	5.49539	10.00
15 YEAR AMORTIZATION				**20 YEAR AMORTIZATION**			
A	12	$8.33324	15.00	A	12	$7.05190	20.00
B	52	2.08331	13.20	B	52	1.76298	17.23
C	52	1.92305	14.93	C	52	1.62736	19.88
D	52	1.91753	15.00	D	52	1.62225	20.00
E	26	4.16662	13.21	E	26	3.52595	17.25
F	26	3.84611	14.94	F	26	3.25472	19.90
G	26	3.83719	15.00	G	26	3.24630	20.00
H	24	4.51384	13.23	H	24	3.81978	17.28
J	24	4.16662	14.97	J	24	3.52595	19.95
K	24	4.16159	15.00	K	24	3.52170	20.00
25 YEAR AMORTIZATION				**30 YEAR AMORTIZATION**			
A	12	$6.32395	25.00	A	12	$5.87031	30.00
B	52	1.58099	21.01	B	52	1.46758	24.51
C	52	1.45937	24.81	C	52	1.35469	29.71
D	52	1.45445	25.00	D	52	1.34984	30.00
E	26	3.16198	21.03	E	26	2.93515	24.54
F	26	2.91875	24.84	F	26	2.70937	29.76
G	26	2.91052	25.00	G	26	2.70118	30.00
H	24	3.42547	21.09	H	24	3.17975	24.62
J	24	3.16198	24.93	J	24	2.93515	29.90
K	24	3.15816	25.00	K	24	2.93161	30.00

TYPES OF PAYMENTS: A—monthly; B—accelerated weekly; C—regular weekly; D—minimum amortized weekly; E—accelerated bi-weekly; F—regular bi-weekly; G—minimum amortized bi-weekly; H—accelerated semi-monthly; J—regular semi-monthly; K—minimum amortized semi-monthly

6%

BLENDED PAYMENTS IN DOLLARS OF PRINCIPAL AND INTEREST FOR A LOAN OF $1,000 AT **6%** PER YEAR, CALCULATED HALF-YEARLY, NOT IN ADVANCE

TYPE OF PMT	PMTS EACH YEAR	PMT EACH PERIOD	YEARS TO RETIRE LOAN	TYPE OF PMT	PMTS EACH YEAR	PMT EACH PERIOD	YEARS TO RETIRE LOAN
5 YEAR AMORTIZATION				**10 YEAR AMORTIZATION**			
A	12	$19.29857	5.00	A	12	$11.06510	10.00
B	52	4.82464	4.55	B	52	2.76627	8.95
C	52	4.45352	4.99	C	52	2.55348	9.96
D	52	4.44336	5.00	D	52	2.54678	10.00
E	26	9.64929	4.55	E	26	5.53255	8.96
F	26	8.90703	4.99	F	26	5.10697	9.97
G	26	8.89177	5.00	G	26	5.09645	10.00
H	24	10.45339	4.55	H	24	5.99360	8.97
J	24	9.64929	4.99	J	24	5.53255	9.98
K	24	9.63740	5.00	K	24	5.52574	10.00
15 YEAR AMORTIZATION				**20 YEAR AMORTIZATION**			
A	12	$8.39883	15.00	A	12	$7.12188	20.00
B	52	2.09971	13.18	B	52	1.78047	17.19
C	52	1.93819	14.93	C	52	1.64351	19.88
D	52	1.93251	15.00	D	52	1.63825	20.00
E	26	4.19941	13.19	E	26	3.56094	17.21
F	26	3.87638	14.94	F	26	3.28702	19.90
G	26	3.86721	15.00	G	26	3.27836	20.00
H	24	4.54937	13.21	H	24	3.85769	17.25
J	24	4.19941	14.97	J	24	3.56094	19.95
K	24	4.19424	15.00	K	24	3.55656	20.00
25 YEAR AMORTIZATION				**30 YEAR AMORTIZATION**			
A	12	$6.39807	25.00	A	12	$5.94823	30.00
B	52	1.59952	20.95	B	52	1.48706	24.41
C	52	1.47648	24.80	C	52	1.37267	29.70
D	52	1.47140	25.00	D	52	1.36768	30.00
E	26	3.19903	20.97	E	26	2.97412	24.44
F	26	2.95295	24.84	F	26	2.74534	29.75
G	26	2.94448	25.00	G	26	2.73690	30.00
H	24	3.46562	21.04	H	24	3.22196	24.53
J	24	3.19903	24.93	J	24	2.97412	29.90
K	24	3.19509	25.00	K	24	2.97045	30.00

TYPES OF PAYMENTS: A—monthly; B—accelerated weekly; C—regular weekly; D—minimum amortized weekly; E—accelerated bi-weekly; F—regular bi-weekly; G—minimum amortized bi-weekly; H—accelerated semi-monthly; J—regular semi-monthly; K—minimum amortized semi-monthly

6.125%

BLENDED PAYMENTS IN DOLLARS OF PRINCIPAL AND INTEREST FOR A LOAN OF $1,000 AT **6.125%** PER YEAR, CALCULATED HALF-YEARLY, NOT IN ADVANCE

TYPE OF PMT	PMTS EACH YEAR	PMT EACH PERIOD	YEARS TO RETIRE LOAN	TYPE OF PMT	PMTS EACH YEAR	PMT EACH PERIOD	YEARS TO RETIRE LOAN
5 YEAR AMORTIZATION				**10 YEAR AMORTIZATION**			
A	12	$19.35526	5.00	A	12	$11.12631	10.00
B	52	4.83881	4.55	B	52	2.78158	8.95
C	52	4.46660	4.99	C	52	2.56761	9.96
D	52	4.45621	5.00	D	52	2.56074	10.00
E	26	9.67763	4.55	E	26	5.56315	8.95
F	26	8.93320	4.99	F	26	5.13522	9.97
G	26	8.91757	5.00	G	26	5.12444	10.00
H	24	10.48410	4.55	H	24	6.02675	8.96
J	24	9.67763	4.99	J	24	5.56315	9.98
K	24	9.66546	5.00	K	24	5.55616	10.00
15 YEAR AMORTIZATION				**20 YEAR AMORTIZATION**			
A	12	$8.46467	15.00	A	12	$7.19219	20.00
B	52	2.11617	13.16	B	52	1.79805	17.16
C	52	1.95339	14.93	C	52	1.65974	19.87
D	52	1.94755	15.00	D	52	1.65433	20.00
E	26	4.23234	13.18	E	26	3.59609	17.18
F	26	3.90677	14.94	F	26	3.31947	19.90
G	26	3.89736	15.00	G	26	3.31057	20.00
H	24	4.58503	13.20	H	24	3.89577	17.22
J	24	4.23234	14.97	J	24	3.59609	19.95
K	24	4.22702	15.00	K	24	3.59157	20.00
25 YEAR AMORTIZATION				**30 YEAR AMORTIZATION**			
A	12	$6.47256	25.00	A	12	$6.02658	30.00
B	52	1.61814	20.89	B	52	1.50664	24.31
C	52	1.49367	24.80	C	52	1.39075	29.69
D	52	1.48844	25.00	D	52	1.38560	30.00
E	26	3.23628	20.91	E	26	3.01329	24.34
F	26	2.98733	24.83	F	26	2.78150	29.74
G	26	2.97861	25.00	G	26	2.77281	30.00
H	24	3.50597	20.98	H	24	3.26440	24.43
J	24	3.23628	24.93	J	24	3.01329	29.89
K	24	3.23221	25.00	K	24	3.00950	30.00

TYPES OF PAYMENTS: A—monthly; B—accelerated weekly; C—regular weekly; D—minimum amortized weekly; E—accelerated bi-weekly; F—regular bi-weekly; G—minimum amortized bi-weekly; H—accelerated semi-monthly; J—regular semi-monthly; K—minimum amortized semi-monthly

6.25%

BLENDED PAYMENTS IN DOLLARS OF PRINCIPAL AND INTEREST FOR A LOAN OF $1,000 AT **6.25%** PER YEAR, CALCULATED HALF-YEARLY, NOT IN ADVANCE

TYPE OF PMT	PMTS EACH YEAR	PMT EACH PERIOD	YEARS TO RETIRE LOAN	TYPE OF PMT	PMTS EACH YEAR	PMT EACH PERIOD	YEARS TO RETIRE LOAN
5 YEAR AMORTIZATION				**10 YEAR AMORTIZATION**			
A	12	$19.41201	5.00	A	12	$11.18768	10.00
B	52	4.85300	4.54	B	52	2.79692	8.94
C	52	4.47970	4.99	C	52	2.58177	9.96
D	52	4.46907	5.00	D	52	2.57473	10.00
E	26	9.70601	4.55	E	26	5.59384	8.95
F	26	8.95939	4.99	F	26	5.16355	9.97
G	26	8.94341	5.00	G	26	5.15250	10.00
H	24	10.51484	4.55	H	24	6.06000	8.95
J	24	9.70601	4.99	J	24	5.59384	9.98
K	24	9.69356	5.00	K	24	5.58667	10.00
15 YEAR AMORTIZATION				**20 YEAR AMORTIZATION**			
A	12	$8.53076	15.00	A	12	$7.26281	20.00
B	52	2.13269	13.15	B	52	1.81570	17.12
C	52	1.96864	14.93	C	52	1.67603	19.87
D	52	1.96265	15.00	D	52	1.67047	20.00
E	26	4.26538	13.16	E	26	3.63141	17.14
F	26	3.93728	14.94	F	26	3.35207	19.89
G	26	3.92761	15.00	G	26	3.34291	20.00
H	24	4.62083	13.18	H	24	3.93402	17.18
J	24	4.26538	14.97	J	24	3.63141	19.95
K	24	4.25991	15.00	K	24	3.62675	20.00
25 YEAR AMORTIZATION				**30 YEAR AMORTIZATION**			
A	12	$6.54742	25.00	A	12	$6.10533	30.00
B	52	1.63685	20.83	B	52	1.52633	24.21
C	52	1.51094	24.79	C	52	1.40892	29.68
D	52	1.50557	25.00	D	52	1.40362	30.00
E	26	3.27371	20.85	E	26	3.05266	24.25
F	26	3.02188	24.82	F	26	2.81784	29.73
G	26	3.01291	25.00	G	26	2.80890	30.00
H	24	3.54652	20.92	H	24	3.30705	24.34
J	24	3.27371	24.92	J	24	3.05266	29.89
K	24	3.26951	25.00	K	24	3.04875	30.00

TYPES OF PAYMENTS: A—monthly; B—accelerated weekly; C—regular weekly; D—minimum amortized weekly; E—accelerated bi-weekly; F—regular bi-weekly; G—minimum amortized bi-weekly; H—accelerated semi-monthly; J—regular semi-monthly; K—minimum amortized semi-monthly

6.375%

BLENDED PAYMENTS IN DOLLARS OF PRINCIPAL AND IN-
TEREST FOR A LOAN OF $1,000 AT **6.375%** PER YEAR, CALCU-
LATED HALF-YEARLY, NOT IN ADVANCE

TYPE OF PMT	PMTS EACH YEAR	PMT EACH PERIOD	YEARS TO RETIRE LOAN	TYPE OF PMT	PMTS EACH YEAR	PMT EACH PERIOD	YEARS TO RETIRE LOAN
5 YEAR AMORTIZATION				**10 YEAR AMORTIZATION**			
A	12	$19.46884	5.00	A	12	$11.24922	10.00
B	52	4.86721	4.54	B	52	2.81231	8.93
C	52	4.49281	4.99	C	52	2.59597	9.96
D	52	4.48194	5.00	D	52	2.58876	10.00
E	26	9.73442	4.55	E	26	5.62461	8.94
F	26	8.98562	4.99	F	26	5.19195	9.97
G	26	8.96928	5.00	G	26	5.18063	10.00
H	24	10.54562	4.55	H	24	6.09333	8.95
J	24	9.73442	4.99	J	24	5.62461	9.98
K	24	9.72169	5.00	K	24	5.61726	10.00
15 YEAR AMORTIZATION				**20 YEAR AMORTIZATION**			
A	12	$8.59711	15.00	A	12	$7.33375	20.00
B	52	2.14928	13.13	B	52	1.83344	17.09
C	52	1.98395	14.92	C	52	1.69240	19.87
D	52	1.97780	15.00	D	52	1.68669	20.00
E	26	4.29855	13.14	E	26	3.66688	17.11
F	26	3.96790	14.94	F	26	3.38481	19.89
G	26	3.95798	15.00	G	26	3.37541	20.00
H	24	4.65677	13.16	H	24	3.97245	17.15
J	24	4.29855	14.97	J	24	3.66688	19.95
K	24	4.29293	15.00	K	24	3.66208	20.00
25 YEAR AMORTIZATION				**30 YEAR AMORTIZATION**			
A	12	$6.62265	25.00	A	12	$6.18448	30.00
B	52	1.65566	20.77	B	52	1.54612	24.11
C	52	1.52830	24.78	C	52	1.42719	29.67
D	52	1.52277	25.00	D	52	1.42173	30.00
E	26	3.31132	20.79	E	26	3.09224	24.15
F	26	3.05661	24.82	F	26	2.85437	29.72
G	26	3.04738	25.00	G	26	2.84518	30.00
H	24	3.58727	20.86	H	24	3.34993	24.24
J	24	3.31132	24.92	J	24	3.09224	29.88
K	24	3.30699	25.00	K	24	3.08820	30.00

TYPES OF PAYMENTS: A—monthly; B—accelerated weekly; C—
regular weekly; D—minimum amortized weekly; E—accelerated
bi-weekly; F—regular bi-weekly; G—minimum amortized bi-
weekly; H—accelerated semi-monthly; J—regular semi-monthly;
K—minimum amortized semi-monthly

6.5%

BLENDED PAYMENTS IN DOLLARS OF PRINCIPAL AND IN-TEREST FOR A LOAN OF $1,000 AT **6.5%** PER YEAR, CALCULATED HALF-YEARLY, NOT IN ADVANCE

TYPE OF PMT	PMTS EACH YEAR	PMT EACH PERIOD	YEARS TO RETIRE LOAN	TYPE OF PMT	PMTS EACH YEAR	PMT EACH PERIOD	YEARS TO RETIRE LOAN
5 YEAR AMORTIZATION				**10 YEAR AMORTIZATION**			
A	12	$19.52575	5.00	A	12	$11.31093	10.00
B	52	4.88144	4.54	B	52	2.82773	8.92
C	52	4.50594	4.99	C	52	2.61021	9.96
D	52	4.49483	5.00	D	52	2.60282	10.00
E	26	9.76287	4.54	E	26	5.65547	8.93
F	26	9.01188	4.99	F	26	5.22043	9.97
G	26	8.99519	5.00	G	26	5.20884	10.00
H	24	10.57645	4.55	H	24	6.12675	8.94
J	24	9.76287	4.99	J	24	5.65547	9.98
K	24	9.74986	5.00	K	24	5.64793	10.00
15 YEAR AMORTIZATION				**20 YEAR AMORTIZATION**			
A	12	$8.66369	15.00	A	12	$7.40500	20.00
B	52	2.16592	13.11	B	52	1.85125	17.05
C	52	1.99931	14.92	C	52	1.70885	19.86
D	52	1.99301	15.00	D	52	1.70298	20.00
E	26	4.33185	13.12	E	26	3.70250	17.07
F	26	3.99863	14.94	F	26	3.41769	19.89
G	26	3.98846	15.00	G	26	3.40804	20.00
H	24	4.69283	13.15	H	24	4.01104	17.11
J	24	4.33185	14.97	J	24	3.70250	19.95
K	24	4.32607	15.00	K	24	3.69757	20.00
25 YEAR AMORTIZATION				**30 YEAR AMORTIZATION**			
A	12	$6.69824	25.00	A	12	$6.26402	30.00
B	52	1.67456	20.70	B	52	1.56601	24.01
C	52	1.54575	24.78	C	52	1.44554	29.65
D	52	1.54006	25.00	D	52	1.43993	30.00
E	26	3.34912	20.73	E	26	3.13201	24.05
F	26	3.09149	24.81	F	26	2.89109	29.71
G	26	3.08202	25.00	G	26	2.88163	30.00
H	24	3.62821	20.80	H	24	3.39301	24.14
J	24	3.34912	24.92	J	24	3.13201	29.88
K	24	3.34466	25.00	K	24	3.12784	30.00

TYPES OF PAYMENTS: A—monthly; B—accelerated weekly; C—regular weekly; D—minimum amortized weekly; E—accelerated bi-weekly; F—regular bi-weekly; G—minimum amortized bi-weekly; H—accelerated semi-monthly; J—regular semi-monthly; K—minimum amortized semi-monthly

6.625%

BLENDED PAYMENTS IN DOLLARS OF PRINCIPAL AND INTEREST FOR A LOAN OF $1,000 AT **6.625%** PER YEAR, CALCULATED HALF-YEARLY, NOT IN ADVANCE

TYPE OF PMT	PMTS EACH YEAR	PMT EACH PERIOD	YEARS TO RETIRE LOAN	TYPE OF PMT	PMTS EACH YEAR	PMT EACH PERIOD	YEARS TO RETIRE LOAN
5 YEAR AMORTIZATION				**10 YEAR AMORTIZATION**			
A	12	$19.58272	5.00	A	12	$11.37280	10.00
B	52	4.89568	4.54	B	52	2.84320	8.92
C	52	4.51909	4.99	C	52	2.62449	9.96
D	52	4.50774	5.00	D	52	2.61692	10.00
E	26	9.79136	4.54	E	26	5.68640	8.93
F	26	9.03818	4.99	F	26	5.24899	9.97
G	26	9.02112	5.00	G	26	5.23712	10.00
H	24	10.60731	4.54	H	24	6.16027	8.94
J	24	9.79136	4.99	J	24	5.68640	9.98
K	24	9.77806	5.00	K	24	5.67868	10.00
15 YEAR AMORTIZATION				**20 YEAR AMORTIZATION**			
A	12	$8.73053	15.00	A	12	$7.47657	20.00
B	52	2.18263	13.09	B	52	1.86914	17.02
C	52	2.01474	14.92	C	52	1.72536	19.86
D	52	2.00827	15.00	D	52	1.71933	20.00
E	26	4.36526	13.11	E	26	3.73828	17.04
F	26	4.02948	14.93	F	26	3.45072	19.88
G	26	4.01905	15.00	G	26	3.44082	20.00
H	24	4.72904	13.13	H	24	4.04981	17.08
J	24	4.36526	14.97	J	24	3.73828	19.94
K	24	4.35934	15.00	K	24	3.73321	20.00
25 YEAR AMORTIZATION				**30 YEAR AMORTIZATION**			
A	12	$6.77419	25.00	A	12	$6.34396	30.00
B	52	1.69355	20.64	B	52	1.58599	23.91
C	52	1.56327	24.77	C	52	1.46399	29.64
D	52	1.55743	25.00	D	52	1.45822	30.00
E	26	3.38709	20.67	E	26	3.17198	23.95
F	26	3.12655	24.81	F	26	2.92798	29.70
G	26	3.11681	25.00	G	26	2.91826	30.00
H	24	3.66935	20.73	H	24	3.43631	24.04
J	24	3.38709	24.91	J	24	3.17198	29.87
K	24	3.38250	25.00	K	24	3.16767	30.00

TYPES OF PAYMENTS: A—monthly; B—accelerated weekly; C—regular weekly; D—minimum amortized weekly; E—accelerated bi-weekly; F—regular bi-weekly; G—minimum amortized bi-weekly; H—accelerated semi-monthly; J—regular semi-monthly; K—minimum amortized semi-monthly

6.75%

BLENDED PAYMENTS IN DOLLARS OF PRINCIPAL AND INTEREST FOR A LOAN OF $1,000 AT **6.75%** PER YEAR, CALCULATED HALF-YEARLY, NOT IN ADVANCE

TYPE OF PMT	PMTS EACH YEAR	PMT EACH PERIOD	YEARS TO RETIRE LOAN	TYPE OF PMT	PMTS EACH YEAR	PMT EACH PERIOD	YEARS TO RETIRE LOAN
5 YEAR AMORTIZATION				**10 YEAR AMORTIZATION**			
A	12	$19.63977	5.00	A	12	$11.43484	10.00
B	52	4.90994	4.54	B	52	2.85871	8.91
C	52	4.53225	4.98	C	52	2.63881	9.96
D	52	4.52066	5.00	D	52	2.63106	10.00
E	26	9.81988	4.54	E	26	5.71742	8.91
F	26	9.06451	4.99	F	26	5.27762	9.97
G	26	9.04709	5.00	G	26	5.26547	10.00
H	24	10.63821	4.54	H	24	6.19387	8.93
J	24	9.81988	4.99	J	24	5.71742	9.98
K	24	9.80630	5.00	K	24	5.70951	10.00
15 YEAR AMORTIZATION				**20 YEAR AMORTIZATION**			
A	12	$8.79761	15.00	A	12	$7.54844	20.00
B	52	2.19940	13.08	B	52	1.88711	16.98
C	52	2.03022	14.92	C	52	1.74195	19.85
D	52	2.02358	15.00	D	52	1.73576	20.00
E	26	4.39880	13.09	E	26	3.77422	17.00
F	26	4.06043	14.93	F	26	3.48390	19.88
G	26	4.04975	15.00	G	26	3.47373	20.00
H	24	4.76537	13.11	H	24	4.08874	17.04
J	24	4.39880	14.96	J	24	3.77422	19.94
K	24	4.39272	15.00	K	24	3.76900	20.00
25 YEAR AMORTIZATION				**30 YEAR AMORTIZATION**			
A	12	$6.85050	25.00	A	12	$6.42428	30.00
B	52	1.71262	20.57	B	52	1.60607	23.81
C	52	1.58088	24.76	C	52	1.48253	29.62
D	52	1.57488	25.00	D	52	1.47659	30.00
E	26	3.42525	20.60	E	26	3.21214	23.84
F	26	3.16177	24.80	F	26	2.96505	29.68
G	26	3.15177	25.00	G	26	2.95507	30.00
H	24	3.71069	20.67	H	24	3.47982	23.94
J	24	3.42525	24.91	J	24	3.21214	29.87
K	24	3.42051	25.00	K	24	3.20770	30.00

TYPES OF PAYMENTS: A—monthly; B—accelerated weekly; C—regular weekly; D—minimum amortized weekly; E—accelerated bi-weekly; F—regular bi-weekly; G—minimum amortized bi-weekly; H—accelerated semi-monthly; J—regular semi-monthly; K—minimum amortized semi-monthly

6.875%

BLENDED PAYMENTS IN DOLLARS OF PRINCIPAL AND INTEREST FOR A LOAN OF $1,000 AT **6.875%** PER YEAR, CALCULATED HALF-YEARLY, NOT IN ADVANCE

TYPE OF PMT	PMTS EACH YEAR	PMT EACH PERIOD	YEARS TO RETIRE LOAN	TYPE OF PMT	PMTS EACH YEAR	PMT EACH PERIOD	YEARS TO RETIRE LOAN
5 YEAR AMORTIZATION				**10 YEAR AMORTIZATION**			
A	12	$19.69688	5.00	A	12	$11.49704	10.00
B	52	4.92422	4.54	B	52	2.87426	8.90
C	52	4.54543	4.98	C	52	2.65316	9.96
D	52	4.53360	5.00	D	52	2.64524	10.00
E	26	9.84844	4.54	E	26	5.74852	8.91
F	26	9.09087	4.99	F	26	5.30632	9.97
G	26	9.07309	5.00	G	26	5.29390	10.00
H	24	10.66915	4.54	H	24	6.22756	8.92
J	24	9.84844	4.99	J	24	5.74852	9.98
K	24	9.83457	5.00	K	24	5.74042	10.00
15 YEAR AMORTIZATION				**20 YEAR AMORTIZATION**			
A	12	$8.86493	15.00	A	12	$7.62062	20.00
B	52	2.21623	13.06	B	52	1.90516	16.94
C	52	2.04575	14.91	C	52	1.75861	19.85
D	52	2.03896	15.00	D	52	1.75226	20.00
E	26	4.43247	13.07	E	26	3.81031	16.96
F	26	4.09151	14.93	F	26	3.51721	19.88
G	26	4.08056	15.00	G	26	3.50679	20.00
H	24	4.80184	13.10	H	24	4.12784	17.01
J	24	4.43247	14.96	J	24	3.81031	19.94
K	24	4.42622	15.00	K	24	3.80495	20.00
25 YEAR AMORTIZATION				**30 YEAR AMORTIZATION**			
A	12	$6.92715	25.00	A	12	$6.50497	30.00
B	52	1.73179	20.51	B	52	1.62624	23.70
C	52	1.59857	24.75	C	52	1.50115	29.61
D	52	1.59241	25.00	D	52	1.49505	30.00
E	26	3.46358	20.54	E	26	3.25248	23.74
F	26	3.19715	24.79	F	26	3.00229	29.67
G	26	3.18689	25.00	G	26	2.99204	30.00
H	24	3.75221	20.61	H	24	3.52353	23.84
J	24	3.46358	24.91	J	24	3.25248	29.86
K	24	3.45870	25.00	K	24	3.24790	30.00

TYPES OF PAYMENTS: A—monthly; B—accelerated weekly; C—regular weekly; D—minimum amortized weekly; E—accelerated bi-weekly; F—regular bi-weekly; G—minimum amortized bi-weekly; H—accelerated semi-monthly; J—regular semi-monthly; K—minimum amortized semi-monthly

7%

BLENDED PAYMENTS IN DOLLARS OF PRINCIPAL AND IN-TEREST FOR A LOAN OF $1,000 AT **7%** PER YEAR, CALCULATED HALF-YEARLY, NOT IN ADVANCE

TYPE OF PMT	PMTS EACH YEAR	PMT EACH PERIOD	YEARS TO RETIRE LOAN	TYPE OF PMT	PMTS EACH YEAR	PMT EACH PERIOD	YEARS TO RETIRE LOAN
5 YEAR AMORTIZATION				**10 YEAR AMORTIZATION**			
A	12	$19.75407	5.00	A	12	$11.55940	10.00
B	52	4.93852	4.53	B	52	2.88985	8.90
C	52	4.55863	4.98	C	52	2.66755	9.96
D	52	4.54656	5.00	D	52	2.65945	10.00
E	26	9.87704	4.54	E	26	5.77970	8.91
F	26	9.11727	4.99	F	26	5.33511	9.97
G	26	9.09912	5.00	G	26	5.32240	10.00
H	24	10.70012	4.54	H	24	6.26134	8.92
J	24	9.87704	4.99	J	24	5.77970	9.98
K	24	9.86288	5.00	K	24	5.77142	10.00
15 YEAR AMORTIZATION				**20 YEAR AMORTIZATION**			
A	12	$8.93249	15.00	A	12	$7.69311	20.00
B	52	2.23312	13.04	B	52	1.92328	16.91
C	52	2.06134	14.91	C	52	1.77533	19.84
D	52	2.05438	15.00	D	52	1.76882	20.00
E	26	4.46625	13.05	E	26	3.84655	16.93
F	26	4.12269	14.93	F	26	3.55066	19.87
G	26	4.11148	15.00	G	26	3.53998	20.00
H	24	4.83843	13.08	H	24	4.16710	16.97
J	24	4.46625	14.96	J	24	3.84655	19.94
K	24	4.45985	15.00	K	24	3.84104	20.00
25 YEAR AMORTIZATION				**30 YEAR AMORTIZATION**			
A	12	$7.00416	25.00	A	12	$6.58603	30.00
B	52	1.75104	20.44	B	52	1.64651	23.60
C	52	1.61634	24.74	C	52	1.51985	29.60
D	52	1.61002	25.00	D	52	1.51359	30.00
E	26	3.50208	20.47	E	26	3.29302	23.64
F	26	3.23269	24.79	F	26	3.03971	29.66
G	26	3.22216	25.00	G	26	3.02919	30.00
H	24	3.79392	20.54	H	24	3.56743	23.74
J	24	3.50208	24.90	J	24	3.29302	29.86
K	24	3.49706	25.00	K	24	3.28830	30.00

TYPES OF PAYMENTS: A—monthly; B—accelerated weekly; C—regular weekly; D—minimum amortized weekly; E—accelerated bi-weekly; F—regular bi-weekly; G—minimum amortized bi-weekly; H—accelerated semi-monthly; J—regular semi-monthly; K—minimum amortized semi-monthly

7.125%

BLENDED PAYMENTS IN DOLLARS OF PRINCIPAL AND INTEREST FOR A LOAN OF $1,000 AT **7.125%** PER YEAR, CALCULATED HALF-YEARLY, NOT IN ADVANCE

TYPE OF PMT	PMTS EACH YEAR	PMT EACH PERIOD	YEARS TO RETIRE LOAN	TYPE OF PMT	PMTS EACH YEAR	PMT EACH PERIOD	YEARS TO RETIRE LOAN
5 YEAR AMORTIZATION				**10 YEAR AMORTIZATION**			
A	12	$19.81134	5.00	A	12	$11.62192	10.00
B	52	4.95283	4.53	B	52	2.90548	8.89
C	52	4.57185	4.98	C	52	2.68198	9.96
D	52	4.55953	5.00	D	52	2.67369	10.00
E	26	9.90567	4.54	E	26	5.81096	8.90
F	26	9.14369	4.99	F	26	5.36396	9.97
G	26	9.12518	5.00	G	26	5.35098	10.00
H	24	10.73114	4.54	H	24	6.29521	8.91
J	24	9.90567	4.99	J	24	5.81096	9.98
K	24	9.89122	5.00	K	24	5.80249	10.00
15 YEAR AMORTIZATION				**20 YEAR AMORTIZATION**			
A	12	$9.00030	15.00	A	12	$7.76589	20.00
B	52	2.25007	13.02	B	52	1.94147	16.87
C	52	2.07699	14.91	C	52	1.79213	19.84
D	52	2.06986	15.00	D	52	1.78545	20.00
E	26	4.50015	13.04	E	26	3.88295	16.89
F	26	4.15398	14.93	F	26	3.58426	19.87
G	26	4.14250	15.00	G	26	3.57330	20.00
H	24	4.87516	13.06	H	24	4.20652	16.94
J	24	4.50015	14.96	J	24	3.88295	19.94
K	24	4.49359	15.00	K	24	3.87728	20.00
25 YEAR AMORTIZATION				**30 YEAR AMORTIZATION**			
A	12	$7.08150	25.00	A	12	$6.66746	30.00
B	52	1.77038	20.38	B	52	1.66686	23.49
C	52	1.63419	24.73	C	52	1.53864	29.58
D	52	1.62770	25.00	D	52	1.53222	30.00
E	26	3.54075	20.41	E	26	3.33373	23.53
F	26	3.26839	24.78	F	26	3.07729	29.65
G	26	3.25759	25.00	G	26	3.06650	30.00
H	24	3.83581	20.48	H	24	3.61154	23.64
J	24	3.54075	24.90	J	24	3.33373	29.85
K	24	3.53559	25.00	K	24	3.32887	30.00

TYPES OF PAYMENTS: A—monthly; B—accelerated weekly; C—regular weekly; D—minimum amortized weekly; E—accelerated bi-weekly; F—regular bi-weekly; G—minimum amortized bi-weekly; H—accelerated semi-monthly; J—regular semi-monthly; K—minimum amortized semi-monthly

7.25%

BLENDED PAYMENTS IN DOLLARS OF PRINCIPAL AND IN-
TEREST FOR A LOAN OF $1,000 AT **7.25%** PER YEAR, CALCU-
LATED HALF-YEARLY, NOT IN ADVANCE

TYPE OF PMT	PMTS EACH YEAR	PMT EACH PERIOD	YEARS TO RETIRE LOAN	TYPE OF PMT	PMTS EACH YEAR	PMT EACH PERIOD	YEARS TO RETIRE LOAN
5 YEAR AMORTIZATION				**10 YEAR AMORTIZATION**			
A	12	$19.86867	5.00	A	12	$11.68461	10.00
B	52	4.96717	4.53	B	52	2.92115	8.88
C	52	4.58508	4.98	C	52	2.69645	9.95
D	52	4.57251	5.00	D	52	2.68798	10.00
E	26	9.93433	4.53	E	26	5.84230	8.89
F	26	9.17016	4.99	F	26	5.39290	9.96
G	26	9.15127	5.00	G	26	5.37963	10.00
H	24	10.76220	4.54	H	24	6.32916	8.90
J	24	9.93433	4.99	J	24	5.84230	9.98
K	24	9.91960	5.00	K	24	5.83364	10.00
15 YEAR AMORTIZATION				**20 YEAR AMORTIZATION**			
A	12	$9.06834	15.00	A	12	$7.83897	20.00
B	52	2.26709	13.00	B	52	1.95974	16.83
C	52	2.09269	14.91	C	52	1.80899	19.83
D	52	2.08540	15.00	D	52	1.80215	20.00
E	26	4.53417	13.02	E	26	3.91949	16.85
F	26	4.18539	14.93	F	26	3.61799	19.86
G	26	4.17364	15.00	G	26	3.60677	20.00
H	24	4.91202	13.04	H	24	4.24611	16.90
J	24	4.53417	14.96	J	24	3.91949	19.93
K	24	4.52744	15.00	K	24	3.91367	20.00
25 YEAR AMORTIZATION				**30 YEAR AMORTIZATION**			
A	12	$7.15919	25.00	A	12	$6.74924	30.00
B	52	1.78980	20.31	B	52	1.68731	23.38
C	52	1.65212	24.72	C	52	1.55752	29.56
D	52	1.64546	25.00	D	52	1.55092	30.00
E	26	3.57959	20.34	E	26	3.37462	23.43
F	26	3.30424	24.77	F	26	3.11504	29.63
G	26	3.29318	25.00	G	26	3.10397	30.00
H	24	3.87789	20.41	H	24	3.65584	23.53
J	24	3.57959	24.90	J	24	3.37462	29.85
K	24	3.57428	25.00	K	24	3.36962	30.00

TYPES OF PAYMENTS: A—monthly; B—accelerated weekly; C—
regular weekly; D—minimum amortized weekly; E—accelerated
bi-weekly; F—regular bi-weekly; G—minimum amortized bi-
weekly; H—accelerated semi-monthly; J—regular semi-monthly;
K—minimum amortized semi-monthly

7.375%

BLENDED PAYMENTS IN DOLLARS OF PRINCIPAL AND IN-TEREST FOR A LOAN OF $1,000 AT **7.375%** PER YEAR, CALCU-LATED HALF-YEARLY, NOT IN ADVANCE

TYPE OF PMT	PMTS EACH YEAR	PMT EACH PERIOD	YEARS TO RETIRE LOAN	TYPE OF PMT	PMTS EACH YEAR	PMT EACH PERIOD	YEARS TO RETIRE LOAN
5 YEAR AMORTIZATION				**10 YEAR AMORTIZATION**			
A	12	$19.92607	5.00	A	12	$11.74746	10.00
B	52	4.98152	4.53	B	52	2.93686	8.88
C	52	4.59832	4.98	C	52	2.71095	9.95
D	52	4.58551	5.00	D	52	2.70230	10.00
E	26	9.96304	4.53	E	26	5.87373	8.88
F	26	9.19665	4.99	F	26	5.42190	9.96
G	26	9.17739	5.00	G	26	5.40835	10.00
H	24	10.79329	4.54	H	24	6.36321	8.90
J	24	9.96304	4.99	J	24	5.87373	9.98
K	24	9.94800	5.00	K	24	5.86487	10.00
15 YEAR AMORTIZATION				**20 YEAR AMORTIZATION**			
A	12	$9.13662	15.00	A	12	$7.91235	20.00
B	52	2.28416	12.98	B	52	1.97809	16.79
C	52	2.10845	14.90	C	52	1.82593	19.83
D	52	2.10098	15.00	D	52	1.81892	20.00
E	26	4.56831	13.00	E	26	3.95618	16.82
F	26	4.21690	14.92	F	26	3.65185	19.86
G	26	4.20488	15.00	G	26	3.64036	20.00
H	24	4.94900	13.03	H	24	4.28586	16.86
J	24	4.56831	14.96	J	24	3.95618	19.93
K	24	4.56142	15.00	K	24	3.95021	20.00
25 YEAR AMORTIZATION				**30 YEAR AMORTIZATION**			
A	12	$7.23720	25.00	A	12	$6.83138	30.00
B	52	1.80930	20.24	B	52	1.70784	23.28
C	52	1.67012	24.72	C	52	1.57647	29.55
D	52	1.66330	25.00	D	52	1.56971	30.00
E	26	3.61860	20.27	E	26	3.41569	23.32
F	26	3.34025	24.76	F	26	3.15294	29.62
G	26	3.32891	25.00	G	26	3.14160	30.00
H	24	3.92015	20.35	H	24	3.70033	23.43
J	24	3.61860	24.89	J	24	3.41569	29.84
K	24	3.61314	25.00	K	24	3.41054	30.00

TYPES OF PAYMENTS: A—monthly; B—accelerated weekly; C—regular weekly; D—minimum amortized weekly; E—accelerated bi-weekly; F—regular bi-weekly; G—minimum amortized bi-weekly; H—accelerated semi-monthly; J—regular semi-monthly; K—minimum amortized semi-monthly

7.5%

BLENDED PAYMENTS IN DOLLARS OF PRINCIPAL AND IN-
TEREST FOR A LOAN OF $1,000 AT **7.5%** PER YEAR, CALCU-
LATED HALF-YEARLY, NOT IN ADVANCE

TYPE OF PMT	PMTS EACH YEAR	PMT EACH PERIOD	YEARS TO RETIRE LOAN	TYPE OF PMT	PMTS EACH YEAR	PMT EACH PERIOD	YEARS TO RETIRE LOAN
5 YEAR AMORTIZATION				**10 YEAR AMORTIZATION**			
A	12	$19.98355	5.00	A	12	$11.81047	10.00
B	52	4.99589	4.53	B	52	2.95262	8.87
C	52	4.61159	4.98	C	52	2.72549	9.95
D	52	4.59852	5.00	D	52	2.71665	10.00
E	26	9.99177	4.53	E	26	5.90523	8.88
F	26	9.22318	4.99	F	26	5.45098	9.96
G	26	9.20355	5.00	G	26	5.43714	10.00
H	24	10.82442	4.53	H	24	6.39734	8.89
J	24	9.99177	4.99	J	24	5.90523	9.98
K	24	9.97645	5.00	K	24	5.89617	10.00
15 YEAR AMORTIZATION				**20 YEAR AMORTIZATION**			
A	12	$9.20514	15.00	A	12	$7.98602	20.00
B	52	2.30128	12.97	B	52	1.99651	16.75
C	52	2.12426	14.90	C	52	1.84293	19.82
D	52	2.11662	15.00	D	52	1.83575	20.00
E	26	4.60257	12.98	E	26	3.99301	16.78
F	26	4.24852	14.92	F	26	3.68586	19.86
G	26	4.23623	15.00	G	26	3.67409	20.00
H	24	4.98612	13.01	H	24	4.32576	16.83
J	24	4.60257	14.96	J	24	3.99301	19.93
K	24	4.59551	15.00	K	24	3.98689	20.00
25 YEAR AMORTIZATION				**30 YEAR AMORTIZATION**			
A	12	$7.31555	25.00	A	12	$6.91386	30.00
B	52	1.82889	20.17	B	52	1.72847	23.17
C	52	1.68820	24.71	C	52	1.59551	29.53
D	52	1.68121	25.00	D	52	1.58857	30.00
E	26	3.65777	20.20	E	26	3.45693	23.21
F	26	3.37641	24.76	F	26	3.19101	29.61
G	26	3.36479	25.00	G	26	3.17938	30.00
H	24	3.96259	20.28	H	24	3.74501	23.32
J	24	3.65777	24.89	J	24	3.45693	29.83
K	24	3.65216	25.00	K	24	3.45163	30.00

TYPES OF PAYMENTS: A—monthly; B—accelerated weekly; C—
regular weekly; D—minimum amortized weekly; E—accelerated
bi-weekly; F—regular bi-weekly; G—minimum amortized bi-
weekly; H—accelerated semi-monthly; J—regular semi-monthly;
K—minimum amortized semi-monthly

7.625%

BLENDED PAYMENTS IN DOLLARS OF PRINCIPAL AND INTEREST FOR A LOAN OF $1,000 AT **7.625%** PER YEAR, CALCULATED HALF-YEARLY, NOT IN ADVANCE

TYPE OF PMT	PMTS EACH YEAR	PMT EACH PERIOD	YEARS TO RETIRE LOAN	TYPE OF PMT	PMTS EACH YEAR	PMT EACH PERIOD	YEARS TO RETIRE LOAN
5 YEAR AMORTIZATION				**10 YEAR AMORTIZATION**			
A	12	$20.04110	5.00	A	12	$11.87363	10.00
B	52	5.01027	4.53	B	52	2.96841	8.86
C	52	4.62487	4.98	C	52	2.74007	9.95
D	52	4.61156	5.00	D	52	2.73104	10.00
E	26	10.02055	4.53	E	26	5.93682	8.87
F	26	9.24974	4.99	F	26	5.48014	9.96
G	26	9.22973	5.00	G	26	5.46600	10.00
H	24	10.85559	4.53	H	24	6.43155	8.88
J	24	10.02055	4.99	J	24	5.93682	9.98
K	24	10.00493	5.00	K	24	5.92756	10.00
15 YEAR AMORTIZATION				**20 YEAR AMORTIZATION**			
A	12	$9.27389	15.00	A	12	$8.05998	20.00
B	52	2.31847	12.95	B	52	2.01500	16.71
C	52	2.14013	14.90	C	52	1.86000	19.82
D	52	2.13231	15.00	D	52	1.85265	20.00
E	26	4.63694	12.96	E	26	4.02999	16.74
F	26	4.28026	14.92	F	26	3.71999	19.85
G	26	4.26769	15.00	G	26	3.70795	20.00
H	24	5.02336	12.99	H	24	4.36582	16.79
J	24	4.63694	14.96	J	24	4.02999	19.93
K	24	4.62971	15.00	K	24	4.02371	20.00
25 YEAR AMORTIZATION				**30 YEAR AMORTIZATION**			
A	12	$7.39422	25.00	A	12	$6.99668	30.00
B	52	1.84855	20.10	B	52	1.74917	23.06
C	52	1.70636	24.70	C	52	1.61462	29.51
D	52	1.69919	25.00	D	52	1.60751	30.00
E	26	3.69711	20.14	E	26	3.49834	23.10
F	26	3.41272	24.75	F	26	3.22924	29.59
G	26	3.40082	25.00	G	26	3.21732	30.00
H	24	4.00520	20.22	H	24	3.78987	23.22
J	24	3.69711	24.89	J	24	3.49834	29.83
K	24	3.69135	25.00	K	24	3.49289	30.00

TYPES OF PAYMENTS: A—monthly; B—accelerated weekly; C—regular weekly; D—minimum amortized weekly; E—accelerated bi-weekly; F—regular bi-weekly; G—minimum amortized bi-weekly; H—accelerated semi-monthly; J—regular semi-monthly; K—minimum amortized semi-monthly

7.75%

BLENDED PAYMENTS IN DOLLARS OF PRINCIPAL AND INTEREST FOR A LOAN OF $1,000 AT **7.75%** PER YEAR, CALCULATED HALF-YEARLY, NOT IN ADVANCE

TYPE OF PMT	PMTS EACH YEAR	PMT EACH PERIOD	YEARS TO RETIRE LOAN	TYPE OF PMT	PMTS EACH YEAR	PMT EACH PERIOD	YEARS TO RETIRE LOAN
5 YEAR AMORTIZATION				**10 YEAR AMORTIZATION**			
A	12	$20.09871	5.00	A	12	$11.93696	10.00
B	52	5.02468	4.52	B	52	2.98424	8.85
C	52	4.63816	4.98	C	52	2.75468	9.95
D	52	4.62460	5.00	D	52	2.74547	10.00
E	26	10.04936	4.53	E	26	5.96848	8.86
F	26	9.27633	4.99	F	26	5.50937	9.96
G	26	9.25595	5.00	G	26	5.49494	10.00
H	24	10.88680	4.53	H	24	6.46585	8.88
J	24	10.04936	4.99	J	24	5.96848	9.98
K	24	10.03344	5.00	K	24	5.95903	10.00
15 YEAR AMORTIZATION				**20 YEAR AMORTIZATION**			
A	12	$9.34287	15.00	A	12	$8.13423	20.00
B	52	2.33572	12.93	B	52	2.03356	16.68
C	52	2.15605	14.90	C	52	1.87713	19.81
D	52	2.14806	15.00	D	52	1.86961	20.00
E	26	4.67144	12.94	E	26	4.06711	16.70
F	26	4.31209	14.92	F	26	3.75426	19.85
G	26	4.29925	15.00	G	26	3.74194	20.00
H	24	5.06072	12.97	H	24	4.40604	16.75
J	24	4.67144	14.96	J	24	4.06711	19.93
K	24	4.66404	15.00	K	24	4.06067	20.00
25 YEAR AMORTIZATION				**30 YEAR AMORTIZATION**			
A	12	$7.47321	25.00	A	12	$7.07983	30.00
B	52	1.86830	20.03	B	52	1.76996	22.95
C	52	1.72459	24.69	C	52	1.63381	29.50
D	52	1.71724	25.00	D	52	1.62652	30.00
E	26	3.73661	20.07	E	26	3.53992	22.99
F	26	3.44917	24.74	F	26	3.26761	29.58
G	26	3.43700	25.00	G	26	3.25541	30.00
H	24	4.04799	20.15	H	24	3.83491	23.11
J	24	3.73661	24.88	J	24	3.53992	29.82
K	24	3.73069	25.00	K	24	3.53431	30.00

TYPES OF PAYMENTS: A—monthly; B—accelerated weekly; C—regular weekly; D—minimum amortized weekly; E—accelerated bi-weekly; F—regular bi-weekly; G—minimum amortized bi-weekly; H—accelerated semi-monthly; J—regular semi-monthly; K—minimum amortized semi-monthly

7.875%

BLENDED PAYMENTS IN DOLLARS OF PRINCIPAL AND IN-TEREST FOR A LOAN OF $1,000 AT **7.875%** PER YEAR, CALCULATED HALF-YEARLY, NOT IN ADVANCE

TYPE OF PMT	PMTS EACH YEAR	PMT EACH PERIOD	YEARS TO RETIRE LOAN	TYPE OF PMT	PMTS EACH YEAR	PMT EACH PERIOD	YEARS TO RETIRE LOAN
5 YEAR AMORTIZATION				**10 YEAR AMORTIZATION**			
A	12	$20.15640	5.00	A	12	$12.00045	10.00
B	52	5.03910	4.52	B	52	3.00011	8.85
C	52	4.65148	4.98	C	52	2.76933	9.95
D	52	4.63766	5.00	D	52	2.75993	10.00
E	26	10.07820	4.53	E	26	6.00022	8.86
F	26	9.30295	4.99	F	26	5.53867	9.96
G	26	9.28220	5.00	G	26	5.52394	10.00
H	24	10.91805	4.53	H	24	6.50024	8.87
J	24	10.07820	4.99	J	24	6.00022	9.98
K	24	10.06198	5.00	K	24	5.99057	10.00
15 YEAR AMORTIZATION				**20 YEAR AMORTIZATION**			
A	12	$9.41208	15.00	A	12	$8.20876	20.00
B	52	2.35302	12.91	B	52	2.05219	16.64
C	52	2.17202	14.89	C	52	1.89433	19.81
D	52	2.16385	15.00	D	52	1.88663	20.00
E	26	4.70604	12.92	E	26	4.10438	16.66
F	26	4.34404	14.91	F	26	3.78866	19.84
G	26	4.33091	15.00	G	26	3.77606	20.00
H	24	5.09821	12.95	H	24	4.44641	16.71
J	24	4.70604	14.95	J	24	4.10438	19.92
K	24	4.69847	15.00	K	24	4.09778	20.00
25 YEAR AMORTIZATION				**30 YEAR AMORTIZATION**			
A	12	$7.55252	25.00	A	12	$7.16331	30.00
B	52	1.88813	19.96	B	52	1.79083	22.84
C	52	1.74289	24.68	C	52	1.65307	29.48
D	52	1.73537	25.00	D	52	1.64561	30.00
E	26	3.77626	20.00	E	26	3.58166	22.88
F	26	3.48578	24.73	F	26	3.30614	29.56
G	26	3.47331	25.00	G	26	3.29365	30.00
H	24	4.09095	20.08	H	24	3.88013	23.00
J	24	3.77626	24.88	J	24	3.58166	29.81
K	24	3.77018	25.00	K	24	3.57589	30.00

TYPES OF PAYMENTS: A—monthly; B—accelerated weekly; C—regular weekly; D—minimum amortized weekly; E—accelerated bi-weekly; F—regular bi-weekly; G—minimum amortized bi-weekly; H—accelerated semi-monthly; J—regular semi-monthly; K—minimum amortized semi-monthly

8%

BLENDED PAYMENTS IN DOLLARS OF PRINCIPAL AND IN-
TEREST FOR A LOAN OF $1,000 AT **8%** PER YEAR, CALCULATED
HALF-YEARLY, NOT IN ADVANCE

TYPE OF PMT	PMTS EACH YEAR	PMT EACH PERIOD	YEARS TO RETIRE LOAN	TYPE OF PMT	PMTS EACH YEAR	PMT EACH PERIOD	YEARS TO RETIRE LOAN
5 YEAR AMORTIZATION				**10 YEAR AMORTIZATION**			
A	12	$20.21416	5.00	A	12	$12.06409	10.00
B	52	5.05354	4.52	B	52	3.01602	8.84
C	52	4.66481	4.98	C	52	2.78402	9.95
D	52	4.65074	5.00	D	52	2.77442	10.00
E	26	10.10708	4.53	E	26	6.03205	8.85
F	26	9.32961	4.99	F	26	5.56804	9.96
G	26	9.30848	5.00	G	26	5.55302	10.00
H	24	10.94934	4.53	H	24	6.53472	8.86
J	24	10.10708	4.99	J	24	6.03205	9.98
K	24	10.09056	5.00	K	24	6.02219	10.00
15 YEAR AMORTIZATION				**20 YEAR AMORTIZATION**			
A	12	$9.48153	15.00	A	12	$8.28357	20.00
B	52	2.37038	12.89	B	52	2.07089	16.60
C	52	2.18805	14.89	C	52	1.91159	19.80
D	52	2.17970	15.00	D	52	1.90372	20.00
E	26	4.74076	12.90	E	26	4.14179	16.62
F	26	4.37609	14.91	F	26	3.82319	19.84
G	26	4.36268	15.00	G	26	3.81031	20.00
H	24	5.13583	12.93	H	24	4.48694	16.67
J	24	4.74076	14.95	J	24	4.14179	19.92
K	24	4.73302	15.00	K	24	4.13502	20.00
25 YEAR AMORTIZATION				**30 YEAR AMORTIZATION**			
A	12	$7.63213	25.00	A	12	$7.24711	30.00
B	52	1.90803	19.89	B	52	1.81178	22.72
C	52	1.76126	24.67	C	52	1.67241	29.46
D	52	1.75357	25.00	D	52	1.66477	30.00
E	26	3.81607	19.93	E	26	3.62356	22.77
F	26	3.52252	24.72	F	26	3.34482	29.55
G	26	3.50977	25.00	G	26	3.33204	30.00
H	24	4.13407	20.01	H	24	3.92552	22.89
J	24	3.81607	24.87	J	24	3.62356	29.80
K	24	3.80983	25.00	K	24	3.61763	30.00

TYPES OF PAYMENTS: A—monthly; B—accelerated weekly; C—
regular weekly; D—minimum amortized weekly; E—accelerated
bi-weekly; F—regular bi-weekly; G—minimum amortized bi-
weekly; H—accelerated semi-monthly; J—regular semi-monthly;
K—minimum amortized semi-monthly

8.125%

BLENDED PAYMENTS IN DOLLARS OF PRINCIPAL AND INTEREST FOR A LOAN OF $1,000 AT **8.125%** PER YEAR, CALCULATED HALF-YEARLY, NOT IN ADVANCE

TYPE OF PMT	PMTS EACH YEAR	PMT EACH PERIOD	YEARS TO RETIRE LOAN	TYPE OF PMT	PMTS EACH YEAR	PMT EACH PERIOD	YEARS TO RETIRE LOAN
5 YEAR AMORTIZATION				**10 YEAR AMORTIZATION**			
A	12	$20.27199	5.00	A	12	$12.12789	10.00
B	52	5.06800	4.52	B	52	3.03197	8.83
C	52	4.67815	4.98	C	52	2.79874	9.95
D	52	4.66383	5.00	D	52	2.78895	10.00
E	26	10.13599	4.52	E	26	6.06395	8.84
F	26	9.35630	4.99	F	26	5.59749	9.96
G	26	9.33479	5.00	G	26	5.58217	10.00
H	24	10.98066	4.53	H	24	6.56927	8.85
J	24	10.13599	4.99	J	24	6.06395	9.97
K	24	10.11917	5.00	K	24	6.05388	10.00
15 YEAR AMORTIZATION				**20 YEAR AMORTIZATION**			
A	12	$9.55120	15.00	A	12	$8.35867	20.00
B	52	2.38780	12.87	B	52	2.08967	16.55
C	52	2.20412	14.89	C	52	1.92892	19.80
D	52	2.19560	15.00	D	52	1.92087	20.00
E	26	4.77560	12.89	E	26	4.17933	16.58
F	26	4.40825	14.91	F	26	3.85785	19.83
G	26	4.39455	15.00	G	26	3.84468	20.00
H	24	5.17357	12.92	H	24	4.52761	16.63
J	24	4.77560	14.95	J	24	4.17933	19.92
K	24	4.76768	15.00	K	24	4.17240	20.00
25 YEAR AMORTIZATION				**30 YEAR AMORTIZATION**			
A	12	$7.71206	25.00	A	12	$7.33122	30.00
B	52	1.92801	19.82	B	52	1.83281	22.61
C	52	1.77971	24.65	C	52	1.69182	29.44
D	52	1.77183	25.00	D	52	1.68399	30.00
E	26	3.85603	19.86	E	26	3.66561	22.66
F	26	3.55941	24.71	F	26	3.38364	29.53
G	26	3.54637	25.00	G	26	3.37056	30.00
H	24	4.17737	19.94	H	24	3.97108	22.78
J	24	3.85603	24.87	J	24	3.66561	29.80
K	24	3.84963	25.00	K	24	3.65953	30.00

TYPES OF PAYMENTS: A—monthly; B—accelerated weekly; C—regular weekly; D—minimum amortized weekly; E—accelerated bi-weekly; F—regular bi-weekly; G—minimum amortized bi-weekly; H—accelerated semi-monthly; J—regular semi-monthly; K—minimum amortized semi-monthly

8.25%

BLENDED PAYMENTS IN DOLLARS OF PRINCIPAL AND INTEREST FOR A LOAN OF $1,000 AT **8.25%** PER YEAR, CALCULATED HALF-YEARLY, NOT IN ADVANCE

TYPE OF PMT	PMTS EACH YEAR	PMT EACH PERIOD	YEARS TO RETIRE LOAN	TYPE OF PMT	PMTS EACH YEAR	PMT EACH PERIOD	YEARS TO RETIRE LOAN
5 YEAR AMORTIZATION				**10 YEAR AMORTIZATION**			
A	12	$20.32988	5.00	A	12	$12.19185	10.00
B	52	5.08247	4.52	B	52	3.04796	8.82
C	52	4.69151	4.98	C	52	2.81350	9.95
D	52	4.67694	5.00	D	52	2.80352	10.00
E	26	10.16494	4.52	E	26	6.09592	8.83
F	26	9.38302	4.99	F	26	5.62701	9.96
G	26	9.36113	5.00	G	26	5.61139	10.00
H	24	11.01202	4.53	H	24	6.60392	8.85
J	24	10.16494	4.99	J	24	6.09592	9.97
K	24	10.14782	5.00	K	24	6.08566	10.00
15 YEAR AMORTIZATION				**20 YEAR AMORTIZATION**			
A	12	$9.62110	15.00	A	12	$8.43404	20.00
B	52	2.40528	12.85	B	52	2.10851	16.51
C	52	2.22025	14.89	C	52	1.94632	19.79
D	52	2.21155	15.00	D	52	1.93808	20.00
E	26	4.81055	12.87	E	26	4.21702	16.54
F	26	4.44051	14.91	F	26	3.89263	19.83
G	26	4.42653	15.00	G	26	3.87918	20.00
H	24	5.21143	12.90	H	24	4.56844	16.60
J	24	4.81055	14.95	J	24	4.21702	19.92
K	24	4.80245	15.00	K	24	4.20992	20.00
25 YEAR AMORTIZATION				**30 YEAR AMORTIZATION**			
A	12	$7.79229	25.00	A	12	$7.41565	30.00
B	52	1.94807	19.75	B	52	1.85391	22.50
C	52	1.79822	24.64	C	52	1.71130	29.42
D	52	1.79016	25.00	D	52	1.70329	30.00
E	26	3.89614	19.78	E	26	3.70782	22.55
F	26	3.59644	24.70	F	26	3.42261	29.51
G	26	3.58311	25.00	G	26	3.40923	30.00
H	24	4.22082	19.87	H	24	4.01681	22.67
J	24	3.89614	24.86	J	24	3.70782	29.79
K	24	3.88958	25.00	K	24	3.70158	30.00

TYPES OF PAYMENTS: A—monthly; B—accelerated weekly; C—regular weekly; D—minimum amortized weekly; E—accelerated bi-weekly; F—regular bi-weekly; G—minimum amortized bi-weekly; H—accelerated semi-monthly; J—regular semi-monthly; K—minimum amortized semi-monthly

8.375%

BLENDED PAYMENTS IN DOLLARS OF PRINCIPAL AND INTEREST FOR A LOAN OF $1,000 AT **8.375%** PER YEAR, CALCULATED HALF-YEARLY, NOT IN ADVANCE

TYPE OF PMT	PMTS EACH YEAR	PMT EACH PERIOD	YEARS TO RETIRE LOAN	TYPE OF PMT	PMTS EACH YEAR	PMT EACH PERIOD	YEARS TO RETIRE LOAN
5 YEAR AMORTIZATION				**10 YEAR AMORTIZATION**			
A	12	$20.38785	5.00	A	12	$12.25596	10.00
B	52	5.09696	4.52	B	52	3.06399	8.82
C	52	4.70489	4.98	C	52	2.82830	9.94
D	52	4.69006	5.00	D	52	2.81812	10.00
E	26	10.19393	4.52	E	26	6.12798	8.83
F	26	9.40978	4.99	F	26	5.65660	9.96
G	26	9.38750	5.00	G	26	5.64068	10.00
H	24	11.04342	4.52	H	24	6.63865	8.84
J	24	10.19393	4.99	J	24	6.12798	9.97
K	24	10.17650	5.00	K	24	6.11751	10.00
15 YEAR AMORTIZATION				**20 YEAR AMORTIZATION**			
A	12	$9.69123	15.00	A	12	$8.50968	20.00
B	52	2.42281	12.83	B	52	2.12742	16.47
C	52	2.23644	14.88	C	52	1.96377	19.79
D	52	2.22755	15.00	D	52	1.95536	20.00
E	26	4.84561	12.85	E	26	4.25484	16.50
F	26	4.47287	14.91	F	26	3.92754	19.82
G	26	4.45860	15.00	G	26	3.91380	20.00
H	24	5.24942	12.88	H	24	4.60941	16.56
J	24	4.84561	14.95	J	24	4.25484	19.91
K	24	4.83733	15.00	K	24	4.24757	20.00
25 YEAR AMORTIZATION				**30 YEAR AMORTIZATION**			
A	12	$7.87281	25.00	A	12	$7.50037	30.00
B	52	1.96820	19.67	B	52	1.87509	22.38
C	52	1.81680	24.63	C	52	1.73085	29.40
D	52	1.80856	25.00	D	52	1.72266	30.00
E	26	3.93641	19.71	E	26	3.75019	22.43
F	26	3.63361	24.70	F	26	3.46171	29.50
G	26	3.61998	25.00	G	26	3.44803	30.00
H	24	4.26444	19.80	H	24	4.06270	22.56
J	24	3.93641	24.86	J	24	3.75019	29.78
K	24	3.92968	25.00	K	24	3.74378	30.00

TYPES OF PAYMENTS: A—monthly; B—accelerated weekly; C—regular weekly; D—minimum amortized weekly; E—accelerated bi-weekly; F—regular bi-weekly; G—minimum amortized bi-weekly; H—accelerated semi-monthly; J—regular semi-monthly; K—minimum amortized semi-monthly

8.5%

BLENDED PAYMENTS IN DOLLARS OF PRINCIPAL AND INTEREST FOR A LOAN OF $1,000 AT **8.5%** PER YEAR, CALCULATED HALF-YEARLY, NOT IN ADVANCE

TYPE OF PMT	PMTS EACH YEAR	PMT EACH PERIOD	YEARS TO RETIRE LOAN	TYPE OF PMT	PMTS EACH YEAR	PMT EACH PERIOD	YEARS TO RETIRE LOAN
5 YEAR AMORTIZATION				**10 YEAR AMORTIZATION**			
A	12	$20.44589	5.00	A	12	$12.32023	10.00
B	52	5.11147	4.51	B	52	3.08006	8.81
C	52	4.71828	4.98	C	52	2.84313	9.94
D	52	4.70319	5.00	D	52	2.83275	10.00
E	26	10.22294	4.52	E	26	6.16012	8.82
F	26	9.43656	4.99	F	26	5.68626	9.96
G	26	9.41390	5.00	G	26	5.67004	10.00
H	24	11.07486	4.52	H	24	6.67346	8.83
J	24	10.22294	4.99	J	24	6.16012	9.97
K	24	10.20521	5.00	K	24	6.14943	10.00
15 YEAR AMORTIZATION				**20 YEAR AMORTIZATION**			
A	12	$9.76158	15.00	A	12	$8.58559	20.00
B	52	2.44039	12.81	B	52	2.14640	16.43
C	52	2.25267	14.88	C	52	1.98129	19.78
D	52	2.24360	15.00	D	52	1.97269	20.00
E	26	4.88079	12.83	E	26	4.29280	16.46
F	26	4.50534	14.90	F	26	3.96258	19.82
G	26	4.49078	15.00	G	26	3.94854	20.00
H	24	5.28752	12.86	H	24	4.65053	16.52
J	24	4.88079	14.95	J	24	4.29280	19.91
K	24	4.87232	15.00	K	24	4.28535	20.00
25 YEAR AMORTIZATION				**30 YEAR AMORTIZATION**			
A	12	$7.95364	25.00	A	12	$7.58539	30.00
B	52	1.98841	19.60	B	52	1.89635	22.27
C	52	1.83545	24.62	C	52	1.75048	29.38
D	52	1.82703	25.00	D	52	1.74209	30.00
E	26	3.97682	19.64	E	26	3.79270	22.32
F	26	3.67091	24.69	F	26	3.50095	29.48
G	26	3.65698	25.00	G	26	3.48697	30.00
H	24	4.30822	19.73	H	24	4.10875	22.45
J	24	3.97682	24.85	J	24	3.79270	29.77
K	24	3.96992	25.00	K	24	3.78612	30.00

TYPES OF PAYMENTS: A—monthly; B—accelerated weekly; C—regular weekly; D—minimum amortized weekly; E—accelerated bi-weekly; F—regular bi-weekly; G—minimum amortized bi-weekly; H—accelerated semi-monthly; J—regular semi-monthly; K—minimum amortized semi-monthly

8.625%

BLENDED PAYMENTS IN DOLLARS OF PRINCIPAL AND IN-
TEREST FOR A LOAN OF $1,000 AT **8.625%** PER YEAR, CALCU-
LATED HALF-YEARLY, NOT IN ADVANCE

TYPE OF PMT	PMTS EACH YEAR	PMT EACH PERIOD	YEARS TO RETIRE LOAN	TYPE OF PMT	PMTS EACH YEAR	PMT EACH PERIOD	YEARS TO RETIRE LOAN
5 YEAR AMORTIZATION				**10 YEAR AMORTIZATION**			
A	12	$20.50399	5.00	A	12	$12.38466	10.00
B	52	5.12600	4.51	B	52	3.09616	8.80
C	52	4.73169	4.98	C	52	2.85800	9.94
D	52	4.71635	5.00	D	52	2.84742	10.00
E	26	10.25200	4.52	E	26	6.19233	8.81
F	26	9.46338	4.98	F	26	5.71600	9.95
G	26	9.44033	5.00	G	26	5.69946	10.00
H	24	11.10633	4.52	H	24	6.07836	8.83
J	24	10.25200	4.99	J	24	6.19233	9.97
K	24	10.23396	5.00	K	24	6.18144	10.00
15 YEAR AMORTIZATION				**20 YEAR AMORTIZATION**			
A	12	$9.83215	15.00	A	12	$8.66177	20.00
B	52	2.45804	12.79	B	52	2.16544	16.39
C	52	2.26896	14.88	C	52	1.99887	19.77
D	52	2.25970	15.00	D	52	1.99009	20.00
E	26	4.91608	12.81	E	26	4.33089	16.42
F	26	4.53792	14.90	F	26	3.99774	19.81
G	26	4.52306	15.00	G	26	3.98340	20.00
H	24	5.32575	12.84	H	24	4.69179	16.48
J	24	4.91608	14.95	J	24	4.33089	19.91
K	24	4.90743	15.00	K	24	4.32327	20.00
25 YEAR AMORTIZATION				**30 YEAR AMORTIZATION**			
A	12	$8.03475	25.00	A	12	$7.67070	30.00
B	52	2.00869	19.53	B	52	1.91768	22.15
C	52	1.85417	24.61	C	52	1.77016	29.36
D	52	1.84556	25.00	D	52	1.76159	30.00
E	26	4.01737	19.57	E	26	3.83535	22.20
F	26	3.70834	24.68	F	26	3.54032	29.46
G	26	3.69411	25.00	G	26	3.52604	30.00
H	24	4.35215	19.66	H	24	4.15496	22.33
J	24	4.01737	24.85	J	24	3.83535	29.76
K	24	4.01031	25.00	K	24	3.82860	30.00

TYPES OF PAYMENTS: A—monthly; B—accelerated weekly; C—
regular weekly; D—minimum amortized weekly; E—accelerated
bi-weekly; F—regular bi-weekly; G—minimum amortized bi-
weekly; H—accelerated semi-monthly; J—regular semi-monthly;
K—minimum amortized semi-monthly

8.75%

BLENDED PAYMENTS IN DOLLARS OF PRINCIPAL AND INTEREST FOR A LOAN OF $1,000 AT **8.75%** PER YEAR, CALCULATED HALF-YEARLY, NOT IN ADVANCE

TYPE OF PMT	PMTS EACH YEAR	PMT EACH PERIOD	YEARS TO RETIRE LOAN	TYPE OF PMT	PMTS EACH YEAR	PMT EACH PERIOD	YEARS TO RETIRE LOAN
5 YEAR AMORTIZATION				**10 YEAR AMORTIZATION**			
A	12	$20.56217	5.00	A	12	$12.44924	10.00
B	52	5.14054	4.51	B	52	3.11231	8.79
C	52	4.74512	4.98	C	52	2.87290	9.94
D	52	4.72951	5.00	D	52	2.86213	10.00
E	26	10.28109	4.52	E	26	6.22462	8.81
F	26	9.49023	4.98	F	26	5.74580	9.95
G	26	9.46680	5.00	G	26	5.72896	10.00
H	24	11.13784	4.52	H	24	6.74334	8.82
J	24	10.28109	4.99	J	24	6.22462	9.97
K	24	10.26274	5.00	K	24	6.21351	10.00
15 YEAR AMORTIZATION				**20 YEAR AMORTIZATION**			
A	12	$9.90294	15.00	A	12	$8.73822	20.00
B	52	2.47574	12.77	B	52	2.18455	16.35
C	52	2.28529	14.87	C	52	2.01651	19.77
D	52	2.27585	15.00	D	52	2.00754	20.00
E	26	4.95147	12.79	E	26	4.36911	16.38
F	26	4.57059	14.90	F	26	4.03302	19.81
G	26	4.55544	15.00	G	26	4.01839	20.00
H	24	5.36409	12.82	H	24	4.73320	16.43
J	24	4.95147	14.95	J	24	4.36911	19.91
K	24	4.94264	15.00	K	24	4.36131	20.00
25 YEAR AMORTIZATION				**30 YEAR AMORTIZATION**			
A	12	$8.11614	25.00	A	12	$7.75630	30.00
B	52	2.02904	19.45	B	52	1.93908	22.04
C	52	1.87296	24.60	C	52	1.78992	29.33
D	52	1.86416	25.00	D	52	1.78115	30.00
E	26	4.05807	19.49	E	26	3.87815	22.09
F	26	3.74591	24.67	F	26	3.57983	29.44
G	26	3.73138	25.00	G	26	3.56524	30.00
H	24	4.39624	19.59	H	24	4.20133	22.22
J	24	4.05807	24.84	J	24	3.87815	29.75
K	24	4.05083	25.00	K	24	3.87123	30.00

TYPES OF PAYMENTS: A—monthly; B—accelerated weekly; C—regular weekly; D—minimum amortized weekly; E—accelerated bi-weekly; F—regular bi-weekly; G—minimum amortized bi-weekly; H—accelerated semi-monthly; J—regular semi-monthly; K—minimum amortized semi-monthly

8.875%

BLENDED PAYMENTS IN DOLLARS OF PRINCIPAL AND INTEREST FOR A LOAN OF $1,000 AT **8.875%** PER YEAR, CALCULATED HALF-YEARLY, NOT IN ADVANCE

TYPE OF PMT	PMTS EACH YEAR	PMT EACH PERIOD	YEARS TO RETIRE LOAN	TYPE OF PMT	PMTS EACH YEAR	PMT EACH PERIOD	YEARS TO RETIRE LOAN
5 YEAR AMORTIZATION				**10 YEAR AMORTIZATION**			
A	12	$20.62042	5.00	A	12	$12.51397	10.00
B	52	5.15510	4.51	B	52	3.12849	8.79
C	52	4.75856	4.98	C	52	2.88784	9.94
D	52	4.74269	5.00	D	52	2.87687	10.00
E	26	10.31021	4.51	E	26	6.25699	8.80
F	26	9.51711	4.98	F	26	5.77568	9.95
G	26	9.49329	5.00	G	26	5.75853	10.00
H	24	11.16939	4.52	H	24	6.77840	8.81
J	24	10.31021	4.99	J	24	6.25699	9.97
K	24	10.29156	5.00	K	24	6.24567	10.00
15 YEAR AMORTIZATION				**20 YEAR AMORTIZATION**			
A	12	$9.97396	15.00	A	12	$8.81493	20.00
B	52	2.49349	12.75	B	52	2.20373	16.30
C	52	2.30168	14.87	C	52	2.03421	19.76
D	52	2.29205	15.00	D	52	2.02506	20.00
E	26	4.98698	12.77	E	26	4.40746	16.33
F	26	4.60337	14.90	F	26	4.06843	19.80
G	26	4.58791	15.00	G	26	4.05349	20.00
H	24	5.40256	12.80	H	24	4.77475	16.39
J	24	4.98698	14.94	J	24	4.40746	19.90
K	24	4.97796	15.00	K	24	4.39949	20.00
25 YEAR AMORTIZATION				**30 YEAR AMORTIZATION**			
A	12	$8.19782	25.00	A	12	$7.84218	30.00
B	52	2.04945	19.38	B	52	1.96054	21.92
C	52	1.89180	24.58	C	52	1.80973	29.31
D	52	1.88282	25.00	D	52	1.80078	30.00
E	26	4.09891	19.42	E	26	3.92109	21.97
F	26	3.78361	24.66	F	26	3.61947	29.42
G	26	3.76877	25.00	G	26	3.60456	30.00
H	24	4.44049	19.51	H	24	4.24785	22.10
J	24	4.09891	24.84	J	24	3.92109	29.74
K	24	4.09149	25.00	K	24	3.91399	30.00

TYPES OF PAYMENTS: A—monthly; B—accelerated weekly; C—regular weekly; D—minimum amortized weekly; E—accelerated bi-weekly; F—regular bi-weekly; G—minimum amortized bi-weekly; H—accelerated semi-monthly; J—regular semi-monthly; K—minimum amortized semi-monthly

9%

BLENDED PAYMENTS IN DOLLARS OF PRINCIPAL AND IN-
TEREST FOR A LOAN OF $1,000 AT **9%** PER YEAR, CALCULATED
HALF-YEARLY, NOT IN ADVANCE

TYPE OF PMT	PMTS EACH YEAR	PMT EACH PERIOD	YEARS TO RETIRE LOAN	TYPE OF PMT	PMTS EACH YEAR	PMT EACH PERIOD	YEARS TO RETIRE LOAN
5 YEAR AMORTIZATION				**10 YEAR AMORTIZATION**			
A	12	$20.67873	5.00	A	12	$12.57886	10.00
B	52	5.16968	4.51	B	52	3.14471	8.78
C	52	4.77201	4.98	C	52	2.90281	9.94
D	52	4.75589	5.00	D	52	2.89164	10.00
E	26	10.33936	4.51	E	26	6.28943	8.79
F	26	9.54403	4.98	F	26	5.80563	9.95
G	26	9.51981	5.00	G	26	5.78816	10.00
H	24	11.20098	4.52	H	24	6.81355	8.80
J	24	10.33936	4.99	J	24	6.28943	9.97
K	24	10.32040	5.00	K	24	6.27789	10.00
15 YEAR AMORTIZATION				**20 YEAR AMORTIZATION**			
A	12	$10.04519	15.00	A	12	$8.89189	20.00
B	52	2.51130	12.73	B	52	2.22297	16.26
C	52	2.31812	14.87	C	52	2.05198	19.75
D	52	2.30829	15.00	D	52	2.04263	20.00
E	26	5.02259	12.75	E	26	4.44595	16.29
F	26	4.63624	14.89	F	26	4.10395	19.80
G	26	4.62049	15.00	G	26	4.08871	20.00
H	24	5.44114	12.78	H	24	4.81644	16.35
J	24	5.02259	14.94	J	24	4.44595	19.90
K	24	5.01338	15.00	K	24	4.43779	20.00
25 YEAR AMORTIZATION				**30 YEAR AMORTIZATION**			
A	12	$8.27977	25.00	A	12	$7.92833	30.00
B	52	2.06994	19.30	B	52	1.98208	21.80
C	52	1.91072	24.57	C	52	1.82961	29.29
D	52	1.90154	25.00	D	52	1.82047	30.00
E	26	4.13989	19.34	E	26	3.96416	21.86
F	26	3.82143	24.65	F	26	3.65923	29.40
G	26	3.80629	25.00	G	26	3.64401	30.00
H	24	4.48488	19.44	H	24	4.29451	21.99
J	24	4.13989	24.83	J	24	3.96416	29.73
K	24	4.13229	25.00	K	24	3.95689	30.00

TYPES OF PAYMENTS: A—monthly; B—accelerated weekly; C—
regular weekly; D—minimum amortized weekly; E—accelerated
bi-weekly; F—regular bi-weekly; G—minimum amortized bi-
weekly; H—accelerated semi-monthly; J—regular semi-monthly;
K—minimum amortized semi-monthly

9.125%

BLENDED PAYMENTS IN DOLLARS OF PRINCIPAL AND INTEREST FOR A LOAN OF $1,000 AT **9.125%** PER YEAR, CALCULATED HALF-YEARLY, NOT IN ADVANCE

TYPE OF PMT	PMTS EACH YEAR	PMT EACH PERIOD	YEARS TO RETIRE LOAN	TYPE OF PMT	PMTS EACH YEAR	PMT EACH PERIOD	YEARS TO RETIRE LOAN
5 YEAR AMORTIZATION				**10 YEAR AMORTIZATION**			
A	12	$20.73711	5.00	A	12	$12.64389	10.00
B	52	5.18428	4.51	B	52	3.16097	8.77
C	52	4.78549	4.98	C	52	2.91782	9.94
D	52	4.76910	5.00	D	52	2.90644	10.00
E	26	10.36856	4.51	E	26	6.32195	8.78
F	26	9.57097	4.98	F	26	5.83564	9.95
G	26	9.54637	5.00	G	26	5.81786	10.00
H	24	11.23260	4.52	H	24	6.84878	8.80
J	24	10.36856	4.99	J	24	6.32195	9.97
K	24	10.34928	5.00	K	24	6.31019	10.00
15 YEAR AMORTIZATION				**20 YEAR AMORTIZATION**			
A	12	$10.11664	15.00	A	12	$8.96912	20.00
B	52	2.52916	12.71	B	52	2.24228	16.22
C	52	2.33461	14.87	C	52	2.06980	19.75
D	52	2.32459	15.00	D	52	2.06026	20.00
E	26	5.05832	12.73	E	26	4.48456	16.25
F	26	4.66922	14.89	F	26	4.13959	19.79
G	26	4.65316	15.00	G	26	4.12405	20.00
H	24	5.47984	12.76	H	24	4.85827	16.31
J	24	5.05832	14.94	J	24	4.48456	19.90
K	24	5.04891	15.00	K	24	4.47622	20.00
25 YEAR AMORTIZATION				**30 YEAR AMORTIZATION**			
A	12	$8.63200	25.00	A	12	$8.01474	30.00
B	52	2.09050	19.23	B	52	2.00369	21.68
C	52	1.92969	24.56	C	52	1.84956	29.26
D	52	1.92032	25.00	D	52	1.84021	30.00
E	26	4.18100	19.27	E	26	4.00737	21.74
F	26	3.85939	24.63	F	26	3.69911	29.38
G	26	3.84393	25.00	G	26	3.68358	30.00
H	24	4.52942	19.37	H	24	4.34132	21.87
J	24	4.18100	24.83	J	24	4.00737	29.72
K	24	4.17323	25.00	K	24	3.99992	30.00

TYPES OF PAYMENTS: A—monthly; B—accelerated weekly; C—regular weekly; D—minimum amortized weekly; E—accelerated bi-weekly; F—regular bi-weekly; G—minimum amortized bi-weekly; H—accelerated semi-monthly; J—regular semi-monthly; K—minimum amortized semi-monthly

9.25%

BLENDED PAYMENTS IN DOLLARS OF PRINCIPAL AND IN-
TEREST FOR A LOAN OF $1,000 AT **9.25%** PER YEAR, CALCU-
LATED HALF-YEARLY, NOT IN ADVANCE

TYPE OF PMT	PMTS EACH YEAR	PMT EACH PERIOD	YEARS TO RETIRE LOAN	TYPE OF PMT	PMTS EACH YEAR	PMT EACH PERIOD	YEARS TO RETIRE LOAN
5 YEAR AMORTIZATION				**10 YEAR AMORTIZATION**			
A	12	$20.79556	5.00	A	12	$12.70908	10.00
B	52	5.19889	4.51	B	52	3.17727	8.76
C	52	4.79898	4.98	C	52	2.93287	9.94
D	52	4.78232	5.00	D	52	2.92128	10.00
E	26	10.39778	4.51	E	26	6.35454	8.78
F	26	9.59795	4.98	F	26	5.86573	9.95
G	26	9.57295	5.00	G	26	5.84763	10.00
H	24	11.26426	4.51	H	24	6.88409	8.79
J	24	10.39778	4.99	J	24	6.35454	9.97
K	24	10.37819	5.00	K	24	6.34257	10.00
15 YEAR AMORTIZATION				**20 YEAR AMORTIZATION**			
A	12	$10.18830	15.00	A	12	$9.04660	20.00
B	52	2.54707	12.69	B	52	2.26165	16.17
C	52	2.35115	14.86	C	52	2.08768	19.74
D	52	2.34093	15.00	D	52	2.07795	20.00
E	26	5.09415	12.71	E	26	4.52330	16.21
F	26	4.70229	14.89	F	26	4.17535	19.79
G	26	4.68593	15.00	G	26	4.15950	20.00
H	24	5.51866	12.74	H	24	4.90024	16.27
J	24	5.09415	14.94	J	24	4.52330	19.89
K	24	5.08455	15.00	K	24	4.51478	20.00
25 YEAR AMORTIZATION				**30 YEAR AMORTIZATION**			
A	12	$8.44450	25.00	A	12	$8.10142	30.00
B	52	2.11112	19.15	B	52	2.02536	21.57
C	52	1.94873	24.54	C	52	1.86956	29.24
D	52	1.93916	25.00	D	52	1.86002	30.00
E	26	4.22225	19.19	E	26	4.05071	21.62
F	26	3.89746	24.62	F	26	3.73912	29.36
G	26	3.88169	25.00	G	26	3.72326	30.00
H	24	4.57410	19.29	H	24	4.38827	21.76
J	24	4.22225	24.82	J	24	4.05071	29.71
K	24	4.21429	25.00	K	24	4.04348	30.00

TYPES OF PAYMENTS: A—monthly; B—accelerated weekly; C—
regular weekly; D—minimum amortized weekly; E—accelerated
bi-weekly; F—regular bi-weekly; G—minimum amortized bi-
weekly; H—accelerated semi-monthly; J—regular semi-monthly;
K—minimum amortized semi-monthly

9.375%

BLENDED PAYMENTS IN DOLLARS OF PRINCIPAL AND IN-
TEREST FOR A LOAN OF $1,000 AT **9.375%** PER YEAR, CALCU-
LATED HALF-YEARLY, NOT IN ADVANCE

TYPE OF PMT	PMTS EACH YEAR	PMT EACH PERIOD	YEARS TO RETIRE LOAN	TYPE OF PMT	PMTS EACH YEAR	PMT EACH PERIOD	YEARS TO RETIRE LOAN
5 YEAR AMORTIZATION				**10 YEAR AMORTIZATION**			
A	12	$20.85408	5.00	A	12	$12.77442	10.00
B	52	5.21352	4.50	B	52	3.19361	8.76
C	52	4.81248	4.98	C	52	2.94794	9.93
D	52	4.79557	5.00	D	52	2.93615	10.00
E	26	10.42704	4.51	E	26	6.38721	8.77
F	26	9.62496	4.98	F	26	5.89589	9.95
G	26	9.59956	5.00	G	26	5.87747	10.00
H	24	11.29596	4.51	H	24	6.91948	8.78
J	24	10.42704	4.99	J	24	6.38721	9.97
K	24	10.40714	5.00	K	24	6.37502	10.00
15 YEAR AMORTIZATION				**20 YEAR AMORTIZATION**			
A	12	$10.26017	15.00	A	12	$9.12433	20.00
B	52	2.56504	12.66	B	52	2.28108	16.13
C	52	2.36773	14.86	C	52	2.10561	19.73
D	52	2.35732	15.00	D	52	2.09569	20.00
E	26	5.13009	12.69	E	26	4.56216	16.16
F	26	4.73546	14.89	F	26	4.21123	19.78
G	26	4.71879	15.00	G	26	4.19506	20.00
H	24	5.55759	12.72	H	24	4.94234	16.23
J	24	5.13009	14.94	J	24	4.56216	19.89
K	24	5.12030	15.00	K	24	4.55346	20.00
25 YEAR AMORTIZATION				**30 YEAR AMORTIZATION**			
A	12	$8.52726	25.00	A	12	$8.18835	30.00
B	52	2.13181	19.07	B	52	2.04709	21.45
C	52	1.96783	24.53	C	52	1.88962	29.21
D	52	1.95806	25.00	D	52	1.87988	30.00
E	26	4.26363	19.12	E	26	4.09418	21.51
F	26	3.93566	24.61	F	26	3.77924	29.34
G	26	3.91957	25.00	G	26	3.76307	30.00
H	24	4.61893	19.22	H	24	4.43536	21.64
J	24	4.26363	24.82	J	24	4.09418	29.70
K	24	4.25549	25.00	K	24	4.08636	30.00

TYPES OF PAYMENTS: A—monthly; B—accelerated weekly; C—
regular weekly; D—minimum amortized weekly; E—accelerated
bi-weekly; F—regular bi-weekly; G—minimum amortized bi-
weekly; H—accelerated semi-monthly; J—regular semi-monthly;
K—minimum amortized semi-monthly

9.5%

BLENDED PAYMENTS IN DOLLARS OF PRINCIPAL AND INTEREST FOR A LOAN OF $1,000 AT **9.5%** PER YEAR, CALCULATED HALF-YEARLY, NOT IN ADVANCE

TYPE OF PMT	PMTS EACH YEAR	PMT EACH PERIOD	YEARS TO RETIRE LOAN	TYPE OF PMT	PMTS EACH YEAR	PMT EACH PERIOD	YEARS TO RETIRE LOAN
5 YEAR AMORTIZATION				**10 YEAR AMORTIZATION**			
A	12	$20.91267	5.00	A	12	$12.83991	10.00
B	52	5.22817	4.50	B	52	3.20998	8.75
C	52	4.82600	4.98	C	52	2.96306	9.93
D	52	4.80882	5.00	D	52	2.95106	10.00
E	26	10.45633	4.52	E	26	6.41996	8.76
F	26	9.65200	4.98	F	26	5.92611	9.95
G	26	9.62621	5.00	G	26	5.90738	10.00
H	24	11.32770	4.51	H	24	6.95495	8.78
J	24	10.45633	4.99	J	24	6.41996	9.97
K	24	10.43612	5.00	K	24	6.40754	10.00
15 YEAR AMORTIZATION				**20 YEAR AMORTIZATION**			
A	12	$10.33226	15.00	A	12	$9.20231	20.00
B	52	2.58307	12.64	B	52	2.30058	16.09
C	52	2.38437	14.86	C	52	2.12361	19.73
D	52	2.37376	15.00	D	52	2.11349	20.00
E	26	5.16613	12.66	E	26	4.60115	16.12
F	26	4.76874	14.88	F	26	4.24722	19.78
G	26	4.75175	15.00	G	26	4.23074	20.00
H	24	5.59664	12.70	H	24	4.98458	16.18
J	24	5.16613	14.94	J	24	4.60115	19.89
K	24	5.15614	15.00	K	24	4.59226	20.00
25 YEAR AMORTIZATION				**30 YEAR AMORTIZATION**			
A	12	$8.61028	25.00	A	12	$8.27554	30.00
B	52	2.15257	19.00	B	52	2.06889	21.33
C	52	1.98699	24.52	C	52	1.90974	29.18
D	52	1.97702	25.00	D	52	1.89980	30.00
E	26	4.30514	19.04	E	26	4.13777	21.39
F	26	3.97397	24.60	F	26	3.81948	29.32
G	26	3.95756	25.00	G	26	3.80298	30.00
H	24	4.66390	19.14	H	24	4.48258	21.53
J	24	4.30514	24.81	J	24	4.13777	29.69
K	24	4.29681	25.00	K	24	4.12977	30.00

TYPES OF PAYMENTS: A—monthly; B—accelerated weekly; C—regular weekly; D—minimum amortized weekly; E—accelerated bi-weekly; F—regular bi-weekly; G—minimum amortized bi-weekly; H—accelerated semi-monthly; J—regular semi-monthly; K—minimum amortized semi-monthly

9.625%

BLENDED PAYMENTS IN DOLLARS OF PRINCIPAL AND INTEREST FOR A LOAN OF $1,000 AT **9.625%** PER YEAR, CALCULATED HALF-YEARLY, NOT IN ADVANCE

TYPE OF PMT	PMTS EACH YEAR	PMT EACH PERIOD	YEARS TO RETIRE LOAN	TYPE OF PMT	PMTS EACH YEAR	PMT EACH PERIOD	YEARS TO RETIRE LOAN
5 YEAR AMORTIZATION				**10 YEAR AMORTIZATION**			
A	12	$20.97133	5.00	A	12	$12.90555	10.00
B	52	5.24283	4.50	B	52	3.22639	8.74
C	52	4.83954	4.98	C	52	2.97820	9.93
D	52	4.82209	5.00	D	52	2.96600	10.00
E	26	10.48566	4.51	E	26	6.45278	8.75
F	26	9.67907	4.98	F	26	5.95641	9.95
G	26	9.65288	5.00	G	26	5.93735	10.00
H	24	11.35947	4.51	H	24	6.99051	8.77
J	24	10.48566	4.99	J	24	6.45278	9.97
K	24	10.46513	5.00	K	24	6.44014	10.00
15 YEAR AMORTIZATION				**20 YEAR AMORTIZATION**			
A	12	$10.40456	15.00	A	12	$9.28053	20.00
B	52	2.60114	12.62	B	52	2.32013	16.04
C	52	2.40105	14.85	C	52	2.14166	19.72
D	52	2.39025	15.00	D	52	2.13134	20.00
E	26	5.20228	12.64	E	26	4.64026	16.08
F	26	4.80210	14.88	F	26	4.28332	19.77
G	26	4.78481	15.00	G	26	4.26652	20.00
H	24	5.63580	12.68	H	24	5.02695	16.14
J	24	5.20228	14.94	J	24	4.64026	19.88
K	24	5.19209	15.00	K	24	4.63118	20.00
25 YEAR AMORTIZATION				**30 YEAR AMORTIZATION**			
A	12	$8.69355	25.00	A	12	$8.36297	30.00
B	52	2.17339	18.92	B	52	2.09074	21.21
C	52	2.00620	24.50	C	52	1.92992	29.16
D	52	1.99604	25.00	D	52	1.91977	30.00
E	26	4.34678	18.96	E	26	4.18149	21.27
F	26	4.01241	24.59	F	26	3.85983	29.30
G	26	3.99568	25.00	G	26	3.84301	30.00
H	24	4.70901	19.07	H	24	4.52994	21.41
J	24	4.34678	24.80	J	24	4.18149	29.68
K	24	4.33826	25.00	K	24	4.17330	30.00

TYPES OF PAYMENTS: A—monthly; B—accelerated weekly; C—regular weekly; D—minimum amortized weekly; E—accelerated bi-weekly; F—regular bi-weekly; G—minimum amortized bi-weekly; H—accelerated semi-monthly; J—regular semi-monthly; K—minimum amortized semi-monthly

9.75%

BLENDED PAYMENTS IN DOLLARS OF PRINCIPAL AND INTEREST FOR A LOAN OF $1,000 AT **9.75%** PER YEAR, CALCULATED HALF-YEARLY, NOT IN ADVANCE

TYPE OF PMT	PMTS EACH YEAR	PMT EACH PERIOD	YEARS TO RETIRE LOAN	TYPE OF PMT	PMTS EACH YEAR	PMT EACH PERIOD	YEARS TO RETIRE LOAN
5 YEAR AMORTIZATION				**10 YEAR AMORTIZATION**			
A	12	$21.03005	5.00	A	12	$12.97134	10.00
B	52	5.25751	4.50	B	52	3.24284	8.73
C	52	4.85309	4.98	C	52	2.99339	9.93
D	52	4.83537	5.00	D	52	2.98097	10.00
E	26	10.51502	4.50	E	26	6.48567	8.74
F	26	9.70618	4.98	F	26	5.98677	9.95
G	26	9.67958	5.00	G	26	5.96739	10.00
H	24	11.39128	4.51	H	24	7.02614	8.76
J	24	10.51502	4.99	J	24	6.48567	9.97
K	24	10.49417	5.00	K	24	6.47281	10.00
15 YEAR AMORTIZATION				**20 YEAR AMORTIZATION**			
A	12	$10.47707	15.00	A	12	$9.35899	20.00
B	52	2.61927	12.60	B	52	2.33975	16.00
C	52	2.41778	14.85	C	52	2.15977	19.71
D	52	2.40678	15.00	D	52	2.14925	20.00
E	26	5.23853	12.62	E	26	4.67950	16.03
F	26	4.83557	14.88	F	26	4.31954	19.77
G	26	4.81796	15.00	G	26	4.30242	20.00
H	24	5.67508	12.66	H	24	5.06946	16.10
J	24	5.23853	14.93	J	24	4.67950	19.88
K	24	5.22814	15.00	K	24	4.67022	20.00
25 YEAR AMORTIZATION				**30 YEAR AMORTIZATION**			
A	12	$8.77708	25.00	A	12	$8.45064	30.00
B	52	2.19427	18.84	B	52	2.11266	21.09
C	52	2.02548	24.49	C	52	1.95015	29.13
D	52	2.01511	25.00	D	52	1.93980	30.00
E	26	4.38854	18.89	E	26	4.22532	21.15
F	26	4.05096	24.58	F	26	3.90030	29.27
G	26	4.03390	25.00	G	26	3.88314	30.00
H	24	4.75425	18.99	H	24	4.57743	21.29
J	24	4.38854	24.80	J	24	4.22532	29.66
K	24	4.37984	25.00	K	24	4.21694	30.00

TYPES OF PAYMENTS: A—monthly; B—accelerated weekly; C—regular weekly; D—minimum amortized weekly; E—accelerated bi-weekly; F—regular bi-weekly; G—minimum amortized bi-weekly; H—accelerated semi-monthly; J—regular semi-monthly; K—minimum amortized semi-monthly

9.875%

BLENDED PAYMENTS IN DOLLARS OF PRINCIPAL AND IN-
TEREST FOR A LOAN OF $1,000 AT **9.875%** PER YEAR, CALCU-
LATED HALF-YEARLY, NOT IN ADVANCE

TYPE OF PMT	PMTS EACH YEAR	PMT EACH PERIOD	YEARS TO RETIRE LOAN	TYPE OF PMT	PMTS EACH YEAR	PMT EACH PERIOD	YEARS TO RETIRE LOAN
5 YEAR AMORTIZATION				**10 YEAR AMORTIZATION**			
A	12	$21.08884	5.00	A	12	$13.03728	10.00
B	52	5.27221	4.50	B	52	3.25932	8.72
C	52	4.86666	4.98	C	52	3.00860	9.93
D	52	4.84867	5.00	D	52	2.99598	10.00
E	26	10.54442	4.50	E	26	6.51864	8.74
F	26	9.73331	4.98	F	26	6.01721	9.95
G	26	9.70632	5.00	G	26	5.99749	10.00
H	24	11.42312	4.51	H	24	7.06186	8.75
J	24	10.54442	4.99	J	24	6.51864	9.97
K	24	10.52325	5.00	K	24	6.50555	10.00
15 YEAR AMORTIZATION				**20 YEAR AMORTIZATION**			
A	12	$10.54978	15.00	A	12	$9.43770	20.00
B	52	2.63744	12.58	B	52	2.35943	15.95
C	52	2.43456	14.85	C	52	2.17793	19.71
D	52	2.42336	15.00	D	52	2.16721	20.00
E	26	5.27489	12.60	E	26	4.71885	15.99
F	26	4.86913	14.88	F	26	4.35586	19.76
G	26	4.85120	15.00	G	26	4.33842	20.00
H	24	5.71446	12.64	H	24	5.11209	16.05
J	24	5.27489	14.93	J	24	4.71885	19.88
K	24	5.26430	15.00	K	24	4.70937	20.00
25 YEAR AMORTIZATION				**30 YEAR AMORTIZATION**			
A	12	$8.86085	25.00	A	12	$8.53855	30.00
B	52	2.21521	18.76	B	52	2.13464	20.97
C	52	2.04481	24.47	C	52	1.97043	29.10
D	52	2.03424	25.00	D	52	1.95988	30.00
E	26	4.43043	18.81	E	26	4.26927	21.03
F	26	4.08962	24.56	F	26	3.94087	29.25
G	26	4.07224	25.00	G	26	3.92339	30.00
H	24	4.79963	18.91	H	24	4.62505	21.18
J	24	4.43043	24.79	J	24	4.26927	29.65
K	24	4.42153	25.00	K	24	4.26070	30.00

TYPES OF PAYMENTS: A—monthly; B—accelerated weekly; C—
regular weekly; D—minimum amortized weekly; E—accelerated
bi-weekly; F—regular bi-weekly; G—minimum amortized bi-
weekly; H—accelerated semi-monthly; J—regular semi-monthly;
K—minimum amortized semi-monthly

10%

BLENDED PAYMENTS IN DOLLARS OF PRINCIPAL AND IN-
TEREST FOR A LOAN OF $1,000 AT **10%** PER YEAR, CALCU-
LATED HALF-YEARLY, NOT IN ADVANCE

TYPE OF PMT	PMTS EACH YEAR	PMT EACH PERIOD	YEARS TO RETIRE LOAN	TYPE OF PMT	PMTS EACH YEAR	PMT EACH PERIOD	YEARS TO RETIRE LOAN
5 YEAR AMORTIZATION				**10 YEAR AMORTIZATION**			
A	12	$21.14770	5.00	A	12	$13.10337	10.00
B	52	5.28692	4.49	B	52	3.27584	8.72
C	52	4.88024	4.98	C	52	3.02385	9.93
D	52	4.86199	5.00	C	52	3.01101	10.00
E	26	10.57385	4.50	E	26	6.55168	8.73
F	26	9.76048	4.98	F	26	6.04771	9.94
G	26	9.73308	5.00	G	26	6.02767	10.00
H	24	11.45500	4.50	H	24	7.09766	8.74
J	24	10.57385	4.99	J	24	6.55168	9.97
K	24	10.55235	5.00	K	24	6.53836	10.00
15 YEAR AMORTIZATION				**20 YEAR AMORTIZATION**			
A	12	$10.62270	15.00	A	12	$9.51664	20.00
B	52	2.65567	12.56	B	52	2.37916	15.91
C	52	2.45139	14.84	C	52	2.19615	19.70
D	52	2.43998	15.00	D	52	2.18522	20.00
E	26	5.31135	12.58	E	26	4.75832	15.94
F	26	4.90278	14.87	F	26	4.39230	19.75
G	26	4.88453	15.00	G	26	4.37454	20.00
H	24	5.75396	12.62	H	24	5.15485	16.01
J	24	5.31135	14.93	J	24	4.75832	19.87
K	24	5.30055	15.00	K	24	4.74865	20.00
25 YEAR AMORTIZATION				**30 YEAR AMORTIZATION**			
A	12	$8.94487	25.00	A	12	$8.62668	30.00
B	52	2.23622	18.68	B	52	2.15667	20.85
C	52	2.06420	24.46	C	52	1.99077	29.07
D	52	2.05342	25.00	D	52	1.98001	30.00
E	26	4.47244	18.73	E	26	4.31334	20.91
F	26	4.12840	24.55	F	26	3.98154	29.22
G	26	4.11069	25.00	G	26	3.96373	30.00
H	24	4.84514	18.84	H	24	4.67278	21.06
J	24	4.47244	24.78	J	24	4.31334	29.64
K	24	4.46334	25.00	K	24	4.30457	30.00

TYPES OF PAYMENTS: A—monthly; B—accelerated weekly; C—
regular weekly; D—minimum amortized weekly; E—accelerated
bi-weekly; F—regular bi-weekly; G—minimum amortized bi-
weekly; H—accelerated semi-monthly; J—regular semi-monthly;
K—minimum amortized semi-monthly

10.125%

BLENDED PAYMENTS IN DOLLARS OF PRINCIPAL AND IN-
TEREST FOR A LOAN OF $1,000 AT **10.125%** PER YEAR, CAL-
CULATED HALF-YEARLY, NOT IN ADVANCE

TYPE OF PMT	PMTS EACH YEAR	PMT EACH PERIOD	YEARS TO RETIRE LOAN	TYPE OF PMT	PMTS EACH YEAR	PMT EACH PERIOD	YEARS TO RETIRE LOAN
5 YEAR AMORTIZATION				**10 YEAR AMORTIZATION**			
A	12	$21.20662	5.00	A	12	$13.16960	10.00
B	52	5.30166	4.49	B	52	3.29240	8.71
C	52	4.89384	4.98	C	52	3.03914	9.93
D	52	4.87531	5.00	D	52	3.02608	10.00
E	26	10.60331	4.50	E	26	6.58480	8.72
F	26	9.78767	4.98	F	26	6.07828	9.94
G	26	9.75987	5.00	G	26	6.05790	10.00
H	24	11.48692	4.50	H	24	7.13353	8.74
J	24	10.60331	4.99	J	24	6.58480	9.96
K	24	10.58149	5.00	K	24	6.57125	10.00
15 YEAR AMORTIZATION				**20 YEAR AMORTIZATION**			
A	12	$10.69582	15.00	A	12	$9.59582	20.00
B	52	2.67396	12.53	B	52	2.39896	15.86
C	52	2.46827	14.84	C	52	2.21442	19.69
D	52	2.45665	15.00	D	52	2.20329	20.00
E	26	5.34791	12.56	E	26	4.79791	15.90
F	26	4.93653	14.87	F	26	4.42884	19.75
G	26	4.91796	15.00	G	26	4.41075	20.00
H	24	5.79357	12.60	H	24	5.19774	15.97
J	24	5.34791	14.93	J	24	4.79791	19.87
K	24	5.33691	15.00	K	24	4.78804	20.00
25 YEAR AMORTIZATION				**30 YEAR AMORTIZATION**			
A	12	$9.02913	25.00	A	12	$8.71504	30.00
B	52	2.25728	18.60	B	52	2.17876	20.73
C	52	2.08365	24.44	C	52	2.01116	29.04
D	52	2.07266	25.00	D	52	2.00019	30.00
E	26	4.51456	18.65	E	26	4.35752	20.80
F	26	4.16729	24.54	F	26	4.02233	29.20
G	26	4.14925	25.00	G	26	4.00417	30.00
H	24	4.89078	18.76	H	24	4.72065	20.94
J	24	4.51456	24.78	J	24	4.35752	29.62
K	24	4.50528	25.00	K	24	4.34855	30.00

TYPES OF PAYMENTS: A—monthly; B—accelerated weekly; C—
regular weekly; D—minimum amortized weekly; E—accelerated
bi-weekly; F—regular bi-weekly; G—minimum amortized bi-
weekly; H—accelerated semi-monthly; J—regular semi-monthly;
K—minimum amortized semi-monthly

10.25%

BLENDED PAYMENTS IN DOLLARS OF PRINCIPAL AND IN-
TEREST FOR A LOAN OF $1,000 AT **10.25%** PER YEAR, CALCU-
LATED HALF-YEARLY, NOT IN ADVANCE

TYPE OF PMT	PMTS EACH YEAR	PMT EACH PERIOD	YEARS TO RETIRE LOAN	TYPE OF PMT	PMTS EACH YEAR	PMT EACH PERIOD	YEARS TO RETIRE LOAN
5 YEAR AMORTIZATION				**10 YEAR AMORTIZATION**			
A	12	$21.26562	5.00	A	12	$13.23598	10.00
B	52	5.31640	4.49	B	52	3.30899	8.70
C	52	4.90745	4.98	C	52	3.05446	9.93
D	52	4.88866	5.00	D	52	3.04119	10.00
E	26	10.63281	4.50	E	26	6.61799	8.71
F	26	9.81490	4.98	F	26	6.10891	9.94
G	26	9.78669	5.00	G	26	6.08821	10.00
H	24	11.51888	4.50	H	24	7.16949	8.73
J	24	10.63281	4.99	J	24	6.61799	9.96
K	24	10.61067	5.00	K	24	6.60421	10.00
15 YEAR AMORTIZATION				**20 YEAR AMORTIZATION**			
A	12	$10.76915	15.00	A	12	$9.67523	20.00
B	52	2.69229	12.51	B	52	2.41881	15.82
C	52	2.48519	14.84	C	52	2.23275	19.68
D	52	2.47337	15.00	D	52	2.22141	20.00
E	26	5.38457	12.54	E	26	4.83762	15.85
F	26	4.97038	14.87	F	26	4.46549	19.74
G	26	4.95148	15.00	G	26	4.44707	20.00
H	24	5.83329	12.58	H	24	5.24075	15.92
J	24	5.38457	14.93	J	24	4.83762	19.87
K	24	5.37336	15.00	K	24	4.82754	20.00
25 YEAR AMORTIZATION				**30 YEAR AMORTIZATION**			
A	12	$9.11362	25.00	A	12	$8.80361	30.00
B	52	2.27841	18.52	B	52	2.20090	20.61
C	52	2.10314	24.42	C	52	2.03160	29.01
D	52	2.09195	25.00	D	52	2.02042	30.00
E	26	4.55681	18.57	E	26	4.40181	20.68
F	26	4.20629	24.53	F	26	4.06321	29.17
G	26	4.18791	25.00	G	26	4.04472	30.00
H	24	4.93655	18.68	H	24	4.76862	20.82
J	24	4.55681	24.77	J	24	4.40181	29.61
K	24	4.54732	25.00	K	24	4.39264	30.00

TYPES OF PAYMENTS: A—monthly; B—accelerated weekly; C—
regular weekly; D—minimum amortized weekly; E—accelerated
bi-weekly; F—regular bi-weekly; G—minimum amortized bi-
weekly; H—accelerated semi-monthly; J—regular semi-monthly;
K—minimum amortized semi-monthly

10.375%

BLENDED PAYMENTS IN DOLLARS OF PRINCIPAL AND INTEREST FOR A LOAN OF $1,000 AT **10.375%** PER YEAR, CALCULATED HALF-YEARLY, NOT IN ADVANCE

TYPE OF PMT	PMTS EACH YEAR	PMT EACH PERIOD	YEARS TO RETIRE LOAN	TYPE OF PMT	PMTS EACH YEAR	PMT EACH PERIOD	YEARS TO RETIRE LOAN
5 YEAR AMORTIZATION				**10 YEAR AMORTIZATION**			
A	12	$21.32468	5.00	A	12	$13.30250	10.00
B	52	5.33117	4.49	B	52	3.32563	8.69
C	52	4.92108	4.97	C	52	3.06981	9.92
D	52	4.90201	5.00	D	52	3.05632	10.00
E	26	10.66234	4.50	E	26	6.65125	8.71
F	26	9.84216	4.98	F	26	6.13962	9.94
G	26	9.81354	5.00	G	26	6.11857	10.00
H	24	11.55087	4.50	H	24	7.20552	8.72
J	24	10.66234	4.99	J	24	6.65125	9.96
K	24	10.63987	5.00	K	24	6.63724	10.00
15 YEAR AMORTIZATION				**20 YEAR AMORTIZATION**			
A	12	$10.84268	15.00	A	12	$9.75487	20.00
B	52	2.71067	12.49	B	52	2.43872	15.77
C	52	2.50216	14.83	C	52	2.25112	19.67
D	52	2.49012	15.00	D	52	2.23957	20.00
E	26	5.42134	12.51	E	26	4.87743	15.81
F	26	5.00431	14.87	F	26	4.50225	19.73
G	26	4.98508	15.00	G	26	4.48350	20.00
H	24	5.87312	12.55	H	24	5.28389	15.88
J	24	5.42134	14.93	J	24	4.87743	19.86
K	24	5.40991	15.00	K	24	4.86716	20.00
25 YEAR AMORTIZATION				**30 YEAR AMORTIZATION**			
A	12	$9.19835	25.00	A	12	$8.89240	30.00
B	52	2.29959	18.44	B	52	2.22310	20.49
C	52	2.12270	24.41	C	52	2.05209	28.97
D	52	2.11129	25.00	D	52	2.04070	30.00
E	26	4.59917	18.49	E	26	4.44620	20.56
F	26	4.24539	24.51	F	26	4.10419	29.15
G	26	4.22668	25.00	G	26	4.08536	30.00
H	24	4.98244	18.60	H	24	4.81672	20.70
J	24	4.59917	24.76	J	24	4.44620	29.60
K	24	4.58948	25.00	K	24	4.43683	30.00

TYPES OF PAYMENTS: A—monthly; B—accelerated weekly; C—regular weekly; D—minimum amortized weekly; E—accelerated bi-weekly; F—regular bi-weekly; G—minimum amortized bi-weekly; H—accelerated semi-monthly; J—regular semi-monthly; K—minimum amortized semi-monthly

10.5%

BLENDED PAYMENTS IN DOLLARS OF PRINCIPAL AND IN-
TEREST FOR A LOAN OF $1,000 AT **10.5%** PER YEAR, CALCU-
LATED HALF-YEARLY, NOT IN ADVANCE

TYPE OF PMT	PMTS EACH YEAR	PMT EACH PERIOD	YEARS TO RETIRE LOAN	TYPE OF PMT	PMTS EACH YEAR	PMT EACH PERIOD	YEARS TO RETIRE LOAN
5 YEAR AMORTIZATION				**10 YEAR AMORTIZATION**			
A	12	$21.38380	5.00	A	12	$13.36917	10.00
B	52	5.34595	4.49	B	52	3.34229	8.68
C	52	4.93472	4.97	C	52	3.08519	9.92
D	52	4.91538	5.00	D	52	3.07149	10.00
E	26	10.69190	4.49	E	26	6.68459	8.70
F	26	9.86945	4.98	F	26	6.17039	9.94
G	26	9.84042	5.00	G	26	6.14901	10.00
H	24	11.58289	4.50	H	24	7.24164	8.71
J	24	10.69190	4.99	J	24	6.68459	9.96
K	24	10.66911	5.00	K	24	6.67033	10.00
15 YEAR AMORTIZATION				**20 YEAR AMORTIZATION**			
A	12	$10.91640	15.00	A	12	$9.83473	20.00
B	52	2.72910	12.47	B	52	2.45868	15.72
C	52	2.51917	14.83	C	52	2.26955	19.67
D	52	2.50693	15.00	D	52	2.25779	20.00
E	26	5.45820	12.49	E	26	4.91737	15.76
F	26	5.03834	14.86	F	26	4.53911	19.73
G	26	5.01878	15.00	G	26	4.52003	20.00
H	24	5.91305	12.53	H	24	5.32715	15.83
J	24	5.45820	14.92	J	24	4.91737	19.86
K	24	5.44656	15.00	K	24	4.90688	20.00
25 YEAR AMORTIZATION				**30 YEAR AMORTIZATION**			
A	12	$9.28330	25.00	A	12	$8.98140	30.00
B	52	2.32082	18.36	B	52	2.24535	20.37
C	52	2.14230	24.39	C	52	2.07263	28.94
D	52	2.13068	25.00	D	52	2.06102	30.00
E	26	4.64165	18.42	E	26	4.49070	20.44
F	26	4.28460	24.50	F	26	4.14526	29.12
G	26	4.26555	25.00	G	26	4.12609	30.00
H	24	5.02845	18.52	H	24	4.86493	20.59
J	24	4.64165	24.75	J	24	4.49070	29.58
K	24	4.63175	25.00	K	24	4.48113	30.00

TYPES OF PAYMENTS: A—monthly; B—accelerated weekly; C—
regular weekly; D—minimum amortized weekly; E—accelerated
bi-weekly; F—regular bi-weekly; G—minimum amortized bi-
weekly; H—accelerated semi-monthly; J—regular semi-monthly;
K—minimum amortized semi-monthly

10.625%

BLENDED PAYMENTS IN DOLLARS OF PRINCIPAL AND IN-
TEREST FOR A LOAN OF $1,000 AT **10.625%** PER YEAR, CAL-
CULATED HALF-YEARLY, NOT IN ADVANCE

TYPE OF PMT	PMTS EACH YEAR	PMT EACH PERIOD	YEARS TO RETIRE LOAN	TYPE OF PMT	PMTS EACH YEAR	PMT EACH PERIOD	YEARS TO RETIRE LOAN
5 YEAR AMORTIZATION				**10 YEAR AMORTIZATION**			
A	12	$21.44300	5.00	A	12	$13.43599	10.00
B	52	5.36075	4.49	B	52	3.35900	8.68
C	52	4.94838	4.97	C	52	3.10061	9.92
D	52	4.92877	5.00	D	52	3.08669	10.00
E	26	10.72150	4.49	E	26	6.71799	8.69
F	26	9.89677	4.98	F	26	6.20122	9.94
G	26	9.86733	5.00	G	26	6.17951	10.00
H	24	11.61496	4.50	H	24	7.27783	8.71
J	24	10.72150	5.99	J	24	6.71799	9.96
K	24	10.69837	5.00	K	24	6.70350	10.00
15 YEAR AMORTIZATION				**20 YEAR AMORTIZATION**			
A	12	$10.99033	15.00	A	12	$9.91482	20.00
B	52	2.74758	12.45	B	52	2.47871	15.68
C	52	2.53623	14.83	C	52	2.28804	19.66
D	52	2.52378	15.00	D	52	2.27606	20.00
E	26	5.49516	12.47	E	26	4.95741	15.71
F	26	5.07246	14.86	F	26	4.57607	19.72
G	26	5.05257	15.00	G	26	4.55665	20.00
H	24	5.95309	12.51	H	24	5.37053	15.79
J	24	5.49516	14.92	J	24	4.95741	19.86
K	24	5.48331	15.00	K	24	4.94672	20.00
25 YEAR AMORTIZATION				**30 YEAR AMORTIZATION**			
A	12	$9.36847	25.00	A	12	$9.07060	30.00
B	52	2.34212	18.28	B	52	2.26765	20.25
C	52	2.16195	24.37	C	52	2.09322	28.91
D	52	2.15012	25.00	D	52	2.08139	30.00
E	26	4.68424	18.34	E	26	4.53530	20.32
F	26	4.32391	24.48	F	26	4.18643	29.09
G	26	4.30451	25.00	G	26	4.16691	30.00
H	24	5.07459	18.45	H	24	4.91324	20.47
J	24	4.68424	24.75	J	24	4.53530	29.57
K	24	4.67413	25.00	K	24	4.52552	30.00

TYPES OF PAYMENTS: A—monthly; B—accelerated weekly; C—
regular weekly; D—minimum amortized weekly; E—accelerated
bi-weekly; F—regular bi-weekly; G—minimum amortized bi-
weekly; H—accelerated semi-monthly; J—regular semi-monthly;
K—minimum amortized semi-monthly

10.75%

BLENDED PAYMENTS IN DOLLARS OF PRINCIPAL AND IN-
TEREST FOR A LOAN OF $1,000 AT **10.75%** PER YEAR, CALCU-
LATED HALF-YEARLY, NOT IN ADVANCE

TYPE OF PMT	PMTS EACH YEAR	PMT EACH PERIOD	YEARS TO RETIRE LOAN	TYPE OF PMT	PMTS EACH YEAR	PMT EACH PERIOD	YEARS TO RETIRE LOAN
5 YEAR AMORTIZATION				**10 YEAR AMORTIZATION**			
A	12	$21.50226	5.00	A	12	$13.50294	10.00
B	52	5.37556	4.48	B	52	3.37574	8.67
C	52	4.96206	4.97	C	52	3.11606	9.92
D	52	4.94217	5.00	D	52	3.10192	10.00
E	26	10.75113	4.49	E	26	6.75147	8.68
F	26	9.92412	4.98	F	26	6.23213	9.94
G	26	9.89427	5.00	G	26	6.21007	10.00
H	24	11.64705	4.49	H	24	7.31409	8.70
J	24	10.75113	4.99	J	24	6.75147	9.96
K	24	10.72767	5.00	K	24	6.73674	10.00
15 YEAR AMORTIZATION				**20 YEAR AMORTIZATION**			
A	12	$11.06445	15.00	A	12	$9.99513	20.00
B	52	2.76611	12.42	B	52	2.49878	15.63
C	52	2.55333	14.82	C	52	2.30657	19.65
D	52	2.54067	15.00	D	52	2.29438	20.00
E	26	5.53222	12.45	E	26	4.99756	15.67
F	26	5.10667	14.86	F	26	4.61314	19.71
G	26	5.08644	15.00	G	26	4.59338	20.00
H	24	5.99324	12.49	H	24	5.41403	15.74
J	24	5.53222	14.92	J	24	4.99756	19.85
K	24	5.52015	15.00	K	24	4.98666	20.00
25 YEAR AMORTIZATION				**30 YEAR AMORTIZATION**			
A	12	$9.45386	25.00	A	12	$9.16000	30.00
B	52	2.36347	18.20	B	52	2.29000	20.13
C	52	2.18166	24.36	C	52	2.11385	28.87
D	52	2.16961	25.00	D	52	2.10180	30.00
E	26	4.72693	18.26	E	26	4.58000	20.20
F	26	4.36332	24.47	F	26	4.22769	29.06
G	26	4.34358	25.00	G	26	4.20783	30.00
H	24	5.12084	18.37	H	24	4.96167	20.35
J	24	4.72693	24.74	J	24	4.58000	29.55
K	24	4.71662	25.00	K	24	4.57001	30.00

TYPES OF PAYMENTS: A—monthly; B—accelerated weekly; C—
regular weekly; D—minimum amortized weekly; E—accelerated
bi-weekly; F—regular bi-weekly; G—minimum amortized bi-
weekly; H—accelerated semi-monthly; J—regular semi-monthly;
K—minimum amortized semi-monthly

10.875%

BLENDED PAYMENTS IN DOLLARS OF PRINCIPAL AND IN-
TEREST FOR A LOAN OF $1,000 AT **10.875%** PER YEAR, CAL-
CULATED HALF-YEARLY, NOT IN ADVANCE

TYPE OF PMT	PMTS EACH YEAR	PMT EACH PERIOD	YEARS TO RETIRE LOAN	TYPE OF PMT	PMTS EACH YEAR	PMT EACH PERIOD	YEARS TO RETIRE LOAN
5 YEAR AMORTIZATION				**10 YEAR AMORTIZATION**			
A	12	$21.56158	5.00	A	12	$13.57004	10.00
B	52	5.39040	4.48	B	52	3.39251	8.66
C	52	4.97575	4.97	C	52	3.13155	9.92
D	52	4.95558	5.00	D	52	3.11718	10.00
E	26	10.78079	4.49	E	26	6.78502	8.67
F	26	9.95150	4.98	F	26	6.26310	9.94
G	26	9.92124	5.00	G	26	6.24069	10.00
H	24	11.67919	4.49	H	24	7.35044	8.67
J	24	10.78079	4.99	J	24	6.78502	9.96
K	24	10.75701	5.00	K	24	6.77005	10.00
15 YEAR AMORTIZATION				**20 YEAR AMORTIZATION**			
A	12	$11.13876	15.00	A	12	$10.07566	20.00
B	52	2.78469	12.40	B	52	2.51891	15.58
C	52	2.57048	14.82	C	52	2.32515	19.64
D	52	2.55760	15.00	D	52	2.31275	20.00
E	26	5.56938	12.43	E	26	5.03783	15.62
F	26	5.14097	14.85	F	26	4.65030	19.71
G	26	5.12041	15.00	G	26	4.63020	20.00
H	24	6.03350	12.47	H	24	5.45765	15.70
J	24	5.56938	14.92	J	24	5.03783	19.85
K	24	5.55709	15.00	K	24	5.02671	20.00
25 YEAR AMORTIZATION				**30 YEAR AMORTIZATION**			
A	12	$9.53947	25.00	A	12	$9.24960	30.00
B	52	2.38487	18.12	B	52	2.31240	20.01
C	52	2.20142	24.34	C	52	2.13452	28.84
D	52	2.18915	25.00	D	52	2.12226	30.00
E	26	4.76974	18.18	E	26	4.62480	20.08
F	26	4.40283	24.45	F	26	4.26904	29.03
G	26	4.38275	25.00	G	26	4.24883	30.00
H	24	5.16721	18.29	H	24	5.01020	20.23
J	24	4.76974	24.73	J	24	4.62480	29.53
K	24	4.75921	25.00	K	24	4.61460	30.00

TYPES OF PAYMENTS: A—monthly; B—accelerated weekly; C—
regular weekly; D—minimum amortized weekly; E—accelerated
bi-weekly; F—regular bi-weekly; G—minimum amortized bi-
weekly; H—accelerated semi-monthly; J—regular semi-monthly;
K—minimum amortized semi-monthly

11%

BLENDED PAYMENTS IN DOLLARS OF PRINCIPAL AND IN-
TEREST FOR A LOAN OF $1,000 AT **11%** PER YEAR, CALCU-
LATED HALF-YEARLY, NOT IN ADVANCE

TYPE OF PMT	PMTS EACH YEAR	PMT EACH PERIOD	YEARS TO RETIRE LOAN	TYPE OF PMT	PMTS EACH YEAR	PMT EACH PERIOD	YEARS TO RETIRE LOAN
5 YEAR AMORTIZATION				**10 YEAR AMORTIZATION**			
A	12	$21.62097	5.00	A	12	$13.63729	10.00
B	52	5.40524	4.48	B	52	3.40932	8.65
C	52	4.98946	4.97	C	52	3.14707	9.92
D	52	4.96901	5.00	D	52	3.13247	10.00
E	26	10.81049	4.49	E	26	6.81864	8.66
F	26	9.97891	4.98	F	26	6.29413	9.94
G	26	9.94823	5.00	G	26	6.27138	10.00
H	24	11.71136	4.49	H	24	7.38686	8.68
J	24	10.81049	4.99	J	24	6.81864	9.96
K	24	10.78637	5.00	K	24	6.80343	10.00
15 YEAR AMORTIZATION				**20 YEAR AMORTIZATION**			
A	12	$11.21327	15.00	A	12	$10.15640	20.00
B	52	2.80332	12.38	B	52	2.53910	15.53
C	52	2.58768	14.81	C	52	2.34378	19.63
D	52	2.57458	15.00	D	52	2.33117	20.00
E	26	5.60663	12.40	E	26	5.07820	15.57
F	26	5.17536	14.85	F	26	4.68757	19.70
G	26	5.15445	15.00	G	26	4.66712	20.00
H	24	6.07385	12.45	H	24	5.50138	15.65
J	24	5.60663	14.92	J	24	5.07820	19.84
K	24	5.59413	15.00	K	24	5.06687	20.00
25 YEAR AMORTIZATION				**30 YEAR AMORTIZATION**			
A	12	$9.62529	25.00	A	12	$9.33938	30.00
B	52	2.40632	18.04	B	52	2.33484	19.89
C	52	2.22122	24.32	C	52	2.15524	28.80
D	52	2.20873	25.00	D	52	2.14275	30.00
E	26	4.81265	18.09	E	26	4.66969	19.96
F	26	4.44244	24.44	F	26	4.31048	29.00
G	26	4.42201	25.00	G	26	4.28991	30.00
H	24	5.21370	18.21	H	24	5.05883	20.11
J	24	4.81265	24.72	J	24	4.66969	29.52
K	24	4.80191	25.00	K	24	4.65927	30.00

TYPES OF PAYMENTS: A—monthly; B—accelerated weekly; C—
regular weekly; D—minimum amortized weekly; E—accelerated
bi-weekly; F—regular bi-weekly; G—minimum amortized bi-
weekly; H—accelerated semi-monthly; J—regular semi-monthly;
K—minimum amortized semi-monthly

11.125%

BLENDED PAYMENTS IN DOLLARS OF PRINCIPAL AND INTEREST FOR A LOAN OF $1,000 AT **11.125%** PER YEAR, CALCULATED HALF-YEARLY, NOT IN ADVANCE

TYPE OF PMT	PMTS EACH YEAR	PMT EACH PERIOD	YEARS TO RETIRE LOAN	TYPE OF PMT	PMTS EACH YEAR	PMT EACH PERIOD	YEARS TO RETIRE LOAN
5 YEAR AMORTIZATION				**10 YEAR AMORTIZATION**			
A	12	$21.68043	5.00	A	12	$13.70467	10.00
B	52	5.42011	4.48	B	52	3.42617	8.64
C	52	5.00318	4.97	C	52	3.16262	9.92
D	52	4.98245	5.00	D	52	3.14780	10.00
E	26	10.84021	4.49	E	26	6.85234	8.66
F	26	10.00635	4.98	F	26	6.32523	9.93
G	26	9.97526	5.00	G	26	6.30214	10.00
H	24	11.74357	4.49	H	24	7.42336	8.67
J	24	10.84021	4.99	J	24	6.85234	9.96
K	24	10.81576	5.00	K	24	6.83688	10.00
15 YEAR AMORTIZATION				**20 YEAR AMORTIZATION**			
A	12	$11.28797	15.00	A	12	$10.23735	20.00
B	52	2.82199	12.35	B	52	2.55934	15.49
C	52	2.60492	14.81	C	52	2.36247	19.62
D	52	2.59160	15.00	D	52	2.34963	20.00
E	26	5.64398	12.38	E	26	5.11867	15.53
F	26	5.20983	14.85	F	26	4.72493	19.69
G	26	5.18859	15.00	G	26	4.70414	20.00
H	24	6.11432	12.42	H	24	5.54523	15.60
J	24	5.64398	14.92	J	26	5.11867	19.84
K	24	5.63125	15.00	K	26	5.10713	20.00
25 YEAR AMORTIZATION				**30 YEAR AMORTIZATION**			
A	12	$9.71132	25.00	A	12	$9.42935	30.00
B	52	2.42783	17.96	B	52	2.35734	19.77
C	52	2.24107	24.30	C	52	2.17600	28.76
D	52	2.22836	25.00	D	52	2.16329	30.00
E	26	4.85566	18.01	E	26	4.71467	19.84
F	26	4.48215	24.42	F	26	4.35201	28.97
G	26	4.46136	25.00	G	26	4.33108	30.00
H	24	5.26030	18.13	H	24	5.10756	19.99
J	24	4.85566	24.71	J	24	4.71467	29.50
K	24	4.84471	25.00	K	24	4.70404	30.00

TYPES OF PAYMENTS: A—monthly; B—accelerated weekly; C—regular weekly; D—minimum amortized weekly; E—accelerated bi-weekly; F—regular bi-weekly; G—minimum amortized bi-weekly; H—accelerated semi-monthly; J—regular semi-monthly; K—minimum amortized semi-monthly

11.25%

BLENDED PAYMENTS IN DOLLARS OF PRINCIPAL AND IN-
TEREST FOR A LOAN OF $1,000 AT **11.25%** PER YEAR, CALCU-
LATED HALF-YEARLY, NOT IN ADVANCE

TYPE OF PMT	PMTS EACH YEAR	PMT EACH PERIOD	YEARS TO RETIRE LOAN	TYPE OF PMT	PMTS EACH YEAR	PMT EACH PERIOD	YEARS TO RETIRE LOAN
5 YEAR AMORTIZATION				**10 YEAR AMORTIZATION**			
A	12	$21.73995	5.00	A	12	$13.77220	10.00
B	52	5.43499	4.48	B	52	3.44305	8.63
C	52	5.01691	4.97	C	52	3.17820	9.91
D	52	4.99591	5.00	D	52	3.16315	10.00
E	26	10.86998	4.48	E	26	6.88610	8.65
F	26	10.03382	4.98	F	26	6.35640	9.93
G	26	10.00231	5.00	G	26	6.33295	10.00
H	24	11.77581	4.49	H	24	7.45994	8.67
J	24	10.86998	4.98	J	24	6.88610	9.96
K	24	10.84519	5.00	K	24	6.87040	10.00
15 YEAR AMORTIZATION				**20 YEAR AMORTIZATION**			
A	12	$11.36286	15.00	A	12	$10.31851	20.00
B	52	2.84071	12.33	B	52	2.57963	15.44
C	52	2.62220	14.81	C	52	2.38120	19.61
D	52	2.60866	15.00	D	52	2.36814	20.00
E	26	5.68143	12.36	E	26	5.15926	15.48
F	26	5.24440	14.85	F	26	4.76239	19.69
G	26	5.22281	15.00	G	26	4.74125	20.00
H	24	6.15488	12.40	H	24	5.58919	15.56
J	24	5.68143	14.91	J	24	5.15926	19.84
K	24	5.66847	15.00	K	24	5.14749	20.00
25 YEAR AMORTIZATION				**30 YEAR AMORTIZATION**			
A	12	$9.79755	25.00	A	12	$9.51949	30.00
B	52	2.44939	17.87	B	52	2.37987	19.65
C	52	2.26097	24.28	C	52	2.19681	28.72
D	52	2.24804	25.00	D	52	2.18387	30.00
E	26	4.89877	17.93	E	26	4.75975	19.72
F	26	4.52195	24.41	F	26	4.39361	28.94
G	26	4.50081	25.00	G	26	4.37233	30.00
H	24	5.30701	18.05	H	24	5.15639	19.88
J	24	4.89877	24.70	J	24	4.75975	29.48
K	24	4.88760	25.00	K	24	4.74889	30.00

TYPES OF PAYMENTS: A—monthly; B—accelerated weekly; C—
regular weekly; D—minimum amortized weekly; E—accelerated
bi-weekly; F—regular bi-weekly; G—minimum amortized bi-
weekly; H—accelerated semi-monthly; J—regular semi-monthly;
K—minimum amortized semi-monthly

11.375%

BLENDED PAYMENTS IN DOLLARS OF PRINCIPAL AND IN-
TEREST FOR A LOAN OF $1,000 AT **11.375%** PER YEAR, CAL-
CULATED HALF-YEARLY, NOT IN ADVANCE

TYPE OF PMT	PMTS EACH YEAR	PMT EACH PERIOD	YEARS TO RETIRE LOAN	TYPE OF PMT	PMTS EACH YEAR	PMT EACH PERIOD	YEARS TO RETIRE LOAN
5 YEAR AMORTIZATION				**10 YEAR AMORTIZATION**			
A	12	$21.79954	5.00	A	12	$13.83986	10.00
B	52	5.44989	4.48	B	52	3.45997	8.62
C	52	5.03066	4.97	C	52	3.19381	9.91
D	52	5.00938	5.00	D	52	3.17854	10.00
E	26	10.89977	4.48	E	26	6.91993	8.64
F	26	10.06133	4.98	F	26	6.38763	9.93
G	26	10.02939	5.00	G	26	6.36383	10.00
H	24	11.80808	4.49	H	24	7.49659	8.66
J	24	10.89977	4.98	J	24	6.91993	9.96
K	24	10.87465	5.00	K	24	6.90398	10.00
15 YEAR AMORTIZATION				**20 YEAR AMORTIZATION**			
A	12	$11.43794	15.00	A	12	$10.39988	20.00
B	52	2.85948	12.31	B	52	2.59997	15.39
C	52	2.63952	14.80	C	52	2.39997	19.60
D	52	2.62577	15.00	D	52	2.38669	20.00
E	26	5.71897	12.33	E	26	5.19994	15.43
F	26	5.27905	14.84	F	26	4.79995	19.68
G	26	5.25712	15.00	G	26	4.77846	20.00
H	24	6.19555	12.38	H	24	5.63327	15.51
J	24	5.71897	14.91	J	24	5.19994	19.83
K	24	5.70579	15.00	K	24	5.18796	20.00
25 YEAR AMORTIZATION				**30 YEAR AMORTIZATION**			
A	12	$9.88398	25.00	A	12	$9.60981	30.00
B	52	2.47099	17.79	B	52	2.40245	19.53
C	52	2.28092	24.26	C	52	2.21765	28.68
D	52	2.26776	25.00	D	52	2.20449	30.00
E	26	4.94199	17.85	E	26	4.80491	19.61
F	26	4.56184	24.39	F	26	4.43530	28.90
G	26	4.54034	25.00	G	26	4.41366	30.00
H	24	5.35382	17.97	H	24	5.20531	19.76
J	24	4.94199	24.69	J	24	4.80481	29.46
K	24	4.93060	25.00	K	24	4.79383	30.00

TYPES OF PAYMENTS: A—monthly; B—accelerated weekly; C—
regular weekly; D—minimum amortized weekly; E—accelerated
bi-weekly; F—regular bi-weekly; G—minimum amortized bi-
weekly; H—accelerated semi-monthly; J—regular semi-monthly;
K—minimum amortized semi-monthly

11.5%

BLENDED PAYMENTS IN DOLLARS OF PRINCIPAL AND IN-
TEREST FOR A LOAN OF $1,000 AT **11.5%** PER YEAR, CALCU-
LATED HALF-YEARLY, NOT IN ADVANCE

TYPE OF PMT	PMTS EACH YEAR	PMT EACH PERIOD	YEARS TO RETIRE LOAN	TYPE OF PMT	PMTS EACH YEAR	PMT EACH PERIOD	YEARS TO RETIRE LOAN
5 YEAR AMORTIZATION				**10 YEAR AMORTIZATION**			
A	12	$21.85919	5.00	A	12	$13.90767	10.00
B	52	5.46480	4.47	B	52	3.47692	8.62
C	52	5.04443	4.97	C	52	3.20946	9.91
D	52	5.02286	5.00	D	52	3.19396	10.00
E	26	10.92960	4.48	E	26	6.95383	8.63
F	26	10.08886	4.98	F	26	6.41892	9.93
G	26	10.05650	5.00	G	26	6.39477	10.00
H	24	11.84040	4.49	H	24	7.53332	8.65
J	24	10.92960	4.98	J	24	6.95383	9.96
K	24	10.90414	5.00	K	24	6.93763	10.00
15 YEAR AMORTIZATION				**20 YEAR AMORTIZATION**			
A	12	$11.51320	15.00	A	12	$10.48146	20.00
B	52	2.87830	12.28	B	52	2.62036	15.34
C	52	2.65689	14.80	C	52	2.41880	19.59
D	52	2.64292	15.00	D	52	2.40529	20.00
E	26	5.75660	12.31	E	26	5.24073	15.38
F	26	5.31379	14.84	F	26	4.83760	19.67
G	26	5.29150	15.00	G	26	4.81575	20.00
H	24	6.23632	12.36	H	24	5.67746	15.46
J	24	5.75660	14.91	J	24	5.24073	19.83
K	24	5.74319	15.00	K	24	5.22852	20.00
25 YEAR AMORTIZATION				**30 YEAR AMORTIZATION**			
A	12	$9.97061	25.00	A	12	$9.70030	30.00
B	52	2.49265	17.71	B	52	2.42508	19.41
C	52	2.30091	24.24	C	52	2.23853	28.64
D	52	2.28753	25.00	D	52	2.22514	30.00
E	26	4.98530	17.77	E	26	4.85015	19.49
F	26	4.60182	24.37	F	26	4.47706	28.87
G	26	4.57996	25.00	G	26	4.45506	30.00
H	24	5.40074	17.89	H	24	5.25433	19.64
J	24	4.98530	24.69	J	24	4.85015	29.44
K	24	4.97369	25.00	K	24	4.83885	30.00

TYPES OF PAYMENTS: A—monthly; B—accelerated weekly; C—
regular weekly; D—minimum amortized weekly; E—accelerated
bi-weekly; F—regular bi-weekly; G—minimum amortized bi-
weekly; H—accelerated semi-monthly; J—regular semi-monthly;
K—minimum amortized semi-monthly

11.625%

BLENDED PAYMENTS IN DOLLARS OF PRINCIPAL AND IN-
TEREST FOR A LOAN OF $1,000 AT **11.625%** PER YEAR, CAL-
CULATED HALF-YEARLY, NOT IN ADVANCE

TYPE OF PMT	PMTS EACH YEAR	PMT EACH PERIOD	YEARS TO RETIRE LOAN	TYPE OF PMT	PMTS EACH YEAR	PMT EACH PERIOD	YEARS TO RETIRE LOAN
5 YEAR AMORTIZATION				**10 YEAR AMORTIZATION**			
A	12	$21.91891	5.00	A	12	$13.97561	10.00
B	52	5.47973	4.47	B	52	3.49390	8.61
C	52	5.05821	4.97	C	52	3.22514	9.91
D	52	5.03636	5.00	D	52	3.20941	10.00
E	26	10.95946	4.48	E	26	6.98781	8.62
F	26	10.11642	4.98	F	26	6.45028	9.93
G	26	10.08364	5.00	G	26	6.42577	10.00
H	24	11.87274	4.48	H	24	7.57012	8.64
J	24	10.95946	4.98	J	24	6.98781	9.96
K	24	10.93366	5.00	K	24	6.97136	10.00
15 YEAR AMORTIZATION				**20 YEAR AMORTIZATION**			
A	12	$11.58865	15.00	A	12	$10.56323	20.00
B	52	2.89716	12.26	B	52	2.64081	15.29
C	52	2.67430	14.79	C	52	2.43767	19.58
D	52	2.66010	15.00	D	52	2.42394	20.00
E	26	5.79433	12.29	E	26	5.28162	15.34
F	26	5.34861	14.84	F	26	4.87534	19.66
G	26	5.32598	15.00	G	26	4.85314	20.00
H	24	6.27719	12.33	H	24	5.72175	15.41
J	24	5.79433	14.91	J	24	5.28162	19.82
K	24	5.78069	15.00	K	24	5.26918	20.00
25 YEAR AMORTIZATION				**30 YEAR AMORTIZATION**			
A	12	$10.05742	25.00	A	12	$9.79096	30.00
B	52	2.51436	17.63	B	52	2.44774	19.29
C	52	2.32094	24.22	C	52	2.25945	28.60
D	52	2.30733	25.00	D	52	2.24583	30.00
E	26	5.02871	17.69	E	26	4.89548	19.37
F	26	4.64189	24.36	F	26	4.51890	28.83
G	26	4.61967	25.00	G	26	4.49654	30.00
H	24	5.44777	17.81	H	24	5.30343	19.52
J	24	5.02871	24.68	J	24	4.89548	29.42
K	24	5.01687	25.00	K	24	4.88395	30.00

TYPES OF PAYMENTS: A—monthly; B—accelerated weekly; C—
regular weekly; D—minimum amortized weekly; E—accelerated
bi-weekly; F—regular bi-weekly; G—minimum amortized bi-
weekly; H—accelerated semi-monthly; J—regular semi-monthly;
K—minimum amortized semi-monthly

11.75%

BLENDED PAYMENTS IN DOLLARS OF PRINCIPAL AND IN-
TEREST FOR A LOAN OF $1,000 AT **11.75%** PER YEAR, CALCU-
LATED HALF-YEARLY, NOT IN ADVANCE

TYPE OF PMT	PMTS EACH YEAR	PMT EACH PERIOD	YEARS TO RETIRE LOAN	TYPE OF PMT	PMTS EACH YEAR	PMT EACH PERIOD	YEARS TO RETIRE LOAN
5 YEAR AMORTIZATION				**10 YEAR AMORTIZATION**			
A	12	$21.97870	5.00	A	12	$14.04369	10.00
B	52	5.49467	4.47	B	52	3.51092	8.60
C	52	5.07201	4.97	C	52	3.24085	9.91
D	52	5.04987	5.00	D	52	3.22488	10.00
E	26	10.98935	4.48	E	26	7.02185	8.62
F	26	10.14401	4.98	F	26	6.48170	9.93
G	26	10.11081	5.00	G	26	6.45684	10.00
H	24	11.90513	4.48	H	24	7.60700	8.63
J	24	10.98935	4.98	J	24	7.02185	9.96
K	24	10.96321	5.00	K	24	7.00514	10.00
15 YEAR AMORTIZATION				**20 YEAR AMORTIZATION**			
A	12	$11.66428	15.00	A	12	$10.64521	20.00
B	52	2.91607	12.24	B	52	2.66130	15.24
C	52	2.69176	14.79	C	52	2.45659	19.57
D	52	2.67733	15.00	D	52	2.44263	20.00
E	26	5.83214	12.27	E	26	5.32260	15.29
F	26	5.38352	14.83	F	26	4.91317	19.65
G	26	5.36053	15.00	G	26	4.89062	20.00
H	24	6.31815	12.31	H	24	5.76615	15.37
J	24	5.83214	14.91	J	24	5.32260	19.82
K	24	5.81827	15.00	K	24	5.30994	20.00
25 YEAR AMORTIZATION				**30 YEAR AMORTIZATION**			
A	12	$10.14443	25.00	A	12	$9.88177	30.00
B	52	2.53611	17.54	B	52	2.47044	19.17
C	52	2.34102	24.20	C	52	2.28041	28.55
D	52	2.32718	25.00	D	52	2.26656	30.00
E	26	5.07222	17.61	E	26	4.94089	19.25
F	26	4.68205	24.34	F	26	4.56082	28.80
G	26	4.65947	25.00	G	26	4.53809	30.00
H	24	5.49490	17.73	H	24	5.35263	19.41
J	24	5.07222	24.67	J	24	4.94089	29.40
K	24	5.06015	25.00	K	24	4.92913	30.00

TYPES OF PAYMENTS: A—monthly; B—accelerated weekly; C—
regular weekly; D—minimum amortized weekly; E—accelerated
bi-weekly; F—regular bi-weekly; G—minimum amortized bi-
weekly; H—accelerated semi-monthly; J—regular semi-monthly;
K—minimum amortized semi-monthly

11.875%

BLENDED PAYMENTS IN DOLLARS OF PRINCIPAL AND IN-
TEREST FOR A LOAN OF $1,000 AT **11.875%** PER YEAR, CAL-
CULATED HALF-YEARLY, NOT IN ADVANCE

TYPE OF PMT	PMTS EACH YEAR	PMT EACH PERIOD	YEARS TO RETIRE LOAN	TYPE OF PMT	PMTS EACH YEAR	PMT EACH PERIOD	YEARS TO RETIRE LOAN
5 YEAR AMORTIZATION				**10 YEAR AMORTIZATION**			
A	12	$22.03854	5.00	A	12	$14.11191	10.00
B	52	5.50964	4.47	B	52	3.52798	8.59
C	52	5.08582	4.97	C	52	3.25660	9.91
D	52	5.06339	5.00	D	52	3.24039	10.00
E	26	11.01927	4.48	E	26	7.05596	8.61
F	26	10.17164	4.98	F	26	6.51319	9.93
G	26	10.13800	5.00	G	26	6.48796	10.00
H	24	11.93754	4.48	H	24	7.64395	8.63
J	24	11.01927	4.98	J	24	7.05596	9.95
K	24	10.99279	5.00	K	24	7.03900	10.00
15 YEAR AMORTIZATION				**20 YEAR AMORTIZATION**			
A	12	$11.74010	15.00	A	12	$10.72738	20.00
B	52	2.93503	12.21	B	52	2.68184	15.19
C	52	2.70925	14.79	C	52	2.47555	19.56
D	52	2.69460	15.00	D	52	2.46136	20.00
E	26	5.87005	12.24	E	26	5.36369	15.24
F	26	5.41851	14.83	F	26	4.95110	19.65
G	26	5.39517	15.00	G	26	4.92818	20.00
H	24	6.35922	12.29	H	24	5.81066	15.32
J	24	5.87005	14.90	J	24	5.36369	19.81
K	24	5.85594	15.00	K	24	5.35080	20.00
25 YEAR AMORTIZATION				**30 YEAR AMORTIZATION**			
A	12	$10.23162	25.00	A	12	$9.97275	30.00
B	52	2.55791	17.46	B	52	2.49319	19.06
C	52	2.36114	24.17	C	52	2.30140	28.51
D	52	2.34707	25.00	D	52	2.28732	30.00
E	26	5.11581	17.52	E	26	4.98637	19.13
F	26	4.72229	24.32	F	26	4.60281	28.76
G	26	4.69934	25.00	G	26	4.57970	30.00
H	24	5.54213	17.64	H	24	5.40190	19.29
J	24	5.11581	24.66	J	24	4.98637	29.38
K	24	5.10352	25.00	K	24	4.97439	30.00

TYPES OF PAYMENTS: A—monthly; B—accelerated weekly; C—
regular weekly; D—minimum amortized weekly; E—accelerated
bi-weekly; F—regular bi-weekly; G—minimum amortized bi-
weekly; H—accelerated semi-monthly; J—regular semi-monthly;
K—minimum amortized semi-monthly

BLENDED PAYMENTS IN DOLLARS OF PRINCIPAL AND IN-TEREST FOR A LOAN OF $1,000 AT **12%** PER YEAR, CALCU-LATED HALF-YEARLY, NOT IN ADVANCE

TYPE OF PMT	PMTS EACH YEAR	PMT EACH PERIOD	YEARS TO RETIRE LOAN	TYPE OF PMT	PMTS EACH YEAR	PMT EACH PERIOD	YEARS TO RETIRE LOAN
5 YEAR AMORTIZATION				**10 YEAR AMORTIZATION**			
A	12	$22.09846	5.00	A	12	$14.18027	10.00
B	52	5.52461	4.47	B	52	3.54507	8.58
C	52	5.09964	4.97	C	52	3.27237	9.91
D	52	5.07693	5.00	D	52	3.25593	10.00
E	26	11.04923	4.47	E	26	7.09013	8.60
F	26	10.19929	4.98	F	26	6.54474	9.93
G	26	10.16523	5.00	G	26	6.51915	10.00
H	24	11.97000	4.48	H	24	7.68098	8.62
J	24	11.04923	4.98	J	24	7.09013	9.95
K	24	11.02240	5.00	K	24	7.07292	10.00
15 YEAR AMORTIZATION				**20 YEAR AMORTIZATION**			
A	12	$11.81610	15.00	A	12	$10.80974	20.00
B	52	2.95402	12.19	B	52	2.70244	15.14
C	52	2.72679	14.78	C	52	2.49456	19.55
D	52	2.71191	15.00	D	52	2.48014	20.00
E	26	5.90805	12.22	E	26	5.40487	15.19
F	26	5.45358	14.83	F	26	4.98911	19.64
G	26	5.42989	15.00	G	26	4.96583	20.00
H	24	6.40039	12.26	H	24	5.85528	15.27
J	24	5.90805	14.90	J	24	5.40487	19.81
K	24	5.89370	15.00	K	24	5.39175	20.00
25 YEAR AMORTIZATION				**30 YEAR AMORTIZATION**			
A	12	$10.31900	25.00	A	12	$10.06387	30.00
B	52	2.57975	17.38	B	52	2.51597	18.94
C	52	2.38131	24.15	C	52	2.32243	28.47
D	52	2.36700	25.00	D	52	2.30811	30.00
E	26	5.15950	17.44	E	26	5.03194	19.02
F	26	4.76261	24.30	F	26	4.64486	28.72
G	26	4.73930	25.00	G	26	4.62139	30.00
H	24	5.58946	17.56	H	24	5.45127	19.17
J	24	5.15950	24.64	J	24	5.03194	29.36
K	24	5.14697	25.00	K	24	5.01972	30.00

TYPES OF PAYMENTS: A—monthly; B—accelerated weekly; C—regular weekly; D—minimum amortized weekly; E—accelerated bi-weekly; F—regular bi-weekly; G—minimum amortized bi-weekly; H—accelerated semi-monthly; J—regular semi-monthly; K—minimum amortized semi-monthly

12.125%

BLENDED PAYMENTS IN DOLLARS OF PRINCIPAL AND IN-
TEREST FOR A LOAN OF $1,000 AT **12.125%** PER YEAR, CAL-
CULATED HALF-YEARLY, NOT IN ADVANCE

TYPE OF PMT	PMTS EACH YEAR	PMT EACH PERIOD	YEARS TO RETIRE LOAN	TYPE OF PMT	PMTS EACH YEAR	PMT EACH PERIOD	YEARS TO RETIRE LOAN
5 YEAR AMORTIZATION				**10 YEAR AMORTIZATION**			
A	12	$22.15843	5.00	A	12	$14.24876	10.00
B	52	5.53961	4.47	B	52	3.56219	8.57
C	52	5.11348	4.97	C	52	3.28818	9.90
D	52	5.09049	5.00	D	52	3.27150	10.00
E	26	11.07922	4.47	E	26	7.12438	8.59
F	26	10.22697	4.98	F	26	6.57635	9.93
G	26	10.19248	5.00	G	26	6.55040	10.00
H	24	12.00249	4.48	H	24	7.71808	8.61
J	24	11.07922	4.98	J	24	7.12438	9.95
K	24	11.05205	5.00	K	24	7.10691	10.00
15 YEAR AMORTIZATION				**20 YEAR AMORTIZATION**			
A	12	$11.89227	15.00	A	12	$10.89230	20.00
B	52	2.97307	12.16	B	52	2.72307	15.09
C	52	2.74437	14.78	C	52	2.51361	19.54
D	52	2.72926	15.00	D	52	2.49896	20.00
E	26	5.94614	12.19	E	26	5.44615	15.14
F	26	5.48874	14.82	F	26	5.02721	19.63
G	26	5.46468	15.00	G	26	5.00357	20.00
H	24	6.44165	12.24	H	24	5.89999	15.22
J	24	5.94614	14.90	J	24	5.44615	19.80
K	24	5.93155	15.00	K	24	5.43279	20.00
25 YEAR AMORTIZATION				**30 YEAR AMORTIZATION**			
A	12	$10.40655	25.00	A	12	$10.15515	30.00
B	52	2.60164	17.30	B	52	2.53879	18.82
C	52	2.40151	24.13	C	52	2.34350	28.42
D	52	2.38697	25.00	D	52	2.32894	30.00
E	26	5.20327	17.36	E	26	5.07757	18.90
F	26	4.80302	24.28	F	26	4.68699	28.68
G	26	4.77934	25.00	G	26	4.66314	30.00
H	24	5.63688	17.48	H	24	5.50071	19.05
J	24	5.20327	24.63	J	24	5.07757	29.34
K	24	5.19051	25.00	K	24	5.06512	30.00

TYPES OF PAYMENTS: A—monthly; B—accelerated weekly; C—
regular weekly; D—minimum amortized weekly; E—accelerated
bi-weekly; F—regular bi-weekly; G—minimum amortized bi-
weekly; H—accelerated semi-monthly; J—regular semi-monthly;
K—minimum amortized semi-monthly

12.25%

BLENDED PAYMENTS IN DOLLARS OF PRINCIPAL AND INTEREST FOR A LOAN OF $1,000 AT **12.25%** PER YEAR, CALCULATED HALF-YEARLY, NOT IN ADVANCE

TYPE OF PMT	PMTS EACH YEAR	PMT EACH PERIOD	YEARS TO RETIRE LOAN	TYPE OF PMT	PMTS EACH YEAR	PMT EACH PERIOD	YEARS TO RETIRE LOAN
5 YEAR AMORTIZATION				**10 YEAR AMORTIZATION**			
A	12	$22.21848	5.00	A	12	$14.31739	10.00
B	52	5.55462	4.46	B	52	3.57935	8.56
C	52	5.12734	4.97	C	52	3.30401	9.90
D	52	5.10405	5.00	D	52	3.28710	10.00
E	26	11.10924	4.47	E	26	7.15869	8.58
F	26	10.25468	4.98	F	26	6.60803	9.92
G	26	10.21976	5.00	G	26	6.58171	10.00
H	24	12.03501	4.48	H	24	7.75525	8.60
J	24	11.10924	4.98	J	24	7.15869	9.95
K	24	11.08172	5.00	K	24	7.14096	10.00
15 YEAR AMORTIZATION				**20 YEAR AMORTIZATION**			
A	12	$11.96862	15.00	A	12	$10.97504	20.00
B	52	2.99216	12.14	B	52	2.74376	15.04
C	52	2.76199	14.77	C	52	2.53270	19.53
D	52	2.74665	15.00	D	52	2.51782	20.00
E	26	5.98431	12.17	E	26	5.48752	15.09
F	26	5.52398	14.82	F	26	5.06540	19.62
G	26	5.49956	15.00	G	26	5.04139	20.00
H	24	6.48300	12.22	H	24	5.94481	15.17
J	24	5.98431	14.90	J	24	5.48752	19.80
K	24	5.96949	15.00	K	24	5.47393	20.00
25 YEAR AMORTIZATION				**30 YEAR AMORTIZATION**			
A	12	$10.49427	25.00	A	12	$10.24657	30.00
B	52	2.62357	17.21	B	52	2.56164	18.70
C	52	2.42175	24.10	C	52	2.36459	28.37
D	52	2.40698	25.00	D	52	2.34980	30.00
E	26	5.24714	17.28	E	26	5.12328	18.78
F	26	4.84351	24.26	F	26	4.72918	28.64
G	26	4.81945	25.00	G	26	4.70496	30.00
H	24	5.68440	17.40	H	24	5.55022	18.94
J	24	5.24714	24.62	J	24	5.12328	29.31
K	24	5.23414	25.00	K	24	5.11059	30.00

TYPES OF PAYMENTS: A—monthly; B—accelerated weekly; C—regular weekly; D—minimum amortized weekly; E—accelerated bi-weekly; F—regular bi-weekly; G—minimum amortized bi-weekly; H—accelerated semi-monthly; J—regular semi-monthly; K—minimum amortized semi-monthly

12.375%

BLENDED PAYMENTS IN DOLLARS OF PRINCIPAL AND IN-
TEREST FOR A LOAN OF $1,000 AT **12.375%** PER YEAR, CAL-
CULATED HALF-YEARLY, NOT IN ADVANCE

TYPE OF PMT	PMTS EACH YEAR	PMT EACH PERIOD	YEARS TO RETIRE LOAN	TYPE OF PMT	PMTS EACH YEAR	PMT EACH PERIOD	YEARS TO RETIRE LOAN
5 YEAR AMORTIZATION				**10 YEAR AMORTIZATION**			
A	12	$22.27858	5.00	A	12	$14.38615	10.00
B	52	5.56965	4.46	B	52	3.59654	8.56
C	52	5.14121	4.97	C	52	3.31988	9.90
D	52	5.11763	5.00	D	52	3.30273	10.00
E	26	11.13929	4.47	E	26	7.19308	8.57
F	26	10.28242	4.98	F	26	6.63976	9.92
G	26	10.24707	5.00	G	26	6.61308	10.00
H	24	12.06756	4.47	H	24	7.79250	8.59
J	24	11.13929	4.98	J	24	7.19308	9.95
K	24	11.11143	5.00	K	24	7.17508	10.00
15 YEAR AMORTIZATION				**20 YEAR AMORTIZATION**			
A	12	$12.04515	15.00	A	12	$11.05797	20.00
B	52	3.01129	12.11	B	52	2.76449	14.99
C	52	2.77965	14.77	C	52	2.55184	19.52
D	52	2.76407	15.00	D	52	2.53672	20.00
E	26	6.02258	12.15	E	26	5.52898	15.04
F	26	5.55930	14.81	F	26	5.10368	19.61
G	26	5.53452	15.00	G	25	5.07929	20.00
H	24	6.52446	12.19	H	24	5.98973	15.13
J	24	6.02258	14.90	J	24	5.52898	19.79
K	24	6.00751	15.00	K	24	5.51515	20.00
25 YEAR AMORTIZATION				**30 YEAR AMORTIZATION**			
A	12	$10.58217	25.00	A	12	$10.33813	30.00
B	52	2.64554	17.13	B	52	2.58453	18.59
C	52	2.44204	24.08	C	52	2.38572	28.32
D	52	2.42702	25.00	D	52	2.37069	30.00
E	26	5.29108	17.20	E	26	5.16906	18.67
F	26	4.88408	24.24	F	26	4.77144	28.60
G	26	4.85964	25.00	G	26	4.74684	30.00
H	24	5.73201	17.32	H	24	5.59982	18.82
J	24	5.29108	24.61	J	24	5.16906	29.29
K	24	5.27785	25.00	K	24	5.15613	30.00

TYPES OF PAYMENTS: A—monthly; B—accelerated weekly; C—
regular weekly; D—minimum amortized weekly; E—accelerated
bi-weekly; F—regular bi-weekly; G—minimum amortized bi-
weekly; H—accelerated semi-monthly; J—regular semi-monthly;
K—minimum amortized semi-monthly

12.5%

BLENDED PAYMENTS IN DOLLARS OF PRINCIPAL AND INTEREST FOR A LOAN OF $1,000 AT **12.5%** PER YEAR, CALCULATED HALF-YEARLY, NOT IN ADVANCE

TYPE OF PMT	PMTS EACH YEAR	PMT EACH PERIOD	YEARS TO RETIRE LOAN	TYPE OF PMT	PMTS EACH YEAR	PMT EACH PERIOD	YEARS TO RETIRE LOAN
5 YEAR AMORTIZATION				**10 YEAR AMORTIZATION**			
A	12	$22.33875	5.00	A	12	$14.45505	10.00
B	52	5.58469	4.46	B	52	3.61376	8.55
C	52	5.15510	4.97	C	52	3.33578	9.90
D	52	5.13123	5.00	D	52	3.31839	10.00
E	26	11.16937	4.47	E	26	7.22752	8.56
F	26	10.31019	4.98	F	26	6.67156	9.92
G	26	10.27440	5.00	G	26	6.64450	10.00
H	24	12.10016	4.47	H	24	7.82982	8.58
J	24	11.16937	4.98	J	24	7.22752	9.95
K	24	11.14116	5.00	K	24	7.20927	10.00
15 YEAR AMORTIZATION				**20 YEAR AMORTIZATION**			
A	12	$12.12185	15.00	A	12	$11.14108	20.00
B	52	3.03046	12.09	B	52	2.78527	14.94
C	52	2.79735	14.76	C	52	2.57102	19.51
D	52	2.78154	15.00	D	52	2.55566	20.00
E	26	6.06093	12.12	E	26	5.57054	14.99
F	26	5.59470	14.81	F	26	5.14204	19.60
G	26	5.56955	15.00	G	26	5.11728	20.00
H	24	6.56600	12.17	H	24	6.03475	15.08
J	24	6.06093	14.89	J	24	5.57054	19.79
K	24	6.04562	15.00	K	24	5.55647	20.00
25 YEAR AMORTIZATION				**30 YEAR AMORTIZATION**			
A	12	$10.67023	25.00	A	12	$10.42982	30.00
B	52	2.66756	17.05	B	52	2.60746	18.47
C	52	2.46236	24.05	C	52	2.40688	28.27
D	52	2.44711	25.00	D	52	2.39161	30.00
E	26	5.33511	17.11	E	26	5.21491	18.55
F	26	4.92472	24.22	F	26	4.81376	28.56
G	26	4.89991	25.00	G	26	4.78878	30.00
H	24	5.77971	17.24	H	24	5.64949	18.71
J	24	5.33511	24.60	J	24	5.21491	29.26
K	24	5.32164	25.00	K	24	5.20174	30.00

TYPES OF PAYMENTS: A—monthly; B—accelerated weekly; C—regular weekly; D—minimum amortized weekly; E—accelerated bi-weekly; F—regular bi-weekly; G—minimum amortized bi-weekly; H—accelerated semi-monthly; J—regular semi-monthly; K—minimum amortized semi-monthly

12.625%

BLENDED PAYMENTS IN DOLLARS OF PRINCIPAL AND IN-
TEREST FOR A LOAN OF $1,000 AT **12.625%** PER YEAR, CAL-
CULATED HALF-YEARLY, NOT IN ADVANCE

TYPE OF PMT	PMTS EACH YEAR	PMT EACH PERIOD	YEARS TO RETIRE LOAN	TYPE OF PMT	PMTS EACH YEAR	PMT EACH PERIOD	YEARS TO RETIRE LOAN
5 YEAR AMORTIZATION				**10 YEAR AMORTIZATION**			
A	12	$22.39898	5.00	A	12	$14.52408	10.00
B	52	5.59975	4.46	B	52	3.63102	8.54
C	52	5.16900	4.97	C	52	3.35171	9.90
D	52	5.14484	5.00	D	52	3.33408	10.00
E	26	11.19949	4.47	E	26	7.26204	8.56
F	26	10.33799	4.98	F	26	6.70342	9.92
G	26	10.30177	5.00	G	26	6.67599	10.00
H	24	12.13278	4.47	H	24	7.86721	8.58
J	24	11.19949	4.98	J	24	7.26204	9.95
K	24	11.17093	5.00	K	24	7.24352	10.00
15 YEAR AMORTIZATION				**20 YEAR AMORTIZATION**			
A	12	$12.19873	15.00	A	12	$11.22437	20.00
B	52	3.04968	12.07	B	52	2.80609	14.89
C	52	2.81509	14.76	C	52	2.59024	19.50
D	52	2.79904	15.00	D	52	2.57465	20.00
E	26	6.09936	12.10	E	26	5.61219	14.94
F	26	5.63018	14.81	F	26	5.18048	19.59
G	26	5.60466	15.00	G	26	5.15535	20.00
H	24	6.60764	12.15	H	24	6.07987	15.03
J	24	6.09936	14.89	J	24	5.61219	19.78
K	24	6.08381	15.00	K	24	5.59787	20.00
25 YEAR AMORTIZATION				**30 YEAR AMORTIZATION**			
A	12	$10.75845	25.00	A	12	$10.52165	30.00
B	52	2.68961	16.96	B	52	2.63041	18.35
C	52	2.48272	24.03	C	52	2.42807	28.22
D	52	2.46722	25.00	D	52	2.41256	30.00
E	26	5.37923	17.03	E	26	5.26082	18.44
F	26	4.96544	24.20	F	26	4.85615	28.52
G	26	4.94025	25.00	G	26	4.83078	30.00
H	24	5.82749	17.16	H	24	5.69923	18.59
J	24	5.37923	24.59	J	24	5.26082	29.24
K	24	5.36551	25.00	K	24	5.24741	30.00

TYPES OF PAYMENTS: A—monthly; B—accelerated weekly; C—
regular weekly; D—minimum amortized weekly; E—accelerated
bi-weekly; F—regular bi-weekly; G—minimum amortized bi-
weekly; H—accelerated semi-monthly; J—regular semi-monthly;
K—minimum amortized semi-monthly

12.75%

BLENDED PAYMENTS IN DOLLARS OF PRINCIPAL AND IN-
TEREST FOR A LOAN OF $1,000 AT **12.75%** PER YEAR, CALCU-
LATED HALF-YEARLY, NOT IN ADVANCE

TYPE OF PMT	PMTS EACH YEAR	PMT EACH PERIOD	YEARS TO RETIRE LOAN	TYPE OF PMT	PMTS EACH YEAR	PMT EACH PERIOD	YEARS TO RETIRE LOAN
5 YEAR AMORTIZATION				**10 YEAR AMORTIZATION**			
A	12	$22.45928	5.00	A	12	$14.59324	10.00
B	52	5.61482	4.46	B	52	3.64831	8.53
C	52	5.18291	4.97	C	52	3.36767	9.90
D	52	5.15846	5.00	D	52	3.34979	10.00
E	26	11.22964	4.46	E	26	7.29662	8.55
F	26	10.36582	4.98	F	26	6.73534	9.92
G	26	10.32916	5.00	G	26	6.70754	10.00
H	24	12.16544	4.47	H	24	7.90467	8.57
J	24	11.22964	4.98	J	24	7.29662	9.95
K	24	11.20072	5.00	K	24	7.27783	10.00
15 YEAR AMORTIZATION				**20 YEAR AMORTIZATION**			
A	12	$12.27577	15.00	A	12	$11.30784	20.00
B	52	3.06894	12.04	B	52	2.82696	14.84
C	52	2.83287	14.75	C	52	2.60950	19.49
D	52	2.81658	15.00	D	52	2.59367	20.00
E	26	6.13789	12.07	E	26	5.65392	14.89
F	26	5.66574	14.80	F	26	5.21900	19.58
G	26	5.63985	15.00	G	26	5.19349	20.00
H	24	6.64938	12.12	H	24	6.12508	14.98
J	24	6.13789	14.89	J	24	5.65392	19.78
K	24	6.12208	15.00	K	24	5.63936	20.00
25 YEAR AMORTIZATION				**30 YEAR AMORTIZATION**			
A	12	$10.84684	25.00	A	12	$10.61360	30.00
B	52	2.71171	16.88	B	52	2.65340	18.24
C	52	2.50312	24.00	C	52	2.44929	28.17
D	52	2.48738	25.00	D	52	2.43353	30.00
E	26	5.42342	16.95	E	26	5.30680	18.32
F	26	5.00623	24.18	F	26	4.89859	28.47
G	26	4.98066	25.00	G	26	4.87284	30.00
H	24	5.87537	17.07	H	24	5.74904	18.48
J	24	5.42342	24.57	J	24	5.30680	29.21
K	24	5.40945	25.00	K	24	5.29314	30.00

TYPES OF PAYMENTS: A—monthly; B—accelerated weekly; C—
regular weekly; D—minimum amortized weekly; E—accelerated
bi-weekly; F—regular bi-weekly; G—minimum amortized bi-
weekly; H—accelerated semi-monthly; J—regular semi-monthly;
K—minimum amortized semi-monthly

12.875%

BLENDED PAYMENTS IN DOLLARS OF PRINCIPAL AND INTEREST FOR A LOAN OF $1,000 AT **12.875%** PER YEAR, CALCULATED HALF-YEARLY, NOT IN ADVANCE

TYPE OF PMT	PMTS EACH YEAR	PMT EACH PERIOD	YEARS TO RETIRE LOAN	TYPE OF PMT	PMTS EACH YEAR	PMT EACH PERIOD	YEARS TO RETIRE LOAN
5 YEAR AMORTIZATION				**10 YEAR AMORTIZATION**			
A	12	$22.51964	5.00	A	12	$14.66254	10.00
B	52	5.62991	4.45	B	52	3.66563	8.52
C	52	5.19684	4.97	C	52	3.38366	9.89
D	52	5.17209	5.00	D	52	3.36554	10.00
E	26	11.25982	4.46	E	26	7.33127	8.54
F	26	10.39368	4.98	F	26	6.76732	9.92
G	26	10.35858	5.00	G	26	6.73914	10.00
H	24	12.19814	4.47	H	24	7.94221	8.56
J	24	11.25982	4.98	J	24	7.33127	9.95
K	24	11.23055	5.00	K	24	7.31221	10.00
15 YEAR AMORTIZATION				**20 YEAR AMORTIZATION**			
A	12	$12.35299	15.00	A	12	$11.39149	20.00
B	52	3.08825	12.02	B	52	2.84787	14.79
C	52	2.85069	14.75	C	52	2.62880	19.47
D	52	2.83416	15.00	D	52	2.61273	20.00
E	26	6.17649	12.05	E	26	5.69574	14.84
F	26	5.70138	14.80	F	26	5.25761	19.57
G	26	5.67511	15.00	G	26	5.23172	20.00
H	24	6.69120	12.10	H	24	6.17039	14.93
J	24	6.17649	14.89	J	24	5.69574	19.77
K	24	6.16044	15.00	K	24	5.68094	20.00
25 YEAR AMORTIZATION				**30 YEAR AMORTIZATION**			
A	12	$10.93538	25.00	A	12	$10.70568	20.00
B	52	2.73384	16.80	B	52	2.67642	18.12
C	52	2.52355	23.98	C	52	2.47054	28.11
D	52	2.50757	25.00	D	52	2.45454	30.00
E	26	5.46769	16.87	E	26	5.35284	18.21
F	26	5.04710	24.16	F	26	4.94108	28.43
G	26	5.02114	25.00	G	26	4.91495	30.00
H	24	5.92333	16.99	H	24	5.79891	18.36
J	24	5.46769	24.56	J	24	5.35284	29.18
K	24	5.45348	25.00	K	24	5.33893	30.00

TYPES OF PAYMENTS: A—monthly; B—accelerated weekly; C—regular weekly; D—minimum amortized weekly; E—accelerated bi-weekly; F—regular bi-weekly; G—minimum amortized bi-weekly; H—accelerated semi-monthly; J—regular semi-monthly; K—minimum amortized semi-monthly

13%

BLENDED PAYMENTS IN DOLLARS OF PRINCIPAL AND IN-
TEREST FOR A LOAN OF $1,000 AT **13%** PER YEAR, CALCU-
LATED HALF-YEARLY, NOT IN ADVANCE

TYPE OF PMT	PMTS EACH YEAR	PMT EACH PERIOD	YEARS TO RETIRE LOAN	TYPE OF PMT	PMTS EACH YEAR	PMT EACH PERIOD	YEARS TO RETIRE LOAN
5 YEAR AMORTIZATION				**10 YEAR AMORTIZATION**			
A	12	$22.58006	5.00	A	12	$14.73196	10.00
B	52	5.64501	4.45	B	52	3.68299	8.51[1]
C	52	5.21078	4.97	C	52	3.39968	9.89
D	52	5.18574	5.00	D	52	3.38132	10.00
E	26	11.29003	4.46	E	26	7.36598	8.53
F	26	10.42157	4.97	F	26	6.79937	9.92
G	26	10.38402	5.00	G	26	6.77081	10.00
H	24	12.23087	4.47	H	24	7.97981	8.55
J	24	11.29003	4.98	J	24	7.36598	9.95
K	24	11.26041	5.00	K	24	7.34665	10.00
15 YEAR AMORTIZATION				**20 YEAR AMORTIZATION**			
A	12	$12.43037	15.00	A	12	$11.47530	20.00
B	52	3.10759	11.99	B	52	2.86883	14.74
C	52	2.86855	14.74	C	52	2.64815	19.46
D	52	2.85178	15.00	D	52	2.63183	20.00
E	26	6.21519	12.02	E	26	5.73765	14.79
F	26	5.73710	14.80	F	26	5.29629	19.56
G	26	5.71045	15.00	G	26	5.27002	20.00
H	24	6.73312	12.07	H	24	6.21579	14.88
J	24	6.21519	14.88	J	24	5.73765	19.77
K	24	6.19888	15.00	K	24	5.72260	20.00
25 YEAR AMORTIZATION				**30 YEAR AMORTIZATION**			
A	12	$11.02407	25.00	A	12	$10.79788	30.00
B	52	2.75602	16.72	B	52	2.69947	18.01
C	52	2.54402	23.95	C	52	2.49182	28.06
D	52	2.52779	25.00	D	52	2.47556	30.00
E	26	5.51204	16.79	E	26	5.39894	18.09
F	26	5.08803	24.14	F	26	4.98364	28.38
G	26	5.06169	25.00	G	26	4.95712	30.00
H	24	5.97137	16.91	H	24	5.84885	18.25
J	24	5.51204	24.55	J	24	5.39894	29.16
K	24	5.49757	25.00	K	24	5.38478	30.00

TYPES OF PAYMENTS: A—monthly; B—accelerated weekly; C—
regular weekly; D—minimum amortized weekly; E—accelerated
bi-weekly; F—regular bi-weekly; G—minimum amortized bi-
weekly; H—accelerated semi-monthly; J—regular semi-monthly;
K—minimum amortized semi-monthly

13.125%

BLENDED PAYMENTS IN DOLLARS OF PRINCIPAL AND INTEREST FOR A LOAN OF $1,000 AT **13.125%** PER YEAR, CALCULATED HALF-YEARLY, NOT IN ADVANCE

TYPE OF PMT	PMTS EACH YEAR	PMT EACH PERIOD	YEARS TO RETIRE LOAN	TYPE OF PMT	PMTS EACH YEAR	PMT EACH PERIOD	YEARS TO RETIRE LOAN
5 YEAR AMORTIZATION				**10 YEAR AMORTIZATION**			
A	12	$22.64054	5.00	A	12	$14.80152	10.00
B	52	5.66014	4.45	B	52	3.70038	8.50
C	52	5.22474	4.97	C	52	3.41573	9.89
D	52	5.19940	5.00	D	52	3.39712	10.00
E	26	11.32027	4.46	E	26	7.40076	8.52
F	26	10.44948	4.97	F	26	6.83147	9.92
G	26	10.41150	5.00	G	26	6.80253	10.00
H	24	12.26363	4.46	H	24	8.01749	8.54
J	24	11.32027	4.98	J	24	7.40076	9.95
K	24	11.29029	5.00	K	24	7.38116	10.00
15 YEAR AMORTIZATION				**20 YEAR AMORTIZATION**			
A	12	$12.50792	15.00	A	12	$11.55929	20.00
B	52	3.12698	11.97	B	52	2.88982	14.69
C	52	2.88644	14.74	C	52	2.66753	19.45
D	52	2.86943	15.00	D	52	2.65097	20.00
E	26	6.25396	12.00	E	26	5.77965	14.74
F	26	5.77289	14.79	F	26	5.33506	19.55
G	26	5.74587	15.00	G	26	5.30840	20.00
H	24	6.77512	12.05	H	24	6.26128	14.83
J	24	6.25396	14.88	J	24	5.77965	19.76
K	24	6.23740	15.00	K	24	5.76434	20.00
25 YEAR AMORTIZATION				**30 YEAR AMORTIZATION**			
A	12	$11.11292	25.00	A	12	$10.89020	30.00
B	52	2.77823	16.63	B	52	2.72255	17.90
C	52	2.56452	23.92	C	52	2.51312	28.00
D	52	2.54804	25.00	D	52	2.49662	30.00
E	26	5.55646	16.70	E	26	5.44510	17.98
F	26	5.12904	24.11	F	26	5.02625	28.34
G	26	5.10231	25.00	G	26	4.99933	30.00
H	24	6.01950	16.83	H	24	5.89886	18.14
J	24	5.55646	24.53	J	24	5.44510	29.13
K	24	5.54174	25.00	K	24	5.43068	30.00

TYPES OF PAYMENTS: A—monthly; B—accelerated weekly; C—regular weekly; D—minimum amortized weekly; E—accelerated bi-weekly; F—regular bi-weekly; G—minimum amortized bi-weekly; H—accelerated semi-monthly; J—regular semi-monthly; K—minimum amortized semi-monthly

13.25%

BLENDED PAYMENTS IN DOLLARS OF PRINCIPAL AND IN-TEREST FOR A LOAN OF $1,000 AT **13.25%** PER YEAR, CALCU-LATED HALF-YEARLY, NOT IN ADVANCE

TYPE OF PMT	PMTS EACH YEAR	PMT EACH PERIOD	YEARS TO RETIRE LOAN	TYPE OF PMT	PMTS EACH YEAR	PMT EACH PERIOD	YEARS TO RETIRE LOAN
5 YEAR AMORTIZATION				**10 YEAR AMORTIZATION**			
A	12	$22.70109	5.00	A	12	$14.87120	10.00
B	52	5.67527	4.45	B	52	3.71780	8.49
C	52	5.23871	4.97	C	52	3.43182	9.89
D	52	5.21308	5.00	D	52	3.41295	10.00
E	26	11.35055	4.46	E	26	7.43560	8.51
F	26	10.47743	4.97	F	26	6.86363	9.91
G	26	10.43900	5.00	G	26	6.83431	10.00
H	24	12.29643	4.46	H	24	8.05523	8.53
J	24	11.35055	4.98	J	24	7.43560	9.95
K	24	11.32021	5.00	K	24	7.41573	10.00
15 YEAR AMORTIZATION				**20 YEAR AMORTIZATION**			
A	12	$12.58564	15.00	A	12	$11.64345	20.00
B	52	3.14641	11.94	B	52	2.91086	14.64
C	52	2.90438	14.73	C	52	2.68695	19.44
D	52	2.88712	15.00	D	52	2.67014	20.00
E	26	6.29282	11.97	E	26	5.83172	14.69
F	26	5.80876	14.79	F	26	5.37390	19.54
G	26	5.78135	15.00	G	26	5.34686	20.00
H	24	6.81722	12.03	H	24	6.30687	14.78
J	24	6.29282	14.88	J	24	5.82172	19.75
K	24	6.27600	15.00	K	24	5.80616	20.00
25 YEAR AMORTIZATION				**30 YEAR AMORTIZATION**			
A	12	$11.20191	25.00	A	12	$10.98263	30.00
B	52	2.80048	16.55	B	52	2.74566	17.78
C	52	2.58506	23.89	C	52	2.53445	27.95
D	52	2.56833	25.00	D	52	2.51770	30.00
E	26	5.60096	16.62	E	26	5.49132	17.87
F	26	5.17011	24.09	F	26	5.06891	28.29
G	26	5.14299	25.00	G	26	5.04160	30.00
H	24	6.06770	16.75	H	24	5.94893	18.03
J	24	5.60096	24.52	J	24	5.49132	29.10
K	24	5.58599	25.00	K	24	5.47664	30.00

TYPES OF PAYMENTS: A—monthly; B—accelerated weekly; C—regular weekly; D—minimum amortized weekly; E—accelerated bi-weekly; F—regular bi-weekly; G—minimum amortized bi-weekly; H—accelerated semi-monthly; J—regular semi-monthly; K—minimum amortized semi-monthly

13.375%

BLENDED PAYMENTS IN DOLLARS OF PRINCIPAL AND INTEREST FOR A LOAN OF $1,000 AT **13.375%** PER YEAR, CALCULATED HALF-YEARLY, NOT IN ADVANCE

TYPE OF PMT	PMTS EACH YEAR	PMT EACH PERIOD	YEARS TO RETIRE LOAN	TYPE OF PMT	PMTS EACH YEAR	PMT EACH PERIOD	YEARS TO RETIRE LOAN
5 YEAR AMORTIZATION				**10 YEAR AMORTIZATION**			
A	12	$22.76170	5.00	A	12	$14.94102	10.00
B	52	5.69043	4.45	B	52	3.73525	8.48
C	52	5.25270	4.97	C	52	3.44793	9.89
D	52	5.22677	5.00	D	52	3.42881	10.00
E	26	11.38085	4.46	E	26	7.47051	8.50
F	26	10.50540	4.97	F	26	6.89585	9.91
G	26	10.46653	5.00	G	26	6.86615	10.00
H	24	12.32926	4.46	H	24	8.09305	8.52
J	24	11.38085	4.98	J	24	7.47051	9.94
K	24	11.35015	5.00	K	24	7.45036	10.00
15 YEAR AMORTIZATION				**20 YEAR AMORTIZATION**			
A	12	$12.66351	15.00	A	12	$11.72777	20.00
B	52	3.16588	11.91	B	52	2.93194	14.59
C	52	2.92235	14.73	C	52	2.70641	19.42
D	52	2.90485	15.00	D	52	2.68935	20.00
E	26	6.33176	11.95	E	26	5.86388	14.64
F	26	5.84470	14.78	F	26	5.41282	19.53
G	26	5.81691	15.00	G	26	5.38538	20.00
H	24	6.85940	12.00	H	24	6.35254	14.73
J	24	6.33176	14.88	J	24	5.86388	19.75
K	24	6.31468	15.00	K	24	5.84807	20.00
25 YEAR AMORTIZATION				**30 YEAR AMORTIZATION**			
A	12	$11.29105	25.00	A	12	$11.07517	30.00
B	52	2.82276	16.47	B	52	2.76879	17.67
C	52	2.60563	23.86	C	52	2.55581	27.89
D	52	2.58865	25.00	D	52	2.53880	30.00
E	26	5.64552	16.54	E	26	5.53759	17.76
F	26	5.21125	24.07	F	26	5.11162	28.24
G	26	5.18373	25.00	G	26	5.08392	30.00
H	24	6.11598	16.67	H	24	5.99905	17.91
J	24	5.64552	24.51	J	24	5.53759	29.07
K	24	5.63030	25.00	K	24	5.52265	30.00

TYPES OF PAYMENTS: A—monthly; B—accelerated weekly; C—regular weekly; D—minimum amortized weekly; E—accelerated bi-weekly; F—regular bi-weekly; G—minimum amortized bi-weekly; H—accelerated semi-monthly; J—regular semi-monthly; K—minimum amortized semi-monthly

13.5%

BLENDED PAYMENTS IN DOLLARS OF PRINCIPAL AND IN-
TEREST FOR A LOAN OF $1,000 AT **13.5%** PER YEAR, CALCU-
LATED HALF-YEARLY, NOT IN ADVANCE

TYPE OF PMT	PMTS EACH YEAR	PMT EACH PERIOD	YEARS TO RETIRE LOAN	TYPE OF PMT	PMTS EACH YEAR	PMT EACH PERIOD	YEARS TO RETIRE LOAN
5 YEAR AMORTIZATION				**10 YEAR AMORTIZATION**			
A	12	$22.82238	5.00	A	12	$15.01096	10.00
B	52	5.70559	4.45	B	52	3.75274	8.47
C	52	5.26670	4.96	C	52	3.46407	9.89
D	52	5.24047	5.00	D	52	3.44470	10.00
E	26	11.41119	4.45	E	26	7.50548	8.49
F	26	10.53340	4.97	F	26	6.92814	9.91
G	26	10.49408	5.00	G	26	6.89804	10.00
H	24	12.36212	4.46	H	24	8.13094	8.52
J	24	11.41119	4.98	J	24	7.50548	9.94
K	24	11.38013	5.00	K	24	7.48505	10.00
15 YEAR AMORTIZATION				**20 YEAR AMORTIZATION**			
A	12	$12.74155	15.00	A	12	$11.81225	20.00
B	52	3.18539	11.89	B	52	2.95306	14.53
C	52	2.94036	14.72	C	52	2.72590	19.41
D	52	2.92261	15.00	D	52	2.70859	20.00
E	26	6.37078	11.92	E	26	5.90613	14.59
F	26	5.88072	14.78	F	26	5.45181	19.52
G	26	5.85255	15.00	G	26	5.42398	20.00
H	24	6.90168	11.98	H	24	6.39830	14.68
J	24	6.37078	14.87	J	24	5.90613	19.74
K	24	6.35344	15.00	K	24	5.89005	20.00
25 YEAR AMORTIZATION				**30 YEAR AMORTIZATION**			
A	12	$11.38032	25.00	A	12	$11.16782	30.00
B	52	2.84508	16.38	B	52	2.79195	17.56
C	52	2.62623	23.84	C	52	2.57719	27.83
D	52	2.60900	25.00	D	52	2.55993	30.00
E	26	5.69016	16.46	E	26	5.58391	17.64
F	26	5.25246	24.04	F	26	5.15438	28.19
G	26	5.22454	25.00	G	26	5.12628	30.00
H	24	6.16434	16.58	H	24	6.04923	17.80
J	24	5.69016	24.49	J	24	5.58391	29.04
K	24	5.67467	25.00	K	24	5.56871	30.00

TYPES OF PAYMENTS: A—monthly; B—accelerated weekly; C—
regular weekly; D—minimum amortized weekly; E—accelerated
bi-weekly; F—regular bi-weekly; G—minimum amortized bi-
weekly; H—accelerated semi-monthly; J—regular semi-monthly;
K—minimum amortized semi-monthly

13.625%

BLENDED PAYMENTS IN DOLLARS OF PRINCIPAL AND INTEREST FOR A LOAN OF $1,000 AT **13.625%** PER YEAR, CALCULATED HALF-YEARLY, NOT IN ADVANCE

TYPE OF PMT	PMTS EACH YEAR	PMT EACH PERIOD	YEARS TO RETIRE LOAN	TYPE OF PMT	PMTS EACH YEAR	PMT EACH PERIOD	YEARS TO RETIRE LOAN
5 YEAR AMORTIZATION				**10 YEAR AMORTIZATION**			
A	12	$22.88311	5.00	A	12	$15.08103	10.00
B	52	5.72078	4.44	B	52	3.77026	8.46
C	52	5.28072	4.96	C	52	3.48024	9.88
D	52	5.25418	5.00	D	52	3.46062	10.00
E	26	11.44155	4.45	E	26	7.54052	8.48
F	26	10.56144	4.97	F	26	6.96048	9.91
G	26	10.52167	5.00	G	26	6.93000	10.00
H	24	12.39502	4.46	H	24	8.16889	8.51
J	24	11.44155	4.98	J	24	7.54052	9.94
K	24	11.41014	5.00	K	24	7.51981	10.00
15 YEAR AMORTIZATION				**20 YEAR AMORTIZATION**			
A	12	$12.81975	15.00	A	12	$11.89689	20.00
B	52	3.20494	11.86	B	52	2.97422	14.48
C	52	2.95840	14.72	C	52	2.74544	19.40
D	52	2.94040	15.00	D	52	2.72788	20.00
E	26	6.40988	11.90	E	26	5.94845	14.54
F	26	5.91681	14.78	F	26	5.49087	19.51
G	26	5.88825	15.00	G	26	5.46266	20.00
H	24	6.94403	11.95	H	24	6.44415	14.63
J	24	6.40988	14.87	J	24	5.94845	19.73
K	24	6.39228	15.00	K	24	5.93211	20.00
25 YEAR AMORTIZATION				**30 YEAR AMORTIZATION**			
A	12	$11.46974	25.00	A	12	$11.26057	30.00
B	52	2.86743	16.30	B	52	2.81514	17.45
C	52	2.64686	23.81	C	52	2.59859	27.77
D	52	2.62938	25.00	D	52	2.58108	30.00
E	26	5.73487	16.38	E	26	5.63028	17.53
F	26	5.29372	24.02	F	26	5.19719	28.14
G	26	5.26541	25.00	G	26	5.16869	30.00
H	24	6.21277	16.50	H	24	6.09947	17.69
J	24	5.73487	24.48	J	24	5.63028	29.00
K	24	5.71912	25.00	K	24	5.61482	30.00

TYPES OF PAYMENTS: A—monthly; B—accelerated weekly; C—regular weekly; D—minimum amortized weekly; E—accelerated bi-weekly; F—regular bi-weekly; G—minimum amortized bi-weekly; H—accelerated semi-monthly; J—regular semi-monthly; K—minimum amortized semi-monthly

13.75%

BLENDED PAYMENTS IN DOLLARS OF PRINCIPAL AND INTEREST FOR A LOAN OF $1,000 AT **13.75%** PER YEAR, CALCULATED HALF-YEARLY, NOT IN ADVANCE

TYPE OF PMT	PMTS EACH YEAR	PMT EACH PERIOD	YEARS TO RETIRE LOAN	TYPE OF PMT	PMTS EACH YEAR	PMT EACH PERIOD	YEARS TO RETIRE LOAN
5 YEAR AMORTIZATION				**10 YEAR AMORTIZATION**			
A	12	$22.94391	5.00	A	12	$15.15123	10.00
B	52	5.73598	4.44	B	52	3.78781	8.46
C	52	5.29475	4.96	C	52	3.49644	9.88
D	52	5.26791	5.00	D	52	3.47656	10.00
E	26	11.47195	4.45	E	26	7.57562	8.48
F	26	10.58950	4.97	F	26	6.99288	9.91
G	26	10.54928	5.00	G	26	6.96200	10.00
H	24	12.42795	4.46	H	24	8.20692	8.50
J	24	11.47195	4.98	J	24	7.57562	9.94
K	24	11.44017	5.00	K	24	7.55463	10.00
15 YEAR AMORTIZATION				**20 YEAR AMORTIZATION**			
A	12	$12.89811	15.00	A	12	$11.98169	20.00
B	52	3.22453	11.84	B	52	2.99542	14.43
C	52	2.97649	14.71	C	52	2.76501	19.39
D	52	2.95824	15.00	D	52	2.74719	20.00
E	26	6.44906	11.87	E	26	5.99085	14.49
F	26	5.95297	14.77	F	26	5.53001	19.50
G	26	5.92403	15.00	G	26	5.50140	20.00
H	24	6.98648	11.93	H	24	6.49008	14.58
J	24	6.44906	14.87	J	24	5.99085	19.73
K	24	6.43119	15.00	K	24	5.97425	20.00
25 YEAR AMORTIZATION				**30 YEAR AMORTIZATION**			
A	12	$11.55928	25.00	A	12	$11.35342	30.00
B	52	2.88982	16.22	B	52	2.83835	17.34
C	52	2.66753	23.77	C	52	2.62002	27.71
D	52	2.64979	25.00	D	52	2.60225	30.00
E	26	5.77964	16.29	E	26	5.67671	17.42
F	26	5.33505	23.99	F	26	5.24004	28.08
G	26	5.30634	25.00	G	26	5.21114	30.00
H	24	6.26128	16.42	H	24	6.14977	17.58
J	24	5.77964	24.46	J	24	5.67671	28.97
K	24	5.76363	25.00	K	24	5.66098	30.00

TYPES OF PAYMENTS: A—monthly; B—accelerated weekly; C—regular weekly; D—minimum amortized weekly; E—accelerated bi-weekly; F—regular bi-weekly; G—minimum amortized bi-weekly; H—accelerated semi-monthly; J—regular semi-monthly; K—minimum amortized semi-monthly

13.875%

BLENDED PAYMENTS IN DOLLARS OF PRINCIPAL AND IN-
TEREST FOR A LOAN OF $1,000 AT **13.875%** PER YEAR, CAL-
CULATED HALF-YEARLY, NOT IN ADVANCE

TYPE OF PMT	PMTS EACH YEAR	PMT EACH PERIOD	YEARS TO RETIRE LOAN	TYPE OF PMT	PMTS EACH YEAR	PMT EACH PERIOD	YEARS TO RETIRE LOAN
5 YEAR AMORTIZATION				**10 YEAR AMORTIZATION**			
A	12	$23.00476	5.00	A	12	$15.22155	10.00
B	52	5.75119	4.44	B	52	3.80539	8.45
C	52	5.30879	4.96	C	52	3.51267	9.88
D	52	5.28165	5.00	D	52	3.49254	10.00
E	26	11.50238	4.45	E	26	7.61078	8.47
F	26	10.61758	4.97	F	26	7.02533	9.91
G	26	10.57691	5.00	G	26	6.99407	10.00
H	24	12.46091	4.45	H	24	8.24501	8.49
J	24	11.50238	4.98	J	24	7.61078	9.94
K	24	11.47024	5.00	K	24	7.58951	10.00
15 YEAR AMORTIZATION				**20 YEAR AMORTIZATION**			
A	12	$12.97663	15.00	A	12	$12.06665	20.00
B	52	3.24416	11.81	B	52	3.01666	14.38
C	52	2.99461	14.71	C	52	2.78461	19.37
D	52	2.97610	15.00	D	52	2.76654	20.00
E	26	6.48831	11.85	E	26	6.03333	14.44
F	26	5.98921	14.77	F	26	5.56922	19.49
G	26	5.95987	15.00	G	26	5.54021	20.00
H	24	7.02901	11.90	H	24	6.53610	14.53
J	24	6.48831	14.87	J	24	6.03333	19.72
K	24	6.47018	15.00	K	24	6.01646	20.00
25 YEAR AMORTIZATION				**30 YEAR AMORTIZATION**			
A	12	$11.64896	25.00	A	12	$11.44636	30.00
B	52	2.91224	16.14	B	52	2.86159	17.23
C	52	2.68822	23.74	C	52	2.64147	27.64
D	52	2.67022	25.00	D	52	2.62344	30.00
E	26	5.82448	16.21	E	26	5.72318	17.31
F	26	5.37644	23.97	F	26	5.28294	28.03
G	26	5.34733	25.00	G	26	5.25363	30.00
H	24	6.30985	16.34	H	24	6.20011	17.47
J	24	5.82448	24.45	J	24	5.72318	28.94
K	24	5.80820	25.00	K	24	5.70719	30.00

TYPES OF PAYMENTS: A—monthly; B—accelerated weekly; C—
regular weekly; D—minimum amortized weekly; E—accelerated
bi-weekly; F—regular bi-weekly; G—minimum amortized bi-
weekly; H—accelerated semi-monthly; J—regular semi-monthly;
K—minimum amortized semi-monthly

14%

BLENDED PAYMENTS IN DOLLARS OF PRINCIPAL AND IN-
TEREST FOR A LOAN OF $1,000 AT **14%** PER YEAR, CALCU-
LATED HALF-YEARLY, NOT IN ADVANCE

TYPE OF PMT	PMTS EACH YEAR	PMT EACH PERIOD	YEARS TO RETIRE LOAN	TYPE OF PMT	PMTS EACH YEAR	PMT EACH PERIOD	YEARS TO RETIRE LOAN
5 YEAR AMORTIZATION				**10 YEAR AMORTIZATION**			
A	12	$23.06568	5.00	A	12	$15.29200	10.00
B	52	5.76642	4.44	B	52	3.82300	8.44
C	52	5.43385	4.96	C	52	3.52892	9.88
D	52	5.29541	5.00	D	52	3.50854	10.00
E	26	11.53284	4.45	E	26	7.64600	8.46
F	26	10.64570	4.97	F	26	7.05785	9.91
G	26	10.60458	5.00	G	26	7.02619	10.00
H	24	12.49391	4.45	H	24	8.28317	8.48
J	24	11.53284	4.98	J	24	7.64600	9.94
K	24	11.50033	5.00	K	24	7.62445	10.00
15 YEAR AMORTIZATION				**20 YEAR AMORTIZATION**			
A	12	$13.05530	15.00	A	12	$12.15176	20.00
B	52	3.26382	11.79	B	52	3.03794	14.33
C	52	3.01276	14.70	C	52	2.80425	19.36
D	52	2.99400	15.00	D	52	2.78593	20.00
E	26	6.52765	11.82	E	26	6.07588	14.38
F	26	6.02552	14.76	F	25	5.60850	19.48
G	26	5.95579	15.00	G	26	5.57909	20.00
H	24	7.07162	11.88	H	24	6.58220	14.48
J	24	6.52765	14.86	J	24	6.07588	19.71
K	24	6.50925	15.00	K	24	6.05875	20.00
25 YEAR AMORTIZATION				**30 YEAR AMORTIZATION**			
A	12	$11.73876	25.00	A	12	$11.53940	30.00
B	52	2.93469	16.06	B	52	2.88485	17.12
C	52	2.70895	23.71	C	52	2.66294	27.58
D	52	2.69069	25.00	D	52	2.64465	30.00
E	26	5.86938	16.13	E	26	5.76970	17.21
F	26	5.41789	23.94	F	26	5.32588	27.98
G	26	5.38837	25.00	G	26	5.29616	30.00
H	24	6.35850	16.26	H	24	6.25051	17.36
J	24	5.86938	24.43	J	24	5.76970	28.90
K	24	5.85284	25.00	K	24	5.75343	30.00

TYPES OF PAYMENTS: A—monthly; B—accelerated weekly; C—
regular weekly; D—minimum amortized weekly; E—accelerated
bi-weekly; F—regular bi-weekly; G—minimum amortized bi-
weekly; H—accelerated semi-monthly; J—regular semi-monthly;
K—minimum amortized semi-monthly

14.125%

BLENDED PAYMENTS IN DOLLARS OF PRINCIPAL AND IN-
TEREST FOR A LOAN OF $1,000 AT **14.125%** PER YEAR, CAL-
CULATED HALF-YEARLY, NOT IN ADVANCE

TYPE OF PMT	PMTS EACH YEAR	PMT EACH PERIOD	YEARS TO RETIRE LOAN	TYPE OF PMT	PMTS EACH YEAR	PMT EACH PERIOD	YEARS TO RETIRE LOAN
5 YEAR AMORTIZATION				**10 YEAR AMORTIZATION**			
A	12	$23.12667	5.00	A	12	$15.36258	10.00
B	52	5.78167	4.44	B	52	3.84064	8.43
C	52	5.33692	4.96	C	52	3.54521	9.88
D	52	5.30918	5.00	D	52	3.52456	10.00
E	26	11.56333	4.44	E	26	7.68129	8.45
F	26	10.67385	4.97	F	26	7.09042	9.90
G	26	10.63227	5.00	G	26	7.05837	10.00
H	24	12.52694	4.45	H	24	8.32140	8.47
J	24	11.56333	4.98	J	24	7.68129	9.94
K	24	11.53045	5.00	K	24	7.65945	10.00
15 YEAR AMORTIZATION				**20 YEAR AMORTIZATION**			
A	12	$13.13412	15.00	A	12	$12.23702	20.00
B	52	3.28353	11.76	B	52	3.05925	14.28
C	52	3.03095	14.70	C	52	2.82393	19.34
D	52	3.01194	15.00	D	52	2.80534	20.00
E	26	6.56706	11.80	E	26	6.11851	14.33
F	26	6.06190	14.76	F	26	5.64785	19.47
G	26	6.03177	15.00	G	26	5.61804	20.00
H	24	7.11432	11.85	H	24	6.62838	14.43
J	24	6.56706	14.86	J	24	6.11851	19.71
K	24	6.54839	15.00	K	24	6.10111	20.00
25 YEAR AMORTIZATION				**30 YEAR AMORTIZATION**			
A	12	$11.82870	25.00	A	12	$11.63253	30.00
B	52	2.95717	15.97	B	52	2.90813	17.01
C	52	2.72970	23.68	C	52	2.68443	27.51
D	52	2.71118	25.00	D	52	2.66588	30.00
E	26	5.91435	16.05	E	26	5.81626	17.10
F	26	5.45940	23.91	F	26	5.36886	27.92
G	26	5.42947	25.00	G	26	5.33874	30.00
H	24	6.40721	16.18	H	24	6.30095	17.26
J	24	5.91435	24.41	J	24	5.81626	28.86
K	24	5.89753	25.00	K	24	5.79973	30.00

TYPES OF PAYMENTS: A—monthly; B—accelerated weekly; C—
regular weekly; D—minimum amortized weekly; E—accelerated
bi-weekly; F—regular bi-weekly; G—minimum amortized bi-
weekly; H—accelerated semi-monthly; J—regular semi-monthly;
K—minimum amortized semi-monthly

14.25%

BLENDED PAYMENTS IN DOLLARS OF PRINCIPAL AND INTEREST FOR A LOAN OF $1,000 AT **14.25%** PER YEAR, CALCULATED HALF-YEARLY, NOT IN ADVANCE

TYPE OF PMT	PMTS EACH YEAR	PMT EACH PERIOD	YEARS TO RETIRE LOAN	TYPE OF PMT	PMTS EACH YEAR	PMT EACH PERIOD	YEARS TO RETIRE LOAN
5 YEAR AMORTIZATION				**10 YEAR AMORTIZATION**			
A	12	$23.18771	5.00	A	12	$15.43328	10.00
B	52	5.79693	4.43	B	52	3.85832	8.42
C	52	5.35101	4.96	C	52	3.56153	9.88
D	52	5.32296	5.00	D	52	3.54062	10.00
E	26	11.59385	4.44	E	26	7.71664	8.44
F	26	10.70202	4.97	F	26	7.12305	9.90
G	26	10.65998	5.00	G	26	7.09060	10.00
H	24	12.56001	4.45	H	24	8.35969	8.46
J	24	11.59385	4.98	J	24	7.71664	9.94
K	24	11.56061	5.00	K	24	7.69451	10.00
15 YEAR AMORTIZATION				**20 YEAR AMORTIZATION**			
A	12	$13.21310	15.00	A	12	$12.32243	20.00
B	52	3.30327	11.73	B	52	3.08061	14.22
C	52	3.04918	14.69	C	52	2.84364	19.33
D	52	3.02991	15.00	D	52	2.82479	20.00
E	26	6.60655	11.77	E	26	6.16121	14.28
F	26	6.09835	14.75	F	26	5.68727	19.46
G	26	6.06782	15.00	G	26	5.65705	20.00
H	24	7.15709	11.83	H	24	6.67465	14.38
J	24	6.60655	14.86	J	24	6.16121	19.70
K	24	6.58760	15.00	K	24	6.14354	30.00
25 YEAR AMORTIZATION				**30 YEAR AMORTIZATION**			
A	12	$11.91875	25.00	A	12	$11.72574	30.00
B	52	2.97969	15.89	B	52	2.93144	16.90
C	52	2.75048	23.65	C	52	2.70594	27.44
D	52	2.73170	25.00	D	52	2.68712	30.00
E	26	5.95937	15.97	E	26	5.86287	16.99
F	26	5.50096	23.89	F	26	5.41188	27.86
G	26	5.47062	25.00	G	26	5.38135	30.00
H	24	6.45599	16.10	H	24	6.35144	17.15
J	24	5.95937	24.40	J	24	5.86287	28.83
K	24	5.94228	25.00	K	24	5.84606	30.00

TYPES OF PAYMENTS: A—monthly; B—accelerated weekly; C—regular weekly; D—minimum amortized weekly; E—accelerated bi-weekly; F—regular bi-weekly; G—minimum amortized bi-weekly; H—accelerated semi-monthly; J—regular semi-monthly; K—minimum amortized semi-monthly

14.375%

BLENDED PAYMENTS IN DOLLARS OF PRINCIPAL AND IN-
TEREST FOR A LOAN OF $1,000 AT **14.375%** PER YEAR, CAL-
CULATED HALF-YEARLY, NOT IN ADVANCE

TYPE OF PMT	PMTS EACH YEAR	PMT EACH PERIOD	YEARS TO RETIRE LOAN	TYPE OF PMT	PMTS EACH YEAR	PMT EACH PERIOD	YEARS TO RETIRE LOAN
5 YEAR AMORTIZATION				**10 YEAR AMORTIZATION**			
A	12	$23.24881	5.00	A	12	$15.50410	10.00
B	52	5.81220	4.43	B	52	3.87603	8.41
C	52	5.36511	4.96	C	52	3.57787	9.87
D	52	5.33675	5.00	D	52	3.55670	10.00
E	26	11.62441	4.44	E	26	7.75205	8.43
F	26	10.73022	4.97	F	26	7.15574	9.90
G	26	10.68773	5.00	G	26	7.12288	10.00
H	24	12.59311	4.45	H	24	8.39805	8.45
J	24	11.62441	4.98	J	24	7.75205	9.94
K	24	11.59079	5.00	K	24	7.72963	10.00
15 YEAR AMORTIZATION				**20 YEAR AMORTIZATION**			
A	12	$13.29223	15.00	A	12	$12.40798	20.00
B	52	3.32306	11.71	B	52	3.10199	14.17
C	52	3.06744	14.69	C	52	2.86338	19.31
D	52	3.04791	15.00	D	52	2.84427	20.00
E	26	6.64611	11.75	E	26	6.20399	14.23
F	26	6.13487	14.75	F	26	5.72676	19.44
G	26	6.10394	15.00	G	26	5.69613	20.00
H	24	7.19996	11.80	H	24	6.72099	14.32
J	24	6.64611	14.86	J	24	6.20399	19.69
K	24	6.62689	15.00	K	24	6.18605	20.00
25 YEAR AMORTIZATION				**30 YEAR AMORTIZATION**			
A	12	$12.00892	25.00	A	12	$11.81904	30.00
B	52	3.00223	15.81	B	52	2.95476	16.79
C	52	2.77129	23.61	C	52	2.72747	27.38
D	52	2.75225	25.00	D	52	2.70839	30.00
E	26	6.00446	15.89	E	26	5.90952	16.88
F	26	5.54258	23.86	F	26	5.45494	27.80
G	26	5.51183	25.00	G	26	5.42400	30.00
H	24	6.50483	16.02	H	24	6.40198	17.04
J	24	6.00446	24.38	J	24	5.90952	28.79
K	24	5.98709	25.00	K	24	5.89243	30.00

TYPES OF PAYMENTS: A—monthly; B—accelerated weekly; C—
regular weekly; D—minimum amortized weekly; E—accelerated
bi-weekly; F—regular bi-weekly; G—minimum amortized bi-
weekly; H—accelerated semi-monthly; J—regular semi-monthly;
K—minimum amortized semi-monthly

14.5%

BLENDED PAYMENTS IN DOLLARS OF PRINCIPAL AND IN-
TEREST FOR A LOAN OF $1,000 AT **14.5%** PER YEAR, CALCU-
LATED HALF-YEARLY, NOT IN ADVANCE

TYPE OF PMT	PMTS EACH YEAR	PMT EACH PERIOD	YEARS TO RETIRE LOAN	TYPE OF PMT	PMTS EACH YEAR	PMT EACH PERIOD	YEARS TO RETIRE LOAN
5 YEAR AMORTIZATION				**10 YEAR AMORTIZATION**			
A	12	$23.30998	5.00	A	12	$15.57505	10.00
B	52	5.82749	4.43	B	52	3.89376	8.40
C	52	5.37923	4.96	C	52	3.59424	9.87
D	52	5.35056	5.00	D	52	3.57281	10.00
E	26	11.65499	4.44	E	26	7.78752	8.42
F	26	10.75845	4.97	F	26	7.18848	9.90
G	26	10.71550	5.00	G	26	7.15523	10.00
H	24	12.62624	4.45	H	24	8.43648	8.44
J	24	11.65499	4.98	J	24	7.78752	9.94
K	24	11.62100	5.00	K	24	7.76481	10.00
15 YEAR AMORTIZATION				**20 YEAR AMORTIZATION**			
A	12	$13.37150	15.00	A	12	$12.49367	20.00
B	52	3.34288	11.68	B	52	3.12342	14.12
C	52	3.08573	14.68	C	52	2.88316	19.30
D	52	3.06594	15.00	D	52	2.86379	20.00
E	26	6.68575	11.72	E	26	6.24684	14.18
F	26	6.17146	14.75	F	26	5.76631	19.43
G	26	6.14013	15.00	G	26	5.73527	20.00
H	24	7.24290	11.78	H	24	6.76741	14.27
J	24	6.68575	14.85	J	24	6.24684	19.69
K	24	6.66625	15.00	K	24	6.22862	20.00
25 YEAR AMORTIZATION				**30 YEAR AMORTIZATION**			
A	12	$12.09921	25.00	A	12	$11.91242	30.00
B	52	3.02480	15.73	B	52	2.97810	16.69
C	52	2.79212	23.58	C	52	2.74902	27.31
D	52	2.77282	25.00	D	52	2.72967	30.00
E	26	6.04960	15.81	E	26	5.95621	16.78
F	26	5.58425	23.83	F	26	5.49804	27.74
G	26	5.55309	25.00	G	26	5.46668	30.00
H	24	6.55374	15.94	H	24	6.45256	16.93
J	24	6.04960	24.36	J	24	5.95621	28.75
K	24	6.03196	25.00	K	24	5.93884	30.00

TYPES OF PAYMENTS: A—monthly; B—accelerated weekly; C—
regular weekly; D—minimum amortized weekly; E—accelerated
bi-weekly; F—regular bi-weekly; G—minimum amortized bi-
weekly; H—accelerated semi-monthly; J—regular semi-monthly;
K—minimum amortized semi-monthly

14.625%

BLENDED PAYMENTS IN DOLLARS OF PRINCIPAL AND IN-
TEREST FOR A LOAN OF $1,000 AT **14.625%** PER YEAR, CAL-
CULATED HALF-YEARLY, NOT IN ADVANCE

TYPE OF PMT	PMTS EACH YEAR	PMT EACH PERIOD	YEARS TO RETIRE LOAN	TYPE OF PMT	PMTS EACH YEAR	PMT EACH PERIOD	YEARS TO RETIRE LOAN
5 YEAR AMORTIZATION				**10 YEAR AMORTIZATION**			
A	12	$23.37120	5.00	A	12	$15.64611	10.00
B	52	5.84280	4.43	B	52	3.91153	8.39
C	52	5.39335	4.96	C	52	3.61064	9.87
D	52	5.36438	5.00	D	52	3.58895	10.00
E	26	11.68560	4.44	E	26	7.82306	8.41
F	26	10.78671	4.97	F	26	7.22128	9.90
G	26	10.74329	5.00	G	26	7.18762	10.00
H	24	12.65940	4.44	H	24	8.47498	8.44
J	24	11.68560	4.98	J	24	7.82306	9.94
K	24	11.65124	5.00	K	24	7.80005	10.00
15 YEAR AMORTIZATION				**20 YEAR AMORTIZATION**			
A	12	$13.45093	15.00	A	12	$12.57951	20.00
B	52	3.36273	11.65	B	52	3.14488	14.07
C	52	3.10406	14.67	C	52	2.90296	19.28
D	52	3.08401	15.00	D	52	2.88333	20.00
E	26	6.72546	11.69	E	26	6.28976	14.13
F	26	6.20812	14.74	F	26	5.80593	19.42
G	26	6.17638	15.00	G	26	5.77448	20.00
H	24	7.28592	11.75	H	24	6.81390	14.22
J	24	6.72546	14.85	J	24	6.28976	19.68
K	24	6.70569	15.00	K	24	6.27126	20.00
25 YEAR AMORTIZATION				**30 YEAR AMORTIZATION**			
A	12	$12.18961	25.00	A	12	$12.00587	30.00
B	52	3.04740	15.65	B	52	3.00147	16.58
C	52	2.81299	23.54	C	52	2.77059	27.23
D	52	2.79341	25.00	D	52	2.75097	30.00
E	26	6.09480	15.73	E	26	6.00294	16.67
F	26	5.62597	23.80	F	26	5.54117	27.68
G	26	5.59439	25.00	G	26	5.50940	30.00
H	24	6.60270	15.86	H	24	6.50318	16.83
J	24	6.09480	24.34	J	24	6.00294	28.71
K	24	6.07688	25.00	K	24	5.98528	30.00

TYPES OF PAYMENTS: A—monthly; B—accelerated weekly; C—
regular weekly; D—minimum amortized weekly; E—accelerated
bi-weekly; F—regular bi-weekly; G—minimum amortized bi-
weekly; H—accelerated semi-monthly; J—regular semi-monthly;
K—minimum amortized semi-monthly

14.75%

BLENDED PAYMENTS IN DOLLARS OF PRINCIPAL AND IN-
TEREST FOR A LOAN OF $1,000 AT **14.75%** PER YEAR, CALCU-
LATED HALF-YEARLY, NOT IN ADVANCE

TYPE OF PMT	PMTS EACH YEAR	PMT EACH PERIOD	YEARS TO RETIRE LOAN	TYPE OF PMT	PMTS EACH YEAR	PMT EACH PERIOD	YEARS TO RETIRE LOAN
5 YEAR AMORTIZATION				**10 YEAR AMORTIZATION**			
A	12	$23.43249	5.00	A	12	$15.71730	10.00
B	52	5.85812	4.43	B	52	3.92933	8.38
C	52	5.40750	4.96	C	52	3.62707	9.87
D	52	5.37821	5.00	D	52	3.60511	10.00
E	26	11.71624	4.44	E	26	7.85865	8.40
F	26	10.81499	4.97	F	26	7.25414	9.90
G	26	10.77112	5.00	G	26	7.22007	10.00
H	24	12.69260	5.55	H	24	8.51354	8.43
J	24	11.71624	4.98	J	24	7.85865	9.93
K	24	11.68151	5.00	K	24	7.83535	10.00
15 YEAR AMORTIZATION				**20 YEAR AMORTIZATION**			
A	12	$13.53030	15.00	A	12	$12.66549	20.00
B	52	3.38262	11.63	B	52	3.16637	14.01
C	52	3.12242	14.67	C	52	2.92280	19.27
D	52	3.10211	15.00	D	52	2.90291	20.00
E	26	6.76525	11.67	E	26	6.33274	14.07
F	26	6.24485	14.74	F	26	5.84561	19.41
G	26	6.21270	15.00	G	26	5.81374	20.00
H	24	7.32902	11.72	H	24	6.86047	14.17
J	24	6.76525	14.85	J	24	6.33274	19.67
K	24	6.74519	15.00	K	24	6.31397	20.00
25 YEAR AMORTIZATION				**30 YEAR AMORTIZATION**			
A	12	$12.28012	25.00	A	12	$12.09940	30.00
B	52	3.07003	15.57	B	52	3.02485	16.48
C	52	2.83387	23.51	C	52	2.79217	27.16
D	52	2.81403	25.00	D	52	2.77228	30.00
E	26	6.14006	15.65	E	26	6.04970	16.57
F	26	5.66775	23.77	F	26	5.58434	27.62
G	26	5.63575	25.00	G	26	5.55215	30.00
H	24	6.65173	15.78	H	24	6.55384	16.72
J	24	6.14006	24.32	J	24	6.04970	28.67
K	24	6.12185	25.00	K	24	6.03176	30.00

TYPES OF PAYMENTS: A—monthly; B—accelerated weekly; C—
regular weekly; D—minimum amortized weekly; E—accelerated
bi-weekly; F—regular bi-weekly; G—minimum amortized bi-
weekly; H—accelerated semi-monthly; J—regular semi-monthly;
K—minimum amortized semi-monthly

14.875%

BLENDED PAYMENTS IN DOLLARS OF PRINCIPAL AND INTEREST FOR A LOAN OF $1,000 AT **14.875%** PER YEAR, CALCULATED HALF-YEARLY, NOT IN ADVANCE

TYPE OF PMT	PMTS EACH YEAR	PMT EACH PERIOD	YEARS TO RETIRE LOAN	TYPE OF PMT	PMTS EACH YEAR	PMT EACH PERIOD	YEARS TO RETIRE LOAN
5 YEAR AMORTIZATION				**10 YEAR AMORTIZATION**			
A	12	$23.49383	5.00	A	12	$15.78861	10.00
B	52	5.87346	4.43	B	52	3.94715	8.37
C	52	5.42165	4.96	C	52	3.64353	9.87
D	52	5.39205	5.00	D	52	3.62130	10.00
E	26	11.74692	4.43	E	26	7.89431	8.39
F	26	10.84331	4.97	F	26	7.28705	9.90
G	26	10.79897	5.00	G	26	7.25257	10.00
H	24	12.72583	4.44	H	24	8.55216	8.42
J	24	11.74692	4.98	J	24	7.89431	9.93
K	24	11.71180	5.00	K	24	7.87071	10.00
15 YEAR AMORTIZATION				**20 YEAR AMORTIZATION**			
A	12	$13.61021	15.00	A	12	$12.75160	20.00
B	52	3.40255	11.60	B	52	3.18790	13.96
C	52	3.14082	14.66	C	52	2.94268	19.25
D	52	3.12024	15.00	D	52	2.92251	20.00
E	26	6.80511	11.64	E	26	6.37580	14.02
F	26	6.28164	14.73	F	26	5.88535	19.39
G	26	6.24908	15.00	G	26	5.85307	20.00
H	24	7.37220	11.70	H	24	6.90712	14.12
J	24	6.80511	14.84	J	24	6.37580	19.66
K	24	6.78477	15.00	K	24	6.35674	20.00
25 YEAR AMORTIZATION				**30 YEAR AMORTIZATION**			
A	12	$12.37073	25.00	A	12	$12.19301	30.00
B	52	3.09268	15.49	B	52	3.04825	16.37
C	52	2.85478	23.47	C	52	2.81377	27.09
D	52	2.83467	25.00	D	52	2.79361	30.00
E	26	6.18537	15.57	E	26	6.09650	16.46
F	26	5.70957	23.74	F	26	5.62754	27.56
G	26	5.67715	25.00	G	26	5.59493	30.00
H	24	6.70081	15.70	H	24	6.60454	16.62
J	24	6.18537	24.30	J	24	6.09650	28.62
K	24	6.16688	25.00	K	24	6.07828	30.00

TYPES OF PAYMENTS: A—monthly; B—accelerated weekly; C—regular weekly; D—minimum amortized weekly; E—accelerated bi-weekly; F—regular bi-weekly; G—minimum amortized bi-weekly; H—accelerated semi-monthly; J—regular semi-monthly; K—minimum amortized semi-monthly

15%

BLENDED PAYMENTS IN DOLLARS OF PRINCIPAL AND INTEREST FOR A LOAN OF $1,000 AT **15%** PER YEAR, CALCULATED HALF-YEARLY, NOT IN ADVANCE

TYPE OF PMT	PMTS EACH YEAR	PMT EACH PERIOD	YEARS TO RETIRE LOAN	TYPE OF PMT	PMTS EACH YEAR	PMT EACH PERIOD	YEARS TO RETIRE LOAN
5 YEAR AMORTIZATION				**10 YEAR AMORTIZATION**			
A	12	$23.55524	5.00	A	12	$15.86004	10.00
B	52	5.88881	4.42	B	52	3.96501	8.36
C	52	5.43582	4.96	C	52	3.66001	9.86
D	52	5.40591	5.00	D	52	3.63751	10.00
E	26	11.77762	4.43	E	26	7.93002	8.38
F	26	10.87165	4.97	F	26	7.32002	9.89
G	26	10.82684	5.00	G	26	7.28513	10.00
H	24	12.75909	4.44	H	24	8.59086	8.41
J	24	11.77762	4.98	J	24	7.93002	9.93
K	24	11.74213	5.00	K	24	7.90612	10.00
15 YEAR AMORTIZATION				**20 YEAR AMORTIZATION**			
A	12	$13.69007	15.00	A	12	$12.83784	20.00
B	52	3.42252	11.57	B	52	3.20946	13.91
C	52	3.15925	14.66	C	52	2.96258	19.24
D	52	3.13840	15.00	D	52	2.94214	20.00
E	26	6.84504	11.61	E	26	6.41892	13.97
F	26	6.31850	14.73	F	26	5.92516	19.38
G	26	6.28552	15.00	G	26	5.89246	20.00
H	24	7.41546	11.67	H	24	6.95383	14.07
J	24	6.84504	14.84	J	24	6.41892	19.65
K	24	6.82441	15.00	K	24	6.39958	20.00
25 YEAR AMORTIZATION				**30 YEAR AMORTIZATION**			
A	12	$12.46146	25.00	A	12	$12.28668	30.00
B	52	3.11536	15.41	B	52	3.07167	16.27
C	52	2.87572	23.43	C	52	2.83539	27.01
D	52	2.85534	25.00	D	52	2.81496	30.00
E	26	6.23073	15.49	E	26	6.14334	16.36
F	26	5.75144	23.71	F	26	5.67077	27.49
G	26	5.71860	25.00	G	26	5.63774	30.00
H	24	6.74996	15.62	H	24	6.65528	16.52
J	24	6.23073	24.28	J	24	6.14334	28.58
K	24	6.21195	25.00	K	24	6.12483	30.00

TYPES OF PAYMENTS: A—monthly; B—accelerated weekly; C—regular weekly; D—minimum amortized weekly; E—accelerated bi-weekly; F—regular bi-weekly; G—minimum amortized bi-weekly; H—accelerated semi-monthly; J—regular semi-monthly; K—minimum amortized semi-monthly

15.125%

BLENDED PAYMENTS IN DOLLARS OF PRINCIPAL AND IN-
TEREST FOR A LOAN OF $1,000 AT **15.125%** PER YEAR, CAL-
CULATED HALF-YEARLY, NOT IN ADVANCE

TYPE OF PMT	PMTS EACH YEAR	PMT EACH PERIOD	YEARS TO RETIRE LOAN	TYPE OF PMT	PMTS EACH YEAR	PMT EACH PERIOD	YEARS TO RETIRE LOAN
5 YEAR AMORTIZATION				**10 YEAR AMORTIZATION**			
A	12	$23.61670	5.00	A	12	$15.93159	10.00
B	52	5.90418	4.42	B	52	3.98290	8.35
C	52	5.45001	4.96	C	52	3.67652	9.86
D	52	5.41978	5.00	D	52	3.65375	10.00
E	26	11.80835	4.43	E	26	7.96579	8.37
F	26	10.90002	4.97	F	26	7.35304	9.89
G	26	10.85474	5.00	G	26	7.31774	10.00
H	24	12.79238	4.44	H	24	8.62961	8.40
J	24	11.80835	4.98	J	24	7.96579	9.93
K	24	11.77248	5.00	K	24	7.94160	10.00
15 YEAR AMORTIZATION				**20 YEAR AMORTIZATION**			
A	12	$13.77007	15.00	A	12	$12.92422	20.00
B	52	3.44252	11.55	B	52	3.23106	13.86
C	52	3.17771	14.65	C	52	2.98251	19.22
D	52	3.15660	15.00	D	52	2.96181	20.00
E	26	6.88504	11.59	E	26	6.46211	13.92
F	26	6.35542	14.72	F	26	5.96503	19.37
G	26	6.32203	15.00	G	26	5.93190	20.00
H	24	7.45879	11.65	H	24	7.00062	14.02
J	24	6.88504	14.84	J	24	6.46211	19.65
K	24	6.86412	15.00	K	24	6.44248	20.00
25 YEAR AMORTIZATION				**30 YEAR AMORTIZATION**			
A	12	$12.55228	25.00	A	12	$12.38041	30.00
B	52	3.13807	15.33	B	52	3.09510	16.17
C	52	2.89668	23.39	C	52	2.85702	26.94
D	52	2.87602	25.00	D	52	2.83632	30.00
E	26	6.27614	15.41	E	26	6.19021	16.26
F	26	5.79336	23.68	F	26	5.71404	27.43
G	26	5.76010	25.00	G	26	5.68057	30.00
H	24	6.79915	15.54	H	24	6.70606	16.41
J	24	6.27614	24.26	J	24	6.19021	28.54
K	24	6.25708	25.00	K	24	6.17140	30.00

TYPES OF PAYMENTS: A—monthly; B—accelerated weekly; C—
regular weekly; D—minimum amortized weekly; E—accelerated
bi-weekly; F—regular bi-weekly; G—minimum amortized bi-
weekly; H—accelerated semi-monthly; J—regular semi-monthly;
K—minimum amortized semi-monthly

15.25%

BLENDED PAYMENTS IN DOLLARS OF PRINCIPAL AND IN-
TEREST FOR A LOAN OF $1,000 AT **15.25%** PER YEAR, CALCU-
LATED HALF-YEARLY, NOT IN ADVANCE

TYPE OF PMT	PMTS EACH YEAR	PMT EACH PERIOD	YEARS TO RETIRE LOAN	TYPE OF PMT	PMTS EACH YEAR	PMT EACH PERIOD	YEARS TO RETIRE LOAN
5 YEAR AMORTIZATION				**10 YEAR AMORTIZATION**			
A	12	$23.67823	5.00	A	12	$16.00326	10.00
B	52	5.91956	4.42	B	52	4.00081	8.34
C	52	5.46421	4.96	C	52	3.69306	9.86
D	52	5.43367	5.00	D	52	3.67002	10.00
E	26	11.83911	4.43	E	26	8.00163	8.36
F	26	10.92841	4.97	F	26	7.38612	9.89
G	26	10.88267	5.00	G	26	7.35040	10.00
H	24	12.82571	4.44	H	24	8.66843	8.39
J	24	11.83911	4.98	J	24	8.00163	9.93
K	24	11.80287	5.00	K	24	7.97713	10.00
15 YEAR AMORTIZATION				**20 YEAR AMORTIZATION**			
A	12	$13.85022	15.00	A	12	$13.01073	20.00
B	52	3.46255	11.52	B	52	3.25268	13.80
C	52	3.19620	14.64	C	52	3.00248	19.20
D	52	3.17482	15.00	D	52	2.98150	20.00
E	26	6.92511	11.56	E	26	6.50536	13.87
F	26	6.39241	14.72	F	26	6.00495	19.35
G	26	6.35860	15.00	G	26	5.97141	20.00
H	24	7.50220	11.62	H	24	7.04748	13.96
J	24	6.92511	14.83	J	24	6.50536	19.64
K	24	6.90390	15.00	K	24	6.48545	20.00
25 YEAR AMORTIZATION				**30 YEAR AMORTIZATION**			
A	12	$12.64321	25.00	A	12	$12.47422	30.00
B	52	3.16080	15.25	B	52	3.11855	16.07
C	52	2.91766	23.35	C	52	2.87867	26.86
D	52	2.89673	25.00	D	52	2.85769	30.00
E	26	6.32160	15.33	E	26	6.23711	16.16
F	26	5.83533	23.65	F	26	5.75733	27.36
G	26	5.80164	25.00	G	26	5.72344	30.00
H	24	6.84840	15.46	H	24	6.75687	16.31
J	24	6.32160	24.24	J	24	6.23711	28.49
K	24	6.30225	25.00	K	24	6.21801	30.00

TYPES OF PAYMENTS: A—monthly; B—accelerated weekly; C—
regular weekly; D—minimum amortized weekly; E—accelerated
bi-weekly; F—regular bi-weekly; G—minimum amortized bi-
weekly; H—accelerated semi-monthly; J—regular semi-monthly;
K—minimum amortized semi-monthly

15.375%

BLENDED PAYMENTS IN DOLLARS OF PRINCIPAL AND IN-
TEREST FOR A LOAN OF $1,000 AT **15.375%** PER YEAR, CAL-
CULATED HALF-YEARLY, NOT IN ADVANCE

TYPE OF PMT	PMTS EACH YEAR	PMT EACH PERIOD	YEARS TO RETIRE LOAN	TYPE OF PMT	PMTS EACH YEAR	PMT EACH PERIOD	YEARS TO RETIRE LOAN
5 YEAR AMORTIZATION				**10 YEAR AMORTIZATION**			
A	12	$23.73981	5.00	A	12	$16.07504	10.00
B	52	5.93495	4.42	B	52	4.01876	8.33
C	52	5.47842	4.96	C	52	3.70963	9.86
D	52	5.44756	5.00	D	52	3.68631	10.00
E	26	11.86991	4.43	E	26	8.03752	8.35
F	26	10.95684	4.97	F	26	7.41925	9.89
G	26	10.91082	5.00	G	26	7.38311	10.00
H	24	12.85907	4.43	H	24	8.70731	8.38
J	24	11.86991	4.98	J	24	8.03752	9.93
K	24	11.83328	5.00	K	24	8.01272	10.00
15 YEAR AMORTIZATION				**20 YEAR AMORTIZATION**			
A	12	$13.93050	15.00	A	12	$13.09736	20.00
B	52	3.48262	11.49	B	52	3.27434	13.75
C	52	3.21473	14.64	C	52	3.02247	19.19
D	52	3.19308	15.00	D	52	3.00121	20.00
E	26	6.96525	11.53	E	26	6.54868	13.81
F	26	6.42946	14.71	F	26	6.04494	19.34
G	26	6.39524	15.00	G	24	6.01097	20.00
H	24	7.54568	11.59	H	24	7.09440	13.91
J	24	6.96525	14.83	J	24	6.54868	19.63
K	24	6.94375	15.00	K	24	6.52847	20.00
25 YEAR AMORTIZATION				**30 YEAR AMORTIZATION**			
A	12	$12.73423	25.00	A	12	$12.56808	30.00
B	52	3.18356	15.17	B	52	3.14202	15.96
C	52	2.93867	23.31	C	52	2.90033	26.78
D	52	2.91746	25.00	D	52	2.87907	30.00
E	26	6.36711	15.25	E	26	6.28404	16.06
F	26	5.87734	23.61	F	26	5.80065	27.29
G	26	5.84322	25.00	G	26	5.76633	30.00
H	24	6.89771	15.38	H	24	6.80771	16.21
J	24	6.36711	24.22	J	24	6.28404	28.44
K	24	6.34747	25.00	K	24	6.26465	30.00

TYPES OF PAYMENTS: A—monthly; B—accelerated weekly; C—
regular weekly; D—minimum amortized weekly; E—accelerated
bi-weekly; F—regular bi-weekly; G—minimum amortized bi-
weekly; H—accelerated semi-monthly; J—regular semi-monthly;
K—minimum amortized semi-monthly

15.5%

BLENDED PAYMENTS IN DOLLARS OF PRINCIPAL AND IN-
TEREST FOR A LOAN OF $1,000 AT **15.5%** PER YEAR, CALCU-
LATED HALF-YEARLY, NOT IN ADVANCE

TYPE OF PMT	PMTS EACH YEAR	PMT EACH PERIOD	YEARS TO RETIRE LOAN	TYPE OF PMT	PMTS EACH YEAR	PMT EACH PERIOD	YEARS TO RETIRE LOAN
5 YEAR AMORTIZATION				**10 YEAR AMORTIZATION**			
A	12	$23.80146	5.00	A	12	$16.14694	10.00
B	52	5.95036	4.42	B	52	4.03674	8.32
C	52	5.49264	4.96	C	52	3.72622	9.86
D	52	5.46147	5.00	D	52	3.70263	10.00
E	26	11.90073	4.43	E	26	8.07347	8.34
F	26	10.98529	4.97	F	26	7.45244	9.89
G	26	10.93860	5.00	G	26	7.41588	10.00
H	24	12.89246	4.43	H	24	8.74626	8.37
J	24	11.90073	4.98	J	24	8.07347	9.93
K	24	11.86372	5.00	K	24	8.04836	10.00
15 YEAR AMORTIZATION				**20 YEAR AMORTIZATION**			
A	12	$14.01091	15.00	A	12	$13.18412	20.00
B	52	3.50273	11.46	B	52	3.29603	13.70
C	52	3.23329	14.63	C	52	3.04249	19.17
D	52	3.21136	15.00	D	52	3.02096	20.00
E	26	7.00546	11.51	E	26	6.59206	13.76
F	26	6.46657	14.71	F	26	6.08498	19.33
G	26	6.43193	15.00	G	26	6.05058	20.00
H	24	7.58924	11.57	H	24	7.14140	13.86
J	24	7.00546	14.83	J	24	6.59206	19.62
K	24	6.98367	15.00	K	24	6.57156	20.00
25 YEAR AMORTIZATION				**30 YEAR AMORTIZATION**			
A	12	$12.82534	25.00	A	12	$12.66200	30.00
B	52	3.20634	15.09	B	52	3.16550	15.86
C	52	2.95969	23.27	C	52	2.92200	26.70
D	52	2.93821	25.00	D	52	2.90047	30.00
E	26	6.41267	15.17	E	26	6.33100	15.96
F	26	5.91939	23.58	F	26	5.84400	27.22
G	26	5.88484	25.00	G	26	5.80925	30.00
H	24	6.94706	15.30	H	24	6.85858	16.11
J	24	6.41267	24.20	J	24	6.33100	28.39
K	24	6.39273	25.00	K	24	6.31131	30.00

TYPES OF PAYMENTS: A—monthly; B—accelerated weekly; C—
regular weekly; D—minimum amortized weekly; E—accelerated
bi-weekly; F—regular bi-weekly; G—minimum amortized bi-
weekly; H—accelerated semi-monthly; J—regular semi-monthly;
K—minimum amortized semi-monthly

15.625%

BLENDED PAYMENTS IN DOLLARS OF PRINCIPAL AND IN-
TEREST FOR A LOAN OF $1,000 AT **15.625%** PER YEAR, CAL-
CULATED HALF-YEARLY, NOT IN ADVANCE

TYPE OF PMT	PMTS EACH YEAR	PMT EACH PERIOD	YEARS TO RETIRE LOAN	TYPE OF PMT	PMTS EACH YEAR	PMT EACH PERIOD	YEARS TO RETIRE LOAN
5 YEAR AMORTIZATION				**10 YEAR AMORTIZATION**			
A	12	$23.86316	5.00	A	12	$16.21896	10.00
B	52	5.96579	4.41	B	52	4.05474	8.31
C	52	5.50688	4.96	C	52	3.74284	9.85
D	52	5.47539	5.00	D	52	3.71898	10.00
E	26	11.93158	4.42	E	26	8.10948	8.33
F	26	11.01377	4.97	F	26	7.48567	9.89
G	26	10.96661	5.00	G	26	7.44870	10.00
H	24	12.92588	4.43	H	24	8.78527	8.36
J	24	11.93158	4.98	J	24	8.10948	9.93
K	24	11.89418	5.00	K	24	8.08406	10.00
15 YEAR AMORTIZATION				**20 YEAR AMORTIZATION**			
A	12	$14.09147	15.00	A	12	$13.27100	20.00
B	52	3.52287	11.44	B	52	3.31775	13.64
C	52	3.25188	14.62	C	52	3.06254	19.15
D	52	3.22968	15.00	D	52	3.04073	20.00
E	26	7.04573	11.48	E	26	6.63550	13.71
F	26	6.50375	14.70	F	26	6.12508	19.31
G	26	6.46869	15.00	G	26	6.09025	20.00
H	24	7.63288	11.54	H	24	7.18846	13.81
J	24	7.04573	14.82	J	24	6.63550	19.61
K	24	7.02365	15.00	K	24	6.61470	20.00
25 YEAR AMORTIZATION				**30 YEAR AMORTIZATION**			
A	12	$12.91655	25.00	A	12	$12.75598	30.00
B	52	3.22914	15.01	B	52	3.18899	15.76
C	52	2.98074	23.23	C	52	2.94369	26.62
D	52	2.95898	25.00	D	52	2.92187	30.00
E	26	6.45828	15.09	E	26	6.37799	15.86
F	26	5.96149	23.55	F	26	5.88737	27.15
G	26	5.92650	25.00	G	26	5.85219	30.00
H	24	6.99647	15.22	H	24	6.90949	16.01
J	24	6.45828	24.18	J	24	6.37799	28.34
K	24	6.43803	25.00	K	24	6.35800	30.00

TYPES OF PAYMENTS: A—monthly; B—accelerated weekly; C—
regular weekly; D—minimum amortized weekly; E—accelerated
bi-weekly; F—regular bi-weekly; G—minimum amortized bi-
weekly; H—accelerated semi-monthly; J—regular semi-monthly;
K—minimum amortized semi-monthly

15.75%

BLENDED PAYMENTS IN DOLLARS OF PRINCIPAL AND IN-
TEREST FOR A LOAN OF $1,000 AT **15.75%** PER YEAR, CALCU-
LATED HALF-YEARLY, NOT IN ADVANCE

TYPE OF PMT	PMTS EACH YEAR	PMT EACH PERIOD	YEARS TO RETIRE LOAN	TYPE OF PMT	PMTS EACH YEAR	PMT EACH PERIOD	YEARS TO RETIRE LOAN
5 YEAR AMORTIZATION				**10 YEAR AMORTIZATION**			
A	12	$23.92492	5.00	A	12	$16.29110	10.00
B	52	5.98123	4.41	B	52	4.07277	8.30
C	52	5.52114	4.96	C	52	3.75948	9.85
D	52	5.48933	5.00	D	52	3.73535	10.00
E	26	11.96246	4.42	E	26	8.14555	8.33
F	26	11.04227	4.97	F	26	7.51897	9.88
G	26	10.99464	5.00	G	26	7.48157	10.00
H	24	12.95933	4.43	H	24	8.82434	8.35
J	24	11.96246	4.98	J	24	8.14555	9.93
K	24	11.92468	5.00	K	24	8.11982	10.00
15 YEAR AMORTIZATION				**20 YEAR AMORTIZATION**			
A	12	$14.17215	15.00	A	12	$13.35801	20.00
B	52	3.54304	11.41	B	52	3.33950	13.59
C	52	3.27050	14.62	C	52	3.08262	19.13
D	52	3.24802	15.00	D	52	3.06053	20.00
E	26	7.08608	11.45	E	26	6.67900	13.66
F	26	6.54099	14.70	F	26	6.16523	19.30
G	26	6.50550	15.00	G	26	6.12997	20.00
H	24	7.67658	11.52	H	24	7.23559	13.76
J	24	7.08608	14.82	J	24	6.67900	19.60
K	24	7.06370	15.00	K	24	6.65791	20.00
25 YEAR AMORTIZATION				**30 YEAR AMORTIZATION**			
A	12	$13.00785	25.00	A	12	$12.85001	30.00
B	52	3.25196	14.93	B	52	3.21250	15.67
C	52	3.00181	23.19	C	52	2.96539	26.54
D	52	2.97976	25.00	D	52	2.94329	30.00
E	26	6.50392	15.01	E	26	6.42500	15.76
F	26	6.00362	23.51	F	26	5.93077	27.08
G	26	5.96820	25.00	G	26	5.89515	30.00
H	24	7.04592	15.15	H	24	6.96042	15.91
J	24	6.50392	24.16	J	24	6.42500	28.29
K	24	6.48338	25.00	K	24	6.40471	30.00

TYPES OF PAYMENTS: A—monthly; B—accelerated weekly; C—
regular weekly; D—minimum amortized weekly; E—accelerated
bi-weekly; F—regular bi-weekly; G—minimum amortized bi-
weekly; H—accelerated semi-monthly; J—regular semi-monthly;
K—minimum amortized semi-monthly

15.875%

BLENDED PAYMENTS IN DOLLARS OF PRINCIPAL AND IN-TEREST FOR A LOAN OF $1,000 AT **15.875%** PER YEAR, CAL-CULATED HALF-YEARLY, NOT IN ADVANCE

TYPE OF PMT	PMTS EACH YEAR	PMT EACH PERIOD	YEARS TO RETIRE LOAN	TYPE OF PMT	PMTS EACH YEAR	PMT EACH PERIOD	YEARS TO RETIRE LOAN
5 YEAR AMORTIZATION				**10 YEAR AMORTIZATION**			
A	12	$23.98674	5.00	A	12	$16.36335	10.00
B	52	5.99669	4.41	B	52	4.09084	8.29
C	52	5.53540	4.96	C	52	3.77616	9.85
D	52	5.50327	5.00	D	52	3.75174	10.00
E	26	11.99337	4.42	E	26	8.18167	8.32
F	26	11.07080	4.97	F	26	7.55231	9.88
G	26	11.02269	5.00	G	26	7.51449	10.00
H	24	12.99282	4.43	H	24	8.86348	8.34
J	24	11.99337	4.98	J	24	8.18167	9.93
K	24	11.95520	5.00	K	24	8.15563	10.00
15 YEAR AMORTIZATION				**20 YEAR AMORTIZATION**			
A	12	$14.25297	15.00	A	12	$13.44513	20.00
B	52	3.56324	11.38	B	52	3.36128	13.54
C	52	3.28915	14.61	C	52	3.10272	19.11
D	52	3.26640	15.00	D	52	3.08036	20.00
E	26	7.12649	11.43	E	26	6.72256	13.61
F	26	6.57830	14.69	F	26	6.20544	19.28
G	26	6.54237	15.00	G	26	6.16975	20.00
H	24	7.72036	11.49	H	24	7.28278	13.71
J	24	7.12649	14.82	J	24	6.72256	19.59
K	24	7.10381	15.00	K	24	6.70117	20.00
25 YEAR AMORTIZATION				**30 YEAR AMORTIZATION**			
A	12	$13.09923	25.00	A	12	$12.99409	30.00
B	52	3.27481	14.85	B	52	3.23602	15.57
C	52	3.02290	23.15	C	52	2.98710	26.46
D	52	3.00057	25.00	D	52	2.96472	30.00
E	26	6.54962	14.94	E	26	6.47204	15.66
F	26	6.04580	23.48	F	26	5.97420	27.01
G	26	6.00994	25.00	G	26	5.93814	30.00
H	24	7.09542	15.07	H	24	7.01138	15.82
J	24	6.54962	24.13	J	24	6.47204	28.24
K	24	6.52877	25.00	K	24	6.45145	30.00

TYPES OF PAYMENTS: A—monthly; B—accelerated weekly; C—regular weekly; D—minimum amortized weekly; E—accelerated bi-weekly; F—regular bi-weekly; G—minimum amortized bi-weekly; H—accelerated semi-monthly; J—regular semi-monthly; K—minimum amortized semi-monthly

16%

BLENDED PAYMENTS IN DOLLARS OF PRINCIPAL AND IN-
TEREST FOR A LOAN OF $1,000 AT **16%** PER YEAR, CALCU-
LATED HALF-YEARLY, NOT IN ADVANCE

TYPE OF PMT	PMTS EACH YEAR	PMT EACH PERIOD	YEARS TO RETIRE LOAN	TYPE OF PMT	PMTS EACH YEAR	PMT EACH PERIOD	YEARS TO RETIRE LOAN
5 YEAR AMORTIZATION				**10 YEAR AMORTIZATION**			
A	12	$24.04862	5.00	A	12	$16.43571	10.00
B	52	6.01216	4.41	B	52	4.10893	8.28
C	52	5.54968	4.96	C	52	3.79286	9.85
D	52	5.51723	5.00	D	52	3.76816	10.00
E	26	12.02431	4.42	E	26	8.21785	8.31
F	26	11.09936	4.97	F	26	7.58571	9.88
G	26	11.05077	5.00	G	26	7.54746	10.00
H	24	13.02634	4.42	H	24	8.90268	8.33
J	24	12.02431	4.98	J	24	8.21785	9.92
K	24	11.98575	5.00	K	24	8.19150	10.00
15 YEAR AMORTIZATION				**20 YEAR AMORTIZATION**			
A	12	$14.33392	15.00	A	12	$13.53236	20.00
B	52	3.58348	11.35	B	52	3.38309	13.49
C	52	3.30783	14.60	C	52	3.12285	19.10
D	52	3.28480	15.00	D	52	3.10021	20.00
E	26	7.16696	11.40	E	26	6.76618	13.55
F	26	6.61566	14.69	F	26	6.24571	19.27
G	26	6.57931	15.00	G	26	6.20968	20.00
H	24	7.76421	11.46	H	24	7.33003	13.65
J	24	7.16696	14.81	J	24	6.76618	19.58
K	24	7.14398	15.00	K	24	6.74449	20.00
25 YEAR AMORTIZATION				**30 YEAR AMORTIZATION**			
A	12	$13.19070	25.00	A	12	$13.03822	30.00
B	52	3.29767	14.77	B	52	3.25956	15.47
C	52	3.04401	23.11	C	52	3.00882	26.37
D	52	3.02139	25.00	D	52	2.98616	30.00
E	26	6.59535	14.86	E	26	6.51911	15.57
F	26	6.08801	23.44	F	26	6.01764	26.94
G	26	6.05172	25.00	G	26	5.98114	30.00
H	24	7.14496	14.99	H	24	7.06237	15.72
J	24	6.59535	24.11	J	24	6.51911	28.19
K	24	6.57420	25.00	K	24	6.49821	30.00

TYPES OF PAYMENTS: A—monthly; B—accelerated weekly; C—
regular weekly; D—minimum amortized weekly; E—accelerated
bi-weekly; F—regular bi-weekly; G—minimum amortized bi-
weekly; H—accelerated semi-monthly; J—regular semi-monthly;
K—minimum amortized semi-monthly

16.125%

BLENDED PAYMENTS IN DOLLARS OF PRINCIPAL AND IN-
TEREST FOR A LOAN OF $1,000 AT **16.125%** PER YEAR, CAL-
CULATED HALF-YEARLY, NOT IN ADVANCE

TYPE OF PMT	PMTS EACH YEAR	PMT EACH PERIOD	YEARS TO RETIRE LOAN	TYPE OF PMT	PMTS EACH YEAR	PMT EACH PERIOD	YEARS TO RETIRE LOAN
5 YEAR AMORTIZATION				**10 YEAR AMORTIZATION**			
A	12	$24.11056	5.00	A	12	$16.50819	10.00
B	52	6.02764	4.41	B	52	4.12705	8.27
C	52	5.56398	4.96	C	52	3.80958	9.85
D	52	5.53120	5.00	D	52	3.78460	10.00
E	26	12.05528	4.42	E	26	8.25409	8.30
F	26	11.12795	4.97	F	26	7.61916	9.88
G	26	11.07888	5.00	G	26	7.58048	10.00
H	24	13.05989	4.42	H	24	8.94193	8.32
J	24	12.05528	4.98	J	24	8.25409	9.92
K	24	12.01633	5.00	K	24	8.22743	10.00
15 YEAR AMORTIZATION				**20 YEAR AMORTIZATION**			
A	12	$14.41501	15.00	A	12	$13.61972	20.00
B	52	3.60375	11.33	B	52	3.40493	13.43
C	52	3.32654	14.60	C	52	3.14301	19.08
D	52	3.30323	15.00	D	52	3.12008	20.00
E	26	7.20750	11.37	E	26	6.80986	13.50
F	26	6.65308	14.68	F	26	6.28602	19.25
G	26	6.61630	15.00	G	26	6.24945	20.00
H	24	7.80813	11.43	H	24	7.37735	13.60
J	24	7.20750	14.81	J	24	6.80986	19.57
K	24	7.18422	15.00	K	24	6.78786	20.00
25 YEAR AMORTIZATION				**30 YEAR AMORTIZATION**			
A	12	$13.28225	25.00	A	12	$13.13240	30.00
B	52	3.32056	14.70	B	52	3.28310	15.37
C	52	3.06513	23.06	C	52	3.03055	26.29
D	52	3.04224	25.00	D	52	3.00761	30.00
E	26	6.64112	14.78	E	26	6.56620	15.47
F	26	6.13027	23.40	F	26	6.06111	26.86
G	26	6.09353	25.00	G	26	6.02417	30.00
H	24	7.19455	14.91	H	24	7.11338	15.62
J	24	6.64112	24.08	J	24	6.56620	28.13
K	24	6.61967	25.00	K	24	6.54498	30.00

TYPES OF PAYMENTS: A—monthly; B—accelerated weekly; C—
regular weekly; D—minimum amortized weekly; E—accelerated
bi-weekly; F—regular bi-weekly; G—minimum amortized bi-
weekly; H—accelerated semi-monthly; J—regular semi-monthly;
K—minimum amortized semi-monthly

16.25%

BLENDED PAYMENTS IN DOLLARS OF PRINCIPAL AND IN-
TEREST FOR A LOAN OF $1,000 AT **16.25%** PER YEAR, CALCU-
LATED HALF-YEARLY, NOT IN ADVANCE

TYPE OF PMT	PMTS EACH YEAR	PMT EACH PERIOD	YEARS TO RETIRE LOAN	TYPE OF PMT	PMTS EACH YEAR	PMT EACH PERIOD	YEARS TO RETIRE LOAN
5 YEAR AMORTIZATION				**10 YEAR AMORTIZATION**			
A	12	$24.17256	5.00	A	12	$16.58078	10.00
B	52	6.04314	4.40	B	52	4.14519	8.26
C	52	5.57828	4.96	C	52	3.82633	9.84
D	52	5.54519	5.00	D	52	3.80107	10.00
E	26	12.08628	4.41	E	26	8.29039	8.29
F	26	11.15656	4.97	F	26	7.65267	9.88
G	26	11.10701	5.00	G	26	7.61355	10.00
H	24	13.09347	4.42	H	24	8.98125	8.31
J	24	12.08628	4.98	J	24	8.29039	9.92
K	24	12.04694	5.00	K	24	8.26340	10.00
15 YEAR AMORTIZATION				**20 YEAR AMORTIZATION**			
A	12	$14.49622	15.00	A	12	$13.70718	20.00
B	52	3.62405	11.30	B	52	3.42679	13.38
C	52	3.34528	14.59	C	52	3.16320	19.06
D	52	3.32169	15.00	D	52	3.13998	20.00
E	26	7.24811	11.34	E	26	6.85359	13.45
F	26	6.69056	14.67	F	26	6.32639	19.24
G	26	6.65334	15.00	G	26	6.28938	20.00
H	24	7.85212	11.41	H	24	7.42472	13.55
J	24	7.24811	14.81	J	24	6.85359	19.56
K	24	7.22452	15.00	K	24	6.83128	20.00
25 YEAR AMORTIZATION				**30 YEAR AMORTIZATION**			
A	12	$13.37388	25.00	A	12	$13.22662	30.00
B	52	3.34347	14.62	B	52	3.30666	15.28
C	52	3.08628	23.02	C	52	3.05230	26.20
D	52	3.06309	25.00	D	52	3.02906	30.00
E	26	6.68694	14.71	E	26	6.61331	15.37
F	26	6.17256	23.37	F	26	6.10459	26.79
G	26	6.13538	25.00	G	26	6.06721	30.00
H	24	7.24418	14.84	H	24	7.16442	15.53
J	24	6.68694	24.06	J	24	6.61331	28.08
K	24	6.66517	25.00	K	24	6.59178	30.00

TYPES OF PAYMENTS: A—monthly; B—accelerated weekly; C—
regular weekly; D—minimum amortized weekly; E—accelerated
bi-weekly; F—regular bi-weekly; G—minimum amortized bi-
weekly; H—accelerated semi-monthly; J—regular semi-monthly;
K—minimum amortized semi-monthly

16.375%

BLENDED PAYMENTS IN DOLLARS OF PRINCIPAL AND IN-
TEREST FOR A LOAN OF $1,000 AT **16.375%** PER YEAR, CAL-
CULATED HALF-YEARLY, NOT IN ADVANCE

TYPE OF PMT	PMTS EACH YEAR	PMT EACH PERIOD	YEARS TO RETIRE LOAN	TYPE OF PMT	PMTS EACH YEAR	PMT EACH PERIOD	YEARS TO RETIRE LOAN
5 YEAR AMORTIZATION				**10 YEAR AMORTIZATION**			
A	12	$24.23461	5.00	A	12	$16.65348	10.00
B	52	6.05865	4.40	B	52	4.16337	8.25
C	52	5.59260	4.95	C	52	3.84311	9.84
D	52	5.55918	5.00	D	52	3.81757	10.00
E	26	12.11731	4.41	E	26	8.32674	8.28
F	26	11.18520	4.97	F	26	7.68622	9.88
G	26	11.13517	5.00	G	26	7.64667	10.00
H	24	13.12708	4.42	H	24	9.02063	8.30
J	24	12.11731	4.98	J	24	8.32674	9.92
K	24	12.07757	5.00	K	24	8.29944	10.00
15 YEAR AMORTIZATION				**20 YEAR AMORTIZATION**			
A	12	$14.57755	15.00	A	12	$13.79475	20.00
B	52	3.64439	11.27	B	52	3.44869	13.33
C	52	3.36405	14.58	C	52	3.18340	19.04
D	52	3.34017	15.00	D	52	3.15990	20.00
E	26	7.28878	11.32	E	26	6.89738	13.40
F	26	6.72810	14.67	F	26	6.36681	19.22
G	26	6.69045	15.00	G	26	6.32936	20.00
H	24	7.89617	11.38	H	24	7.47216	13.50
J	24	7.28878	14.80	J	24	6.89738	19.55
K	24	7.26488	15.00	K	24	6.87476	20.00
25 YEAR AMORTIZATION				**30 YEAR AMORTIZATION**			
A	12	$13.46558	25.00	A	12	$13.32088	30.00
B	52	3.36640	14.54	B	52	3.33022	15.18
C	52	3.10744	22.97	C	52	3.07405	26.11
D	52	3.08397	25.00	D	52	3.05053	30.00
E	26	6.73279	14.63	E	26	6.66044	15.28
F	26	6.21488	23.33	F	26	6.14810	26.71
G	26	6.17726	25.00	G	26	6.11027	30.00
H	24	7.29386	14.76	H	24	7.21548	15.43
J	24	6.73279	24.03	J	24	6.66044	28.02
K	24	6.71072	25.00	K	24	6.63860	30.00

TYPES OF PAYMENTS: A—monthly; B—accelerated weekly; C—
regular weekly; D—minimum amortized weekly; E—accelerated
bi-weekly; F—regular bi-weekly; G—minimum amortized bi-
weekly; H—accelerated semi-monthly; J—regular semi-monthly;
K—minimum amortized semi-monthly

16.5%

BLENDED PAYMENTS IN DOLLARS OF PRINCIPAL AND IN-
TEREST FOR A LOAN OF $1,000 AT **16.5%** PER YEAR, CALCU-
LATED HALF-YEARLY, NOT IN ADVANCE

TYPE OF PMT	PMTS EACH YEAR	PMT EACH PERIOD	YEARS TO RETIRE LOAN	TYPE OF PMT	PMTS EACH YEAR	PMT EACH PERIOD	YEARS TO RETIRE LOAN
5 YEAR AMORTIZATION				**10 YEAR AMORTIZATION**			
A	12	$24.29672	5.00	A	12	$16.72629	10.00
B	52	6.07418	4.40	B	52	4.18157	8.24
C	52	5.60694	4.95	C	52	3.85991	9.84
D	52	5.57319	5.00	D	52	3.83408	10.00
E	26	12.14836	4.41	E	26	8.36315	8.27
F	26	11.21387	4.97	F	26	7.71983	9.87
G	26	11.16335	5.00	G	26	7.67984	10.00
H	24	13.16072	4.42	H	24	9.06007	8.29
J	24	12.14836	4.97	J	24	8.36315	9.92
K	24	12.10823	5.00	K	24	8.33552	10.00
15 YEAR AMORTIZATION				**20 YEAR AMORTIZATION**			
A	12	$14.65901	15.00	A	12	$13.88244	20.00
B	52	3.66475	11.24	B	52	3.47061	13.28
C	52	3.38285	14.58	C	52	3.20364	19.02
D	52	3.35869	15.00	D	52	3.17985	20.00
E	26	7.32951	11.29	E	26	6.94122	13.35
F	26	6.76570	14.66	F	26	6.40728	19.21
G	26	6.72760	15.00	G	26	6.36938	20.00
H	24	7.94030	11.35	H	24	7.51965	13.45
J	24	7.32951	14.80	J	24	6.94122	19.54
K	24	7.30530	15.00	K	24	6.91829	20.00
25 YEAR AMORTIZATION				**30 YEAR AMORTIZATION**			
A	12	$13.55737	25.00	A	12	$13.41519	30.00
B	52	3.38934	14.47	B	52	3.35380	15.09
C	52	3.12862	22.93	C	52	3.09581	26.02
D	52	3.10486	25.00	D	52	3.07200	30.00
E	26	6.77868	14.55	E	26	6.70759	15.19
F	26	6.25725	23.29	F	26	6.19163	26.63
G	26	6.21917	25.00	G	26	6.15335	30.00
H	24	7.34357	14.69	H	24	7.26656	15.34
J	24	6.77868	24.01	J	24	6.70759	27.96
K	24	6.75629	25.00	K	24	6.68544	30.00

TYPES OF PAYMENTS: A—monthly; B—accelerated weekly; C—
regular weekly; D—minimum amortized weekly; E—accelerated
bi-weekly; F—regular bi-weekly; G—minimum amortized bi-
weekly; H—accelerated semi-monthly; J—regular semi-monthly;
K—minimum amortized semi-monthly

16.625%

BLENDED PAYMENTS IN DOLLARS OF PRINCIPAL AND IN-
TEREST FOR A LOAN OF $1,000 AT **16.625%** PER YEAR, CAL-
CULATED HALF-YEARLY, NOT IN ADVANCE

TYPE OF PMT	PMTS EACH YEAR	PMT EACH PERIOD	YEARS TO RETIRE LOAN	TYPE OF PMT	PMTS EACH YEAR	PMT EACH PERIOD	YEARS TO RETIRE LOAN
5 YEAR AMORTIZATION				**10 YEAR AMORTIZATION**			
A	12	$24.35889	5.00	A	12	$16.79922	10.00
B	52	6.08972	4.40	B	52	4.19980	8.23
C	52	5.62128	4.95	C	52	3.87674	9.84
D	52	5.58721	5.00	D	52	3.85063	10.00
E	26	12.17945	4.41	E	26	8.39961	8.26
F	26	11.24257	4.97	F	26	7.75348	9.87
G	26	11.19156	5.00	G	26	7.71306	10.00
H	24	13.19440	4.42	H	24	9.09957	8.29
J	24	12.17945	4.97	J	24	8.39961	9.92
K	24	12.13892	5.00	K	24	8.37166	10.00
15 YEAR AMORTIZATION				**20 YEAR AMORTIZATION**			
A	12	$14.74060	15.00	A	12	$13.97022	20.00
B	52	3.68515	11.21	B	52	3.49256	13.22
C	52	3.40168	14.57	C	52	3.22390	19.00
D	52	3.37723	15.00	D	52	3.19982	20.00
E	26	7.37030	11.26	E	26	6.98511	13.29
F	26	6.80335	14.66	F	26	6.44780	19.19
G	26	6.76482	15.00	G	26	6.40945	20.00
H	24	7.98449	11.33	H	24	7.56720	13.40
J	24	7.37030	14.80	J	24	6.98511	19.53
K	24	7.34578	15.00	K	24	6.96187	20.00
25 YEAR AMORTIZATION				**30 YEAR AMORTIZATION**			
A	12	$13.64922	25.00	A	12	$13.50953	30.00
B	52	3.41230	14.39	B	52	3.37738	15.00
C	52	3.14982	22.88	C	52	3.11758	25.93
D	52	3.12576	25.00	D	52	3.09348	30.00
E	26	6.82461	14.48	E	26	6.75477	15.09
F	26	6.29964	23.25	F	26	6.23517	26.55
G	26	6.26112	25.00	G	26	6.19644	30.00
H	24	7.39333	14.61	H	24	7.31766	15.24
J	24	6.82461	23.98	J	24	6.75477	27.91
K	24	6.80190	25.00	K	24	6.73229	30.00

TYPES OF PAYMENTS: A—monthly; B—accelerated weekly; C—
regular weekly; D—minimum amortized weekly; E—accelerated
bi-weekly; F—regular bi-weekly; G—minimum amortized bi-
weekly; H—accelerated semi-monthly; J—regular semi-monthly;
K—minimum amortized semi-monthly

16.75%

BLENDED PAYMENTS IN DOLLARS OF PRINCIPAL AND INTEREST FOR A LOAN OF $1,000 AT **16.75%** PER YEAR, CALCULATED HALF-YEARLY, NOT IN ADVANCE

TYPE OF PMT	PMTS EACH YEAR	PMT EACH PERIOD	YEARS TO RETIRE LOAN	TYPE OF PMT	PMTS EACH YEAR	PMT EACH PERIOD	YEARS TO RETIRE LOAN
5 YEAR AMORTIZATION				**10 YEAR AMORTIZATION**			
A	12	$24.42112	5.00	A	12	$16.87225	10.00
B	52	6.10528	4.40	B	52	4.21806	8.22
C	52	5.63564	4.95	C	52	3.89360	9.83
D	52	5.60124	5.00	D	52	3.86719	10.00
E	26	12.21056	4.41	E	26	8.43612	8.25
F	26	11.27129	4.97	F	26	7.78719	9.87
G	26	11.21979	5.00	G	26	7.74633	10.00
H	24	13.22811	4.41	H	24	9.13914	8.28
J	24	12.21056	4.97	J	24	8.43612	9.92
K	24	12.16964	5.00	K	24	8.40785	10.00
15 YEAR AMORTIZATION				**20 YEAR AMORTIZATION**			
A	12	$14.82231	15.00	A	12	$14.05811	20.00
B	52	3.70558	11.19	B	52	3.51453	13.17
C	52	3.42053	14.56	C	52	3.24418	18.98
D	52	3.39580	15.00	D	52	3.21981	20.00
E	26	7.41115	11.23	E	26	7.02906	13.24
F	26	6.84107	14.65	F	26	6.48836	19.17
G	26	6.80209	15.00	G	26	6.44957	20.00
H	24	8.02875	11.30	H	24	7.61481	13.34
J	24	7.41115	14.79	J	24	7.02906	19.52
K	24	7.38632	15.00	K	24	7.00550	20.00
25 YEAR AMORTIZATION				**30 YEAR AMORTIZATION**			
A	12	$13.74114	25.00	A	12	$13.60391	30.00
B	52	3.43529	14.32	B	52	3.40098	14.90
C	52	3.17103	22.83	C	52	3.13936	25.84
D	52	3.14668	25.00	D	52	3.11496	30.00
E	26	6.87057	14.40	E	26	6.80195	15.00
F	26	6.34207	23.21	F	26	6.27873	26.47
G	26	6.30309	25.00	G	26	6.23955	30.00
H	24	7.44312	14.54	H	24	7.36878	15.15
J	24	6.87057	23.95	J	24	6.80195	27.84
K	24	6.84755	25.00	K	24	6.77916	30.00

TYPES OF PAYMENTS: A—monthly; B—accelerated weekly; C—regular weekly; D—minimum amortized weekly; E—accelerated bi-weekly; F—regular bi-weekly; G—minimum amortized bi-weekly; H—accelerated semi-monthly; J—regular semi-monthly; K—minimum amortized semi-monthly

16.875%

BLENDED PAYMENTS IN DOLLARS OF PRINCIPAL AND INTEREST FOR A LOAN OF $1,000 AT **16.875%** PER YEAR, CALCULATED HALF-YEARLY, NOT IN ADVANCE

TYPE OF PMT	PMTS EACH YEAR	PMT EACH PERIOD	YEARS TO RETIRE LOAN	TYPE OF PMT	PMTS EACH YEAR	PMT EACH PERIOD	YEARS TO RETIRE LOAN
5 YEAR AMORTIZATION				**10 YEAR AMORTIZATION**			
A	12	$24.48340	5.00	A	12	$16.94539	10.00
B	52	6.12085	4.40	B	52	4.23635	8.21
C	52	5.65002	4.95	C	52	3.91048	9.83
D	52	5.61529	5.00	D	52	3.88378	10.00
E	26	12.24170	4.41	E	26	8.47270	8.24
F	26	11.30003	4.96	F	26	7.82095	9.87
G	26	11.24805	5.00	G	26	7.77965	10.00
H	24	13.26184	4.41	H	24	9.17875	8.27
J	24	12.24170	4.97	J	24	8.47270	9.92
K	24	12.20038	5.00	K	24	8.44410	10.00
15 YEAR AMORTIZATION				**20 YEAR AMORTIZATION**			
A	12	$14.90414	15.00	A	12	$14.14611	20.00
B	52	3.72604	11.16	B	52	3.53653	13.12
C	52	3.43942	14.55	C	52	3.26449	18.96
D	52	3.41439	15.00	D	52	3.23982	20.00
E	26	7.45207	11.21	E	26	7.07305	13.19
F	26	6.87883	14.65	F	26	6.52897	19.16
G	26	6.83941	15.00	G	26	6.48973	20.00
H	24	8.07308	11.27	H	24	7.66248	13.29
J	24	7.45207	14.79	J	24	7.07305	19.51
K	24	7.42692	15.00	K	24	7.04918	20.00
25 YEAR AMORTIZATION				**30 YEAR AMORTIZATION**			
A	12	$13.83314	25.00	A	12	$13.69832	30.00
B	52	3.45828	14.24	B	52	3.42458	14.81
C	52	3.19226	22.78	C	52	3.16115	25.75
D	52	3.16762	25.00	D	52	3.13646	30.00
E	26	6.91657	14.33	E	26	6.84916	14.91
F	26	6.38452	23.17	F	26	6.32230	26.39
G	26	6.34509	25.00	G	26	6.28267	30.00
H	24	7.49295	14.46	H	24	7.41992	15.06
J	24	6.91657	23.92	J	24	6.84916	27.78
K	24	6.89322	25.00	K	24	6.82604	30.00

TYPES OF PAYMENTS: A—monthly; B—accelerated weekly; C—regular weekly; D—minimum amortized weekly; E—accelerated bi-weekly; F—regular bi-weekly; G—minimum amortized bi-weekly; H—accelerated semi-monthly; J—regular semi-monthly; K—minimum amortized semi-monthly

17%

BLENDED PAYMENTS IN DOLLARS OF PRINCIPAL AND IN-
TEREST FOR A LOAN OF $1,000 AT **17%** PER YEAR, CALCU-
LATED HALF-YEARLY, NOT IN ADVANCE

TYPE OF PMT	PMTS EACH YEAR	PMT EACH PERIOD	YEARS TO RETIRE LOAN	TYPE OF PMT	PMTS EACH YEAR	PMT EACH PERIOD	YEARS TO RETIRE LOAN
5 YEAR AMORTIZATION				**10 YEAR AMORTIZATION**			
A	12	$24.54574	5.00	A	12	$17.01865	10.00
B	52	6.13644	4.39	B	52	4.25466	8.20
C	52	5.66440	4.95	C	52	3.92738	9.83
D	52	5.62934	5.00	D	52	3.90040	10.00
E	26	12.27287	4.40	E	26	8.50932	8.23
F	26	11.32880	4.96	F	26	7.85476	9.87
G	26	11.27633	5.00	G	26	7.81302	10.00
H	24	13.29561	4.41	H	24	9.21843	8.26
J	24	12.27287	4.97	J	24	8.50932	9.91
K	24	12.23115	5.00	K	24	8.48040	10.00
15 YEAR AMORTIZATION				**20 YEAR AMORTIZATION**			
A	12	$14.98609	15.00	A	12	$14.23420	20.00
B	52	3.74652	11.13	B	52	3.55855	13.07
C	52	3.45833	14.55	C	52	3.28482	18.94
D	52	3.43301	15.00	D	52	3.25986	20.00
E	26	7.49305	11.18	E	26	7.11710	13.14
F	26	6.91666	14.64	F	26	6.56963	19.14
G	26	6.87678	15.00	G	26	6.52993	20.00
H	24	8.11747	11.25	H	24	7.71019	13.24
J	24	7.49305	14.78	J	24	7.11710	19.50
K	24	7.46758	15.00	K	24	7.09291	20.00
25 YEAR AMORTIZATION				**30 YEAR AMORTIZATION**			
A	12	$13.92519	25.00	A	12	$13.79276	30.00
B	52	3.48130	14.17	B	52	3.44819	14.72
C	52	3.21351	22.73	C	52	3.18295	25.66
D	52	3.18857	25.00	D	52	3.15705	30.00
E	26	6.96260	14.25	E	26	6.89638	14.82
F	26	6.42701	23.13	F	26	6.36589	26.31
G	26	6.38713	25.00	G	26	6.32580	30.00
H	24	7.54281	14.39	H	24	7.47108	14.97
J	24	6.96260	23.90	J	24	6.89638	27.72
K	24	6.93893	25.00	K	24	6.87294	30.00

TYPES OF PAYMENTS: A—monthly; B—accelerated weekly; C—
regular weekly; D—minimum amortized weekly; E—accelerated
bi-weekly; F—regular bi-weekly; G—minimum amortized bi-
weekly; H—accelerated semi-monthly; J—regular semi-monthly;
K—minimum amortized semi-monthly

17.125%

BLENDED PAYMENTS IN DOLLARS OF PRINCIPAL AND IN-
TEREST FOR A LOAN OF $1,000 AT **17.125%** PER YEAR, CAL-
CULATED HALF-YEARLY, NOT IN ADVANCE

TYPE OF PMT	PMTS EACH YEAR	PMT EACH PERIOD	YEARS TO RETIRE LOAN	TYPE OF PMT	PMTS EACH YEAR	PMT EACH PERIOD	YEARS TO RETIRE LOAN
5 YEAR AMORTIZATION				**10 YEAR AMORTIZATION**			
A	12	$24.60814	5.00	A	12	$17.09201	10.00
B	52	6.15204	4.39	B	52	4.27300	8.19
C	52	5.67880	4.95	C	52	3.94431	9.83
D	52	5.64341	5.00	D	52	3.91703	10.00
E	26	12.30407	4.40	E	26	8.54600	8.22
F	26	11.35760	4.96	F	26	7.88862	9.87
G	26	11.30464	5.00	G	26	7.84643	10.00
H	24	13.32941	4.41	H	24	9.25817	8.25
J	24	12.30407	4.97	J	24	8.54600	9.91
K	24	12.26195	5.00	K	24	8.51675	10.00
15 YEAR AMORTIZATION				**20 YEAR AMORTIZATION**			
A	12	$15.06816	15.00	A	12	$14.32239	20.00
B	52	3.76704	11.10	B	52	3.58060	13.01
C	52	3.47727	14.54	C	52	3.30517	18.91
D	52	3.45166	15.00	D	52	3.27991	20.00
E	26	7.53408	11.15	E	26	7.16120	13.09
F	26	6.95453	14.63	F	26	6.61034	19.12
G	26	6.91421	15.00	G	26	6.57018	20.00
H	24	8.16192	11.22	H	24	7.75796	13.19
J	24	7.53408	14.78	J	24	7.16120	19.49
K	24	7.50829	15.00	K	24	7.13668	20.00
25 YEAR AMORTIZATION				**30 YEAR AMORTIZATION**			
A	12	$14.01732	25.00	A	12	$13.88724	30.00
B	52	3.50433	14.09	B	52	3.47181	14.63
C	52	3.23477	22.68	C	52	3.20475	25.56
D	52	3.20953	25.00	D	52	3.17946	30.00
E	26	7.00866	14.18	E	26	6.94362	14.73
F	26	6.46953	23.08	F	26	6.40949	26.22
G	26	6.42919	25.00	G	26	6.36895	30.00
H	24	7.59271	14.31	H	24	7.52225	14.88
J	24	7.00866	23.87	J	24	6.94362	27.66
K	24	6.98467	25.00	K	24	6.91985	30.00

TYPES OF PAYMENTS: A—monthly; B—accelerated weekly; C—
regular weekly; D—minimum amortized weekly; E—accelerated
bi-weekly; F—regular bi-weekly; G—minimum amortized bi-
weekly; H—accelerated semi-monthly; J—regular semi-monthly;
K—minimum amortized semi-monthly

17.25%

BLENDED PAYMENTS IN DOLLARS OF PRINCIPAL AND IN-
TEREST FOR A LOAN OF $1,000 AT **17.25%** PER YEAR, CALCU-
LATED HALF-YEARLY, NOT IN ADVANCE

TYPE OF PMT	PMTS EACH YEAR	PMT EACH PERIOD	YEARS TO RETIRE LOAN	TYPE OF PMT	PMTS EACH YEAR	PMT EACH PERIOD	YEARS TO RETIRE LOAN
5 YEAR AMORTIZATION				**10 YEAR AMORTIZATION**			
A	12	$24.67060	5.00	A	12	$17.16547	10.00
B	52	6.16765	4.39	B	52	4.29137	8.18
C	52	5.69321	4.95	C	52	3.96126	9.83
D	52	5.65749	5.00	D	52	3.93369	10.00
E	26	12.33530	4.40	E	26	8.58274	8.21
F	26	11.38643	4.96	F	26	7.92253	9.86
G	26	11.33297	5.00	G	26	7.87989	10.00
H	24	13.36324	4.41	H	24	9.29796	8.24
J	24	12.33530	4.97	J	24	8.58274	9.91
K	24	12.29278	5.00	K	24	8.55315	10.00
15 YEAR AMORTIZATION				**20 YEAR AMORTIZATION**			
A	12	$15.15034	15.00	A	12	$14.41068	20.00
B	52	3.78759	11.07	B	52	3.60267	12.96
C	52	3.49623	14.53	C	52	3.32554	18.89
D	52	3.47033	15.00	D	52	3.29999	20.00
E	26	7.57517	11.12	E	26	7.20534	13.03
F	26	6.99247	14.63	F	26	6.65108	19.10
G	26	6.95169	15.00	G	26	6.61047	20.00
H	24	8.20644	11.19	H	24	7.80579	13.14
J	24	7.57517	14.78	J	24	7.20534	19.47
K	24	7.54906	15.00	K	24	7.18050	20.00
25 YEAR AMORTIZATION				**30 YEAR AMORTIZATION**			
A	12	$14.10950	25.00	A	12	$13.98174	30.00
B	52	3.52738	14.02	B	52	3.49543	14.54
C	52	3.25604	22.63	C	52	3.22656	25.47
D	52	3.23050	25.00	D	52	3.20097	30.00
E	26	7.05475	14.11	E	26	6.99087	14.64
F	26	6.51208	23.04	F	26	6.45311	26.14
G	26	6.47127	25.00	G	26	6.41211	30.00
H	24	7.64265	14.24	H	24	7.57344	14.79
J	24	7.05475	23.84	J	24	6.99087	27.59
K	24	7.03043	25.00	K	24	6.96677	30.00

TYPES OF PAYMENTS: A—monthly; B—accelerated weekly; C—
regular weekly; D—minimum amortized weekly; E—accelerated
bi-weekly; F—regular bi-weekly; G—minimum amortized bi-
weekly; H—accelerated semi-monthly; J—regular semi-monthly;
K—minimum amortized semi-monthly

17.375%

BLENDED PAYMENTS IN DOLLARS OF PRINCIPAL AND INTEREST FOR A LOAN OF $1,000 AT **17.375%** PER YEAR, CALCULATED HALF-YEARLY, NOT IN ADVANCE

TYPE OF PMT	PMTS EACH YEAR	PMT EACH PERIOD	YEARS TO RETIRE LOAN	TYPE OF PMT	PMTS EACH YEAR	PMT EACH PERIOD	YEARS TO RETIRE LOAN
5 YEAR AMORTIZATION				**10 YEAR AMORTIZATION**			
A	12	$24.73311	5.00	A	12	$17.23905	10.00
B	52	6.18328	4.39	B	52	4.30976	8.17
C	52	5.70764	4.95	C	52	3.97824	9.82
D	52	5.67159	5.00	D	52	3.95038	10.00
E	26	12.36655	4.40	E	26	8.61952	8.20
F	26	11.41528	4.96	F	26	7.95648	9.86
G	26	11.36132	5.00	G	26	7.91340	10.00
H	24	13.39710	4.41	H	24	9.33782	8.23
J	24	12.36655	4.97	J	24	8.61952	9.91
K	24	12.32363	5.00	K	24	8.58960	10.00
15 YEAR AMORTIZATION				**20 YEAR AMORTIZATION**			
A	12	$15.23265	15.00	A	12	$14.49906	20.00
B	52	3.80816	11.04	B	52	3.62477	12.91
C	52	3.51523	14.52	C	52	3.34594	18.87
D	52	3.48903	15.00	D	52	3.32009	20.00
E	26	7.61632	11.10	E	26	7.24953	12.98
F	26	7.03045	14.62	F	26	6.69188	19.09
G	26	6.98922	15.00	G	26	6.65080	20.00
H	24	8.25102	11.16	H	24	7.85366	13.09
J	24	7.61632	14.77	J	24	7.24953	19.46
K	24	7.58989	15.00	K	24	7.22437	20.00
25 YEAR AMORTIZATION				**30 YEAR AMORTIZATION**			
A	12	$14.20175	25.00	A	12	$14.07627	30.00
B	52	3.55044	13.94	B	52	3.51907	14.46
C	52	3.27733	22.58	C	52	3.24837	25.37
D	52	3.25149	25.00	D	52	3.22248	30.00
E	26	7.10087	14.03	E	26	7.03813	14.55
F	26	6.55465	23.00	F	26	6.49674	26.05
G	26	6.51339	25.00	G	26	6.45527	30.00
H	24	7.69261	14.17	H	24	7.62465	14.70
J	24	7.10087	23.81	J	24	7.03813	27.52
K	24	7.07623	25.00	K	24	7.01370	30.00

TYPES OF PAYMENTS: A—monthly; B—accelerated weekly; C—regular weekly; D—minimum amortized weekly; E—accelerated bi-weekly; F—regular bi-weekly; G—minimum amortized bi-weekly; H—accelerated semi-monthly; J—regular semi-monthly; K—minimum amortized semi-monthly

17.5%

BLENDED PAYMENTS IN DOLLARS OF PRINCIPAL AND IN-
TEREST FOR A LOAN OF $1,000 AT **17.5%** PER YEAR, CALCU-
LATED HALF-YEARLY, NOT IN ADVANCE

TYPE OF PMT	PMTS EACH YEAR	PMT EACH PERIOD	YEARS TO RETIRE LOAN	TYPE OF PMT	PMTS EACH YEAR	PMT EACH PERIOD	YEARS TO RETIRE LOAN
5 YEAR AMORTIZATION				**10 YEAR AMORTIZATION**			
A	12	$24.79568	5.00	A	12	$17.31273	10.00
B	52	6.19892	4.39	B	52	4.32818	8.16
C	52	5.72208	4.95	C	52	3.99524	9.82
D	52	5.68569	5.00	D	52	3.96708	10.00
E	26	12.39784	4.40	E	26	8.65636	8.19
F	26	11.44416	4.96	F	26	7.99049	9.86
G	26	11.38970	5.00	G	26	7.94695	10.00
H	24	13.43099	4.40	H	24	9.37773	8.22
J	24	12.39784	4.97	J	24	8.65636	9.91
K	24	12.35451	5.00	K	24	8.62611	10.00
15 YEAR AMORTIZATION				**20 YEAR AMORTIZATION**			
A	12	$15.31506	15.00	A	12	$14.58754	20.00
B	52	3.82877	11.02	B	52	3.64688	12.86
C	52	3.53424	14.51	C	52	3.36635	18.85
D	52	3.50775	15.00	D	52	3.34020	20.00
E	26	7.65753	11.07	E	26	7.29377	12.93
F	26	7.06849	14.61	F	26	6.73271	19.07
G	26	7.02680	15.00	G	26	6.69117	20.00
H	24	8.29566	11.14	H	24	7.90158	13.04
J	24	7.65753	14.77	J	24	7.29377	19.45
K	24	7.63077	15.00	K	24	7.26828	20.00
25 YEAR AMORTIZATION				**30 YEAR AMORTIZATION**			
A	12	$14.29405	25.00	A	12	$14.17082	30.00
B	52	3.57351	13.87	B	52	3.54271	14.37
C	52	3.29863	22.53	C	52	3.27019	25.28
D	52	3.27249	25.00	D	52	3.24400	30.00
E	26	7.14702	13.96	E	26	7.08541	14.47
F	26	6.59725	22.95	F	26	6.54038	25.97
G	26	6.55552	25.00	G	26	6.49845	30.00
H	24	7.74261	14.09	H	24	7.67586	14.61
J	24	7.14702	23.77	J	24	7.08541	27.46
K	24	7.12205	25.00	K	24	7.06065	30.00

TYPES OF PAYMENTS: A—monthly; B—accelerated weekly; C—
regular weekly; D—minimum amortized weekly; E—accelerated
bi-weekly; F—regular bi-weekly; G—minimum amortized bi-
weekly; H—accelerated semi-monthly; J—regular semi-monthly;
K—minimum amortized semi-monthly

17.625%

BLENDED PAYMENTS IN DOLLARS OF PRINCIPAL AND INTEREST FOR A LOAN OF $1,000 AT **17.625%** PER YEAR, CALCULATED HALF-YEARLY, NOT IN ADVANCE

TYPE OF PMT	PMTS EACH YEAR	PMT EACH PERIOD	YEARS TO RETIRE LOAN	TYPE OF PMT	PMTS EACH YEAR	PMT EACH PERIOD	YEARS TO RETIRE LOAN
5 YEAR AMORTIZATION				**10 YEAR AMORTIZATION**			
A	12	$24.85830	5.00	A	12	$17.38651	10.00
B	52	6.21458	4.38	B	52	4.34663	8.15
C	52	5.73653	4.95	C	52	4.01227	9.82
D	52	5.69981	5.00	D	52	3.98381	10.00
E	26	12.42915	4.39	E	26	8.69326	8.18
F	26	11.47306	4.96	F	26	8.02454	9.86
G	26	11.41811	5.00	G	26	7.98055	10.00
H	24	13.46491	4.40	H	24	9.41769	8.21
J	24	12.42915	4.97	J	24	8.69326	9.91
K	24	12.38541	5.00	K	24	8.66266	10.00
15 YEAR AMORTIZATION				**20 YEAR AMORTIZATION**			
A	12	$15.39759	15.00	A	12	$14.67610	20.00
B	52	3.84940	10.99	B	52	3.66903	12.81
C	52	3.55329	14.51	C	52	3.38679	18.82
D	52	3.52650	15.00	D	52	3.36034	20.00
E	26	7.69879	11.04	E	26	7.33805	12.88
F	26	7.10658	14.61	F	26	6.77359	19.05
G	26	7.06444	15.00	G	26	6.73158	20.00
H	24	8.34036	11.11	H	24	7.94956	12.99
J	24	7.69879	14.76	J	24	7.33805	19.44
K	24	7.67170	15.00	K	24	7.31223	20.00
25 YEAR AMORTIZATION				**30 YEAR AMORTIZATION**			
A	12	$14.38641	25.00	A	12	$14.26540	30.00
B	52	3.59660	13.80	B	52	3.56635	14.28
C	52	3.31994	22.48	C	52	3.29201	25.18
D	52	3.29350	25.00	D	52	3.26552	30.00
E	26	7.19320	13.89	E	26	7.13270	14.38
F	26	6.63988	22.91	F	26	6.58403	25.88
G	26	6.59768	25.00	G	26	6.54163	30.00
H	24	7.79264	14.02	H	24	7.72709	14.53
J	24	7.19320	23.74	J	24	7.13270	27.39
K	24	7.16789	25.00	K	24	7.10760	30.00

TYPES OF PAYMENTS: A—monthly; B—accelerated weekly; C—regular weekly; D—minimum amortized weekly; E—accelerated bi-weekly; F—regular bi-weekly; G—minimum amortized bi-weekly; H—accelerated semi-monthly; J—regular semi-monthly; K—minimum amortized semi-monthly

17.75%

BLENDED PAYMENTS IN DOLLARS OF PRINCIPAL AND INTEREST FOR A LOAN OF $1,000 AT **17.75%** PER YEAR, CALCULATED HALF-YEARLY, NOT IN ADVANCE

TYPE OF PMT	PMTS EACH YEAR	PMT EACH PERIOD	YEARS TO RETIRE LOAN	TYPE OF PMT	PMTS EACH YEAR	PMT EACH PERIOD	YEARS TO RETIRE LOAN
5 YEAR AMORTIZATION				**10 YEAR AMORTIZATION**			
A	12	$24.92098	5.00	A	12	$17.46040	10.00
B	52	6.23025	4.38	B	52	4.36510	8.14
C	52	5.75100	4.95	C	52	4.02932	9.82
D	52	5.71394	5.00	D	52	4.00056	10.00
E	26	12.46049	4.39	E	26	8.73020	8.16
F	26	11.50199	4.96	F	26	8.05865	9.86
G	26	11.44654	5.00	G	52	8.01420	10.00
H	24	13.49886	4.40	H	24	9.45772	8.20
J	24	12.46049	4.97	J	24	8.73020	9.91
K	24	12.41634	5.00	K	24	8.69927	10.00
15 YEAR AMORTIZATION				**20 YEAR AMORTIZATION**			
A	12	$15.48023	15.00	A	12	$14.76476	20.00
B	52	3.87006	10.96	B	52	3.69119	12.75
C	52	3.57236	14.50	C	52	3.40725	18.80
D	52	3.54527	15.00	D	52	3.38050	20.00
E	26	7.74011	11.01	E	26	7.38238	12.83
F	26	7.14472	14.60	F	26	6.81450	19.03
G	26	7.10212	15.00	G	26	6.77203	20.00
H	24	8.38512	11.08	H	24	7.99758	12.93
J	24	7.74011	14.76	J	24	7.38238	19.42
K	24	7.71269	15.00	K	24	7.35622	20.00
25 YEAR AMORTIZATION				**30 YEAR AMORTIZATION**			
A	12	$14.47882	25.00	A	12	$14.35999	30.00
B	52	3.61971	13.73	B	52	3.59000	14.20
C	52	3.34127	22.43	C	52	3.31384	25.08
D	52	3.31452	25.00	D	52	3.28704	30.00
E	26	7.23941	13.82	E	26	7.18000	14.29
F	26	6.68253	22.86	F	26	6.62769	25.79
G	26	6.63987	25.00	G	26	6.58483	30.00
H	24	7.84269	13.95	H	24	7.77833	14.44
J	24	7.23941	23.71	J	24	7.18000	27.32
K	24	7.21376	25.00	K	24	7.15456	30.00

TYPES OF PAYMENTS: A—monthly; B—accelerated weekly; C—regular weekly; D—minimum amortized weekly; E—accelerated bi-weekly; F—regular bi-weekly; G—minimum amortized bi-weekly; H—accelerated semi-monthly; J—regular semi-monthly; K—minimum amortized semi-monthly

17.875%

BLENDED PAYMENTS IN DOLLARS OF PRINCIPAL AND INTEREST FOR A LOAN OF $1,000 AT **17.875%** PER YEAR, CALCULATED HALF-YEARLY, NOT IN ADVANCE

TYPE OF PMT	PMTS EACH YEAR	PMT EACH PERIOD	YEARS TO RETIRE LOAN	TYPE OF PMT	PMTS EACH YEAR	PMT EACH PERIOD	YEARS TO RETIRE LOAN
5 YEAR AMORTIZATION				**10 YEAR AMORTIZATION**			
A	12	$24.98372	5.00	A	12	$17.53439	10.00
B	52	6.24593	4.38	B	52	4.38360	8.13
C	52	5.76547	4.95	C	52	4.04640	9.81
D	52	5.72808	5.00	D	52	4.01734	10.00
E	26	12.49186	4.39	E	26	8.76720	8.15
F	26	11.53095	4.96	F	26	8.09280	9.86
G	26	11.47499	5.00	G	26	8.04789	10.00
H	24	13.53285	4.40	H	24	9.49780	8.19
J	24	12.49186	4.97	J	24	8.76720	9.91
K	24	12.44730	5.00	K	24	8.73593	10.00
15 YEAR AMORTIZATION				**20 YEAR AMORTIZATION**			
A	12	$15.56298	15.00	A	12	$14.85349	20.00
B	52	3.89074	10.93	B	52	3.71337	12.70
C	52	3.59146	14.49	C	52	3.42773	18.78
D	52	3.56406	15.00	D	52	3.40067	20.00
E	26	7.78149	10.98	E	26	7.42675	12.78
F	26	7.18291	14.59	F	26	6.85546	19.01
G	26	7.13985	15.00	G	26	6.81252	20.00
H	24	8.42995	11.05	H	24	8.04564	12.88
J	24	7.78149	14.75	J	24	7.42675	19.41
K	24	7.75373	15.00	K	24	7.40026	20.00
25 YEAR AMORTIZATION				**30 YEAR AMORTIZATION**			
A	12	$14.57128	25.00	A	12	$14.45461	30.00
B	52	3.64282	13.65	B	52	3.61365	14.11
C	52	3.36260	22.37	C	52	3.33568	24.98
D	52	3.33555	25.00	D	52	3.30857	30.00
E	26	7.28564	13.74	E	26	7.22730	14.21
F	26	6.72521	22.82	F	26	6.67136	25.70
G	26	6.68207	25.00	G	26	6.62803	30.00
H	24	7.89278	13.88	H	24	7.82958	14.36
J	24	7.28564	23.68	J	24	7.22730	27.24
K	24	7.25966	25.00	K	24	7.20153	30.00

TYPES OF PAYMENTS: A—monthly; B—accelerated weekly; C—regular weekly; D—minimum amortized weekly; E—accelerated bi-weekly; F—regular bi-weekly; G—minimum amortized bi-weekly; H—accelerated semi-monthly; J—regular semi-monthly; K—minimum amortized semi-monthly

18%

BLENDED PAYMENTS IN DOLLARS OF PRINCIPAL AND IN-
TEREST FOR A LOAN OF $1,000 AT **18%** PER YEAR, CALCU-
LATED HALF-YEARLY, NOT IN ADVANCE

TYPE OF PMT	PMTS EACH YEAR	PMT EACH PERIOD	YEARS TO RETIRE LOAN	TYPE OF PMT	PMTS EACH YEAR	PMT EACH PERIOD	YEARS TO RETIRE LOAN
5 YEAR AMORTIZATION				**10 YEAR AMORTIZATION**			
A	12	$25.04651	5.00	A	12	$17.60849	10.00
B	52	6.26163	4.38	B	52	4.40212	8.11
C	52	5.77996	4.95	C	52	4.06350	9.81
D	52	5.74223	5.00	D	52	4.03414	10.00
E	26	12.52325	4.39	E	26	8.80425	8.14
F	26	11.55993	4.96	F	26	8.12700	9.85
G	26	11.50347	5.00	G	26	8.08163	10.00
H	24	13.56686	4.40	H	24	9.53793	8.18
J	24	12.52325	4.97	J	24	8.80425	9.90
K	24	12.47829	5.00	K	24	8.77263	10.00
15 YEAR AMORTIZATION				**20 YEAR AMORTIZATION**			
A	12	$15.64584	15.00	A	12	$14.49232	20.00
B	52	3.91146	10.90	B	52	3.73558	12.65
C	52	3.61058	14.48	C	52	3.44823	18.75
D	52	3.58288	15.00	D	52	3.42086	20.00
E	26	7.82292	10.96	E	26	7.47116	12.73
F	26	7.22116	14.59	F	26	6.89646	18.99
G	26	7.17762	15.00	G	26	6.85305	20.00
H	24	8.47483	11.02	H	24	8.09376	12.83
J	24	7.82292	14.75	J	24	7.47116	19.40
K	24	7.79483	15.00	K	24	7.44433	20.00
25 YEAR AMORTIZATION				**30 YEAR AMORTIZATION**			
A	12	$14.66380	25.00	A	12	$14.54924	30.00
B	52	3.66595	13.58	B	52	3.63731	14.03
C	52	3.38395	22.32	C	52	3.35752	24.88
D	52	3.35659	25.00	D	52	3.33010	30.00
E	26	7.33190	13.67	E	26	7.27462	14.12
F	26	6.76791	22.77	F	26	6.71504	25.61
G	26	6.72430	25.00	G	26	6.67123	30.00
H	24	7.94289	13.81	H	24	7.88084	14.27
J	24	7.33190	23.64	J	24	7.27462	27.17
K	24	7.30557	25.00	K	24	7.24850	30.00

TYPES OF PAYMENTS: A—monthly; B—accelerated weekly; C—
regular weekly; D—minimum amortized weekly; E—accelerated
bi-weekly; F—regular bi-weekly; G—minimum amortized bi-
weekly; H—accelerated semi-monthly; J—regular semi-monthly;
K—minimum amortized semi-monthly

4

Interest Factors

INTEREST FACTORS IN DOLLARS FOR A LOAN OF $1,000 AT VARIOUS INTEREST RATES, CALCULATED HALF-YEARLY, NOT IN ADVANCE

TYPE OF PMT	4% INT FACTOR	4.125% INT FACTOR	4.25% INT FACTOR	4.375% INT FACTOR
monthly	$3.30589	3.40833	3.51071	3.61304
weekly	0.75984	0.78335	0.80685	0.83034
bi-weekly	1.52026	1.56732	1.61436	1.66137
semi-monthly	1.65158	1.70271	1.75382	1.80489

TYPE OF PMT	4.5% INT FACTOR	4.625% INT FACTOR	4.75% INT FACTOR	4.875% INT FACTOR
monthly	$3.71532	3.81755	3.91972	4.02184
weekly	0.85381	0.87727	0.90071	0.92415
bi-weekly	1.70835	1.75531	1.80224	1.84915
semi-monthly	1.85594	1.90696	1.95794	2.00890

TYPE OF PMT	5% INT FACTOR	5.125% INT FACTOR	5.25% INT FACTOR	5.375% INT FACTOR
monthly	$4.12392	4.22593	4.32790	4.42982
weekly	0.09476	0.97097	0.99436	1.01773
bi-weekly	1.89602	1.94287	1.98967	2.03650
semi-monthly	2.05984	2.11074	2.16161	2.21246

TYPE OF PMT	5.5% INT FACTOR	5.625% INT FACTOR	5.75% INT FACTOR	5.875% INT FACTOR
monthly	$4.53168	4.63349	4.73525	4.83696
weekly	1.04109	1.06444	1.08778	1.11110
bi-weekly	2.08327	2.13002	2.17674	2.22343
semi-monthly	2.26328	2.31407	2.36483	2.41556

TYPE OF PMT	6% INT FACTOR	6.125% INT FACTOR	6.25% INT FACTOR	6.375% INT FACTOR
monthly	$4.93862	5.04023	5.14178	5.24329
weekly	1.13441	1.15770	1.18098	1.20425
bi-weekly	2.27010	2.31674	2.36335	2.40994
semi-monthly	2.46627	2.51695	2.56760	2.61822

TYPE OF PMT	6.5% INT FACTOR	6.625% INT FACTOR	6.75% INT FACTOR	6.875% INT FACTOR
monthly	$5.34474	5.44614	5.54749	5.64879
weekly	1.22750	1.25074	1.27397	1.29718
bi-weekly	2.45651	2.50304	2.54955	2.59604
semi-monthly	2.66881	2.71937	2.76991	2.82042

INTEREST FACTORS IN DOLLARS FOR A LOAN OF $1,000 AT
VARIOUS INTEREST RATES, CALCULATED HALF-YEARLY, NOT
IN ADVANCE

TYPE OF PMT	7% INT FACTOR	7.125% INT FACTOR	7.25% INT FACTOR	7.375% INT FACTOR
monthly	$5.75004	5.85124	5.95238	6.05348
weekly	1.32038	1.34356	1.36674	1.38990
bi-weekly	2.64250	2.68893	2.73534	2.78172
semi-monthly	2.87090	2.92135	2.97178	3.02217

TYPE OF PMT	7.5% INT FACTOR	7.625% INT FACTOR	7.75% INT FACTOR	7.875% INT FACTOR
monthly	$6.15452	6.25552	6.35646	6.45735
weekly	1.41304	1.43617	1.45929	1.48240
bi-weekly	2.82808	2.87441	2.92071	2.96699
semi-monthly	3.07254	3.12288	3.17320	3.22348

TYPE OF PMT	8% INT FACTOR	8.125% INT FACTOR	8.25% INT FACTOR	8.375% INT FACTOR
monthly	$6.55820	6.65899	6.75973	6.86042
weekly	1.50549	1.52857	1.55163	1.57468
bi-weekly	3.01324	3.05947	3.10567	3.15185
semi-monthly	3.27374	3.32397	3.37417	3.42435

TYPE OF PMT	8.5% INT FACTOR	8.625% INT FACTOR	8.75% INT FACTOR	8.875% INT FACTOR
monthly	$6.96106	7.06165	7.16219	7.26268
weekly	1.59772	1.62075	1.64376	1.66676
bi-weekly	3.19800	3.24412	3.29022	3.33630
semi-monthly	3.47450	3.52461	3.57471	3.62477

TYPE OF PMT	9% INT FACTOR	9.125% INT FACTOR	9.25% INT FACTOR	9.375% INT FACTOR
monthly	$7.36312	7.46351	7.56385	7.66414
weekly	1.68974	1.71272	1.73568	1.75862
bi-weekly	3.38235	3.42837	3.47437	3.52034
semi-monthly	3.67481	3.72482	3.77480	3.82476

TYPE OF PMT	9.5% INT FACTOR	9.625% INT FACTOR	9.75% INT FACTOR	9.875% INT FACTOR
monthly	$7.76438	7.86457	7.96471	8.06480
weekly	1.78156	1.80448	1.82738	1.85028
bi-weekly	3.56629	3.61221	3.65810	3.70398
semi-monthly	3.87468	3.92459	3.97446	4.02430

INTEREST FACTORS IN DOLLARS FOR A LOAN OF $1,000 AT VARIOUS INTEREST RATES, CALCULATED HALF-YEARLY, NOT IN ADVANCE

TYPE OF PMT	10% INT FACTOR	10.125% INT FACTOR	10.25% INT FACTOR	10.375% INT FACTOR
monthly	$8.16485	8.26484	8.36478	8.46467
weekly	1.87316	1.89602	1.91888	1.94172
bi-weekly	3.74982	3.79564	3.84144	3.88721
semi-monthly	4.07412	4.12392	4.17368	4.22342

TYPE OF PMT	10.5% INT FACTOR	10.625% INT FACTOR	10.75% INT FACTOR	10.875% INT FACTOR
monthly	$8.56452	8.66431	8.76405	8.86375
weekly	1.96455	1.98736	1.01016	2.03295
bi-weekly	3.93295	3.97867	4.02437	4.07004
semi-monthly	4.27313	4.32281	4.37247	4.42210

TYPE OF PMT	11% INT FACTOR	11.125% INT FACTOR	11.25% INT FACTOR	11.375% INT FACTOR
monthly	$8.96339	9.06299	9.16254	9.26204
weekly	2.05573	2.07849	2.10124	2.12398
bi-weekly	4.11568	4.16130	4.20690	4.25247
semi-monthly	4.47170	4.52127	4.57082	4.62034

TYPE OF PMT	11.5% INT FACTOR	11.625% INT FACTOR	11.75% INT FACTOR	11.875% INT FACTOR
monthly	$9.36149	9.46089	9.56024	9.65954
weekly	2.14670	2.16941	2.19211	2.21480
bi-weekly	4.29801	4.34354	4.38903	4.43450
semi-monthly	4.66984	4.71931	4.76875	4.81816

TYPE OF PMT	12% INT FACTOR	12.125% INT FACTOR	12.25% INT FACTOR	12.375% INT FACTOR
monthly	$9.75879	9.85800	9.95716	10.05626
weekly	2.23747	2.26013	2.28278	2.30541
bi-weekly	4.47995	4.52537	4.57077	4.61614
semi-monthly	4.86755	4.91691	4.96625	5.01555

TYPE OF PMT	12.5% INT FACTOR	12.625% INT FACTOR	12.75% INT FACTOR	12.875% INT FACTOR
monthly	$10.15532	10.25433	10.35330	10.45221
weekly	2.32803	2.35064	2.37324	2.39582
bi-weekly	4.66149	4.70681	4.75211	4.79738
semi-monthly	5.06483	5.11409	5.16332	5.21252

INTEREST FACTORS IN DOLLARS FOR A LOAN OF $1,000 AT VARIOUS INTEREST RATES, CALCULATED HALF-YEARLY, NOT IN ADVANCE

TYPE OF PMT	13% INT FACTOR	13.125% INT FACTOR	13.25% INT FACTOR	13.375% INT FACTOR
monthly	$10.55107	10.64989	10.74866	10.84738
weekly	2.41839	2.44095	2.46349	2.48603
bi-weekly	4.84263	4.88786	4.93306	4.97823
semi-monthly	5.26169	5.31084	5.35997	5.40906

TYPE OF PMT	13.5% INT FACTOR	13.625% INT FACTOR	13.75% INT FACTOR	13.875% INT FACTOR
monthly	$10.94605	11.04468	11.14325	11.24178
weekly	2.50855	2.53105	2.55355	2.57603
bi-weekly	5.02338	5.06851	5.11361	5.15869
semi-monthly	5.45813	5.50717	5.55619	5.60518

TYPE OF PMT	14% INT FACTOR	14.125% INT FACTOR	14.25% INT FACTOR	14.375% INT FACTOR
monthly	$11.34026	11.43869	11.53708	11.63541
weekly	2.59850	2.62095	2.64340	2.66583
bi-weekly	5.20375	5.24877	5.29378	5.33876
semi-monthly	5.65415	5.70308	5.75200	5.80088

TYPE OF PMT	14.5% INT FACTOR	14.625% INT FACTOR	14.75% INT FACTOR	14.875% INT FACTOR
monthly	$11.73370	11.83194	11.93014	12.02828
weekly	2.68825	2.71065	2.73305	2.75543
bi-weekly	5.38372	5.42865	5.47356	5.51844
semi-monthly	5.84974	5.89857	5.94738	5.99616

TYPE OF PMT	15% INT FACTOR	15.125% INT FACTOR	15.25% INT FACTOR	15.375% INT FACTOR
monthly	$12.12638	12.22443	12.32243	12.42039
weekly	2.77779	2.80015	2.82249	2.84482
bi-weekly	5.56330	5.60814	5.65295	5.69774
semi-monthly	6.04492	6.09365	6.14235	6.19103

TYPE OF PMT	15.5% INT FACTOR	15.625% INT FACTOR	15.75% INT FACTOR	15.875% INT FACTOR
monthly	$12.51830	12.61616	12.71397	12.81174
weekly	2.86714	2.88945	2.91174	2.93402
bi-weekly	5.74251	5.78725	5.83196	5.87665
semi-monthly	6.23968	6.28831	6.33691	6.38548

INTEREST FACTORS IN DOLLARS FOR A LOAN OF $1,000 AT VARIOUS INTEREST RATES, CALCULATED HALF-YEARLY, NOT IN ADVANCE

TYPE OF PMT	16% INT FACTOR	16.125% INT FACTOR	16.25% INT FACTOR	16.375% INT FACTOR
monthly	$12.90946	13.00713	13.10475	13.20233
weekly	2.95629	2.97855	3.00080	3.02302
bi-weekly	5.92132	5.96597	6.01059	6.05519
semi-monthly	6.43403	6.48255	6.53105	6.57952

TYPE OF PMT	16.5% INT FACTOR	16.625% INT FACTOR	16.75% INT FACTOR	16.875% INT FACTOR
monthly	$13.29986	13.39735	13.49479	13.59218
weekly	3.04524	3.06745	3.08964	3.11183
bi-weekly	6.09976	6.14431	6.18883	6.23334
semi-monthly	6.62797	6.67639	6.72478	6.77315

TYPE OF PMT	17% INT FACTOR	17.125% INT FACTOR	17.25% INT FACTOR	17.375% INT FACTOR
monthly	$13.68952	13.78682	13.88407	13.98127
weekly	3.13400	3.15615	3.17830	3.20043
bi-weekly	6.27781	6.32227	6.36670	6.41111
semi-monthly	6.82149	6.86981	6.91810	6.96637

TYPE OF PMT	17.5% INT FACTOR	17.625% INT FACTOR	17.75% INT FACTOR	17.875% INT FACTOR
monthly	$14.07843	14.17554	14.27260	14.36962
weekly	3.22255	3.24466	3.26676	3.28884
bi-weekly	6.45549	6.49985	6.54419	6.58850
semi-monthly	7.01461	7.06283	7.11102	7.15918

TYPE OF PMT	18% INT FACTOR
monthly	$14.46659
weekly	3.31091
bi-weekly	6.63279
semi-monthly	7.20732

Appendix
Your Own Customized Payment Schedule

Creating your own customized payment schedule is easy. Start by filling in the blanks below.

a) balance owing _____
b) interest rate _____
c) amount of the blended payment (with no tax component) _____
d) how frequently it's paid _____
e) date of the *next* payment _____
f) interest factor (for the interest rate and type of payment) _____

Formula: $\dfrac{interest\ factor \times balance\ owing}{\$1000}$ = *interest component*

Then complete the following chart by calculating the principal and interest components of each blended payment plus the balance owing after that payment has been made. Before long you'll have a customized payment schedule that reflects your unique mortgage terms:

Payment Number	Date	Payment Made	Interest Component	Principal Component	Balance Owing

Payment Number	Date Payment Made	Interest Component	Principal Component	Balance Owing

Payment Number	Date	Payment Made	Interest Component	Principal Component	Balance Owing

Payment Number	Date Made	Payment	Interest Component	Principal Component	Balance Owing

Payment Number	Date	Payment Made	Interest Component	Principal Component	Balance Owing

Payment Number	Date	Payment Made	Interest Component	Principal Component	Balance Owing

Payment Number	Date	Payment Made	Interest Component	Principal Component	Balance Owing

Payment Number	Date	Payment Made	Interest Component	Principal Component	Balance Owing

Payment Number	Date	Payment Made	Interest Component	Principal Component	Balance Owing

Payment Number	Date	Payment Made	Interest Component	Principal Component	Balance Owing

Payment Number	Date	Payment Made	Interest Component	Principal Component	Balance Owing

Payment Number	Date	Payment Made	Interest Component	Principal Component	Balance Owing

Payment Number	Date	Payment Made	Interest Component	Principal Component	Balance Owing

Payment Number	Date	Payment Made	Interest Component	Principal Component	Balance Owing